Reckoning with the Beast

The Johns Hopkins University Studies in Historical and Political Science

Animals, Pain,
and Humanity
in the Victorian Mind

Reckoning
with
the
Beast

James Turner

The Johns Hopkins University Press ● *Baltimore and London*

This book has been brought to publication with the generous assistance of the Andrew F. Mellon Foundation.

The Johns Hopkins University Press, Baltimore, Maryland 21218
The Johns Hopkins Press Ltd., London

Library of Congress Cataloging in Publication Data

Turner, James Crewdson, 1946-
    Reckoning with the beast.

    (The Johns Hopkins University studies in historical and political science; 98th ser., no. 2)
    Bibliographic Note: p. 181
    Includes index.
    1. Animals, Treatment of. 2. Great Britain—Social conditions. 3. United States—Social conditions.
I. Title. II. Series: Johns Hopkins University. Studies in historical and political science; 98th ser., no. 2.
HV4708.T87   179'.3'0973   80-11559
ISBN 0-8018-2399-4

Nous n'avons pas d'histoire de l'*Amour,* qu'on y pense! Nous n'avons pas d'histoire de la *Mort.* Nous n'avons pas d'histoire de la *Pitié.*

—Lucien Febvre

If we choose to let conjecture run wild, then animals—our fellow brethren in pain, disease, death, suffering and famine, our slaves in the most laborious works, our companions in our amusements,—they may partake from our origin in one common ancestor, we may be all netted together.

—Charles Darwin (1837)

Contents

Preface

This book is about people who changed their minds. And ours. I mean not the discarding of a few outworn opinions, but the outgrowing of a way of thinking and feeling and the emergence of a new, distinctively modern sensibility. I use the indefinite article advisedly, for I do not believe human beings to be so simple, nor ourselves so wise, as to identify such a thing as "the" modern sensibility. Still, our cast of mind distinguishes us from people of other places and times, and it is possible to sketch major elements in our world view, even if we cannot define the whole. That is what I have tried to do—to trace the origins of one complex of attitudes and ideas close to the heart of our own way of dealing with the world.

This may seem an excessively grandiose claim for a book about attitudes toward animals. Granted, the great Victorian societies for prevention of cruelty to animals not only enrolled thousands of members but also attracted the support of the rich and powerful: of church dignitaries, peers, ministers, governors, senators, presidents, and the most eminent Victorian, the queen herself. Granted, too, that even this was only a part of something much greater, that those who spoke up for animals, inside or out of such societies, echoed beliefs that by the century's end reverberated throughout the Anglo-American world. Still, one harbors a certain skepticism. These notions penetrated widely, perhaps, but how deeply? Will the curious reader who bothers to bore into the heart of Victorian fondness for animals find anything there but the sentimentalism of a mawkish age?

It is a commonplace among those interested in the nineteenth century that two revolutionary changes in outlook, among others, helped to transform the Anglo-American mind during those years. One was the realization that human beings are not supranatural but are directly descended from beasts. The other was the rising esteem for science, as a model of intellectual endeavor and as the key to the future of the race. It is not so widely recognized, though much has been written around the edges of this subject, that the nineteenth century was also an era of enhanced sensitiveness about pain. Then, for the first time, men and women developed that dread of pain—that "instinctive" revulsion from the physical suffering even of others—uniquely characteristic of the modern era. It is even less commonly realized, if at all, that all three of these attitudes grew up together, feeding upon and nourishing one another. Yet without appreciating the mutual development of all three, no one can be fully understood. Nor can they be understood apart from the still more fundamental social transformation that cleared their way: the shock of massive industrialization and urbanization, wrenching people loose from old habits of mind and putting the relationship between man and nature on a radically new footing.

At one point all converged. The new acceptance of human animality, the new appreciation of science, the new horror of pain all impinged on one seemingly minor question, raised to public attention chiefly by the traumas of industrialization. How ought people to treat the animals around them? The question did not remain minor, and in answering it the Victorians illuminated much of their interior selves. I think that I see in their answers glimmerings of our own responses to science, to nature, to suffering and death. But now I am getting ahead of the story, which starts with none of these but, more simply, with animals and their masters.

For reasons partly of convenience, partly of realism, but mostly of ignorance, I have limited my horizons to the Anglo-American world. (With apologies to Canadians and West Indians, I will use this term usually to refer only to England and the United States. More accurate alternatives are too clumsy.) There is, fortunately, good reason for this, independent of my limitations. The Anglo-American world comprises still—and more so, a century ago—a separate cultural entity within the larger European civilization. Without denying the differences dividing Americans from the English, no one could fail to distinguish them all as a group from, say, the Germans or Italians. And in this distinctive Anglo-American soil, the values and beliefs that I write about took root earliest and most deeply.

Reckoning with the Beast

I
Introduction

Recorded history, in a sense, begins with the famous cave paintings at Lascaux in southwestern France. The subject of the paleolithic artists was animals. Great bisons stalk the dank limestone walls; a herd of stags fords a stream; shaggy ponies trot out of the lost past.[1]

As hunters and prey, as gods and demons, as workers and parasites, or merely as mobile larders, animals have lived intimately with man since before he was man. No one knows when some hungry proto-human first grew bored with roots and berries and began to stalk about in search of red meat, and only a slightly informed guess puts the domestication of the dog (the first beast to find a rope around its neck) in the Upper Paleolithic era.[2] What *is* known with certainty is that every human culture has grown up around and adapted to the animals it relies on. The sacred cat of the Theban priest and the medieval peasant's village ox both marked their masters' lives, as did Hannibal's elephants, the Welsh miner's pit ponies, the Texan cowboy's longhorns, and presumably even King Charles's spaniels.[3]

Beasts have been feared, loved, beaten, caressed, starved, stuffed, and ignored. Attitudes toward animals have been as diverse as people and animals themselves. But before the modern era all the myriad variations on this theme were usually played in only two keys.

Preindustrial peoples every day faced the blunt fact that animals—wild beasts to be hunted, sheep to be shorn, oxen to draw the plow—were, simply, crucial to survival. Yet disease, rough weather, infertility, and like curses could wreak havoc for the hunter or farmer, while his own hands hung helpless. Caution thus drew men to woo the animal world by the same sorts of magical and religious rites used to charm the corn or coax the rain.[4] Perhaps also, a certain half-conscious sense of gratitude for the food and labor wrested from animals, or of trepidation at the slaying of creatures obviously similar to man, found an outlet in religious ceremony.[5] Animals, as part of the mysterious and ungovernable order of nature, demanded propitiation.

1

This reverence for animals in the abstract typically coexisted with a daily round of careless brutality. The local priest's blessing did not spare the ox his meed of lashes. In the first chapter of Genesis, God gave Adam dominion over the beasts, and Adam's progeny exercised it with a will.[6] Even animals protected from serious injury by their owners' self-interest routinely suffered treatment appalling to modern sensibilities. Thomas Blundevill, an Elizabethan horse fancier actually noted for his gentle hand, repeatedly advised readers of his manual for horsemen to beat their steeds about the head with a cudgel.[7] Less-favored animals did not get off so lightly. From at least Angevin times and probably much earlier, Englishmen of all ranks delighted in watching dogs torn to pieces by equally lacerated bulls, bears, and badgers. Two cocks going at each other talon and spur was a commonplace Sunday diversion.[8]

Yet these bloodied animals were probably not victims of cruelty. Cruelty implies a desire to inflict pain and thus presupposes an empathetic appreciation of the suffering of the object of cruelty. Empathy, however, seems not to have been a highly developed trait in premodern Europeans. People no doubt felt pity or compassion for spouse or children or neighbors, but their sighs apparently stopped there. No generalized humanitarianism evoked fellow feeling with the sufferings of the next village, much less the plight of total strangers fifty miles away.[9] People who walked hand-in-hand with plague, famine, and dying children could ill afford to squander their affective capital on useless emotion. Moreover, moralists insisted that even the scant pity doled out to relatives and neighbors was of doubtful worth. As Sir Thomas Browne pointed out, the proper motive for charity was obedience to God's commands; compassion was self-indulgent.[10] Small wonder that animals scarcely benefited at all from this cramped, hoarded sympathy. Not only were their aches and pains ignored, but they seem to have stood almost completely outside the emotional walls of premodern Europe.[11] Those rare souls who bothered to notice maltreatment of animals felt uneasy only because the habit might extend to abusing human beings.[12] Pity was reserved for people.

This conceptual gap between beasts and higher beings yawned still wider in contemporary theories of the nature of animals. To be sure, Aristotle—until the Renaissance the accepted master of the subject—had declared that human beings and animals share a common "sensitive" soul. He had even gone so far as to ascribe to both the same mechanism of motivation. But he also carefully pointed out that men have a rational soul denied to beasts.[13] When the Schoolmen grafted Christian belief in human immortality onto Aristotle's schema, they sharpened further the distinction between man and "the beasts that perish." Man partook of animal nature, but he was, as Hamlet said, the "paragon of animals," the connecting link between angels and animals, the center and purpose of physical creation. Beasts existed only to serve his needs.[14] Even in imaginative literature, where their presence went back to Aesop and beyond, animals were used mainly as symbols of human vices and virtues.[15] Only an eccentric few showed any interest in animals for their own sake.

This is not to say that people kept animals only for narrow utility. Elephants, lions, camels, and an occasional giraffe swelled the glory and confusion of many a medieval and Renaissance court. But admirers valued these exotic menageries as marvels, not because of any fondness for their inmates.[16] Pet dogs, then as now, rested in the laps of noble ladies; and such *chiens gentilz,* unlike their objectionable impoverished relatives, had free run of fourteenth-century London. These "sybaritical puppies" did not pine for attention ("Yea, they oft feed them of the best, where the poore mans child at their doores can hardlie come by the worst"). But they served mainly as toys or badges of rank, and whatever affection befell them neither extended to other animals nor was mimicked by the lower orders of society.[17]

Affection was hardly to be expected for creatures seldom really looked at. People whose livelihood depended on animals naturally noted the economically valuable traits of their stock, but otherwise animals were rarely observed closely. Medieval writers often merely parroted the descriptions inherited from classical authorities. Not until the sixteenth century did scholars and artists, more sensitive to nature in general and perhaps also inspired by the strange animals brought back to Europe by the great explorers of that seaborne century, begin regularly to depict animals from first-hand observation. Even then many antique errors persisted, and scientific zoology lagged far behind its neighbor, botany.[18]

Clearly, however, these hairline fractures weakened the old cast of mind. A few adventurous (or perverse) writers around 1600, Montaigne the best known, went so far as to question the vanity that separated man from "his fellow members and companions," the animals.[19] Such eccentricity was rare. But during the following century, especially in England, the social and moral status of animals began a slight but steady rise. With the emergence of fox hunting and racing, the county gentleman's horses and hounds became objects of pride, although they continued to receive their allowance of kicks and beatings. The new enthusiasm for country life made people take a second look at animals, even if only as an element of the rural landscape, yearned for in the Horatian mode.[20] Yet merely to state these developments is almost to exaggerate their impact. Not until the latter half of the seventeenth century did attitudes toward animals start to diverge sharply from their traditional mold—and then for very different reasons.

Medieval thinkers had conceded that people shared the strictly physical nature of animals. What really set people apart were their mental, and especially their spiritual, qualities. Henry More, the seventeenth-century English Platonist, voiced this still dominant belief when he warned that "vile epicurism and sensuality will make the soul of man so degenerate and blind, that he will not only be content to slide into brutish immorality, but please himself in this very opinion that he is a real brute already, an ape, satyr, or baboon."[21] Vile epicures who actually believed man to be essentially an animal were certainly scarce among More's contemporaries, so his worries were premature—but prescient. For scientific evidence of man's basic animality was beginning to accumulate.

Particularly in the latter half of the seventeenth century, after the Royal Society gave a new impetus to scientific research, experiments on animals became more common. Investigators year after year uncovered new similarities between men and beasts.[22] It was not merely that comparative anatomy showed the bodies of people and animals to be "similar in principle" and "in many cases identical, organ for organ. . . ." Even Henry More could have accepted that, for, with a certain amount of psychological strain, it could be absorbed into the Aristotelian-Scholastic theory of human nature—especially since physico-theology and Copernican astronomy had begun to humble man's pretensions by undercutting the older anthropocentric cosmology.[23] But the anatomists were edging perilously close to that exclusively human preserve, the mind. Neurological experiment suggested that the senses functioned in people exactly as they did in animals.[24] By the start of the eighteenth century, if not earlier, this was a commonplace belief among the reading public: "That dogs are endued with the Sense of Feeling, is not to be doubted, since they are not without Nerves, which are the most proper Organs of that, as well as the rest of the Senses."[25] Yet, indisputably, sensation seemed in people to be at least partly a mental function. So, if the senses operated through identical physical networks in the bodies of people and animals, what was one to conclude? If brutes could feel, they must have minds; and if they have minds . . . ? Most English writers soon came to believe that beasts had not only feeling but a degree of reason.[26]

Scientific evidence of the similarity of men and animals did not necessarily guarantee the latter a place in the affections of Englishmen. For one thing, even a thoughtful horse was only a soulless brute, created to serve the master's needs.[27] A much more immediate obstacle blocking concern for animals was the continued dearth of compassion for people and beasts alike. It did animals little good to be recognized as distant cousins if man would not lift a hand to help closer relatives. Yet changes were in the air. While scientists labored to unveil the mysteries of anatomy, moral and religious writers were at work whetting the moral sensibilities of their audience, and a benevolent tide of sympathy ushered in the eighteenth century.

The first hints of this appeared around the middle of the seventeenth century. The gentlemen's "courtesy books," popular since Tudor times, now began to enforce "the obligation to be of service to mankind." A "good Heart" became a necessary genteel accessory.[28] More influential were the insistent exhortations of an important section of the Established clergy—determined, from the Restoration onwards, to eradicate the religion that had temporarily turned them out. To the angry predestinarian God of the Puritans, liberal Anglicans opposed divine goodness and mercy; for Puritan splitting of theological hairs, these "Latitude-men" substituted a stress on the universality of the moral law and on the cooperation of all men of good will in doing God's work; and against the Puritan emphasis on faith alone as the agent of salvation, the Latitudinarians vindicated the efficacy of works.[29] Hobbes's egoistic naturalism provided another, less important, victim for the Churchly knives already honed for Calvinist divines.[30] Militant benevolence thus became a major weapon in the Latitudinarian arsenal. Virtue, in fact, was identified with universal benevolence. But benevolence involved more than *doing* good. Its acolytes stressed the tender passions—supposedly natural to human beings—that prompted and accompanied acts of charity. Indeed, God implanted these delicious emotions as an incentive to good deeds.

Preachers therefore urged their congregations to savor the delightful self-congratulatory feelings that welled up in one's bosom as a result of almsgiving or visiting the sick. Sober divines invited their readers to thrill to the "Self-approving Joy."[31] The Reverend Isaac Barrow, one of the greatest melting hearts of the age, nicely caught the spirit of the whole thing in a sermon worth quoting at length:

> We are indispensably obliged to these duties [of charity], because the best of our natural inclinations prompt us to the performance of them, especially those of pity and benignity, which are manifestly discernible in all, but most powerful and vigorous in the best natures; and which, questionless, by the most wise and good Author of our beings were implanted therein both as monitors to direct, and as spurs to incite us to the performance of our duty. . . . Even the stories of calamities, that in ages long since past have happened to persons nowise related to us, yea, the fabulous reports of tragical events, do (even against the bent of our wills, and all resistance of reason) melt our hearts with compassion, and draw tears from our eyes; and thereby evidently signify that general sympathy which naturally intercedes between all men, since we can neither see, nor hear of, nor imagine another's grief, without being afflicted ourselves.[32]

The contrast with the mood of earlier centuries needs no comment.

Soon the spirit of Latitudinarian benevolence had descended upon New England as well.[33] Meanwhile, in England Shaftesbury's influential writings reinforced the doctrines early in the eighteenth century. Especially through his disciple Francis Hutcheson, the new temper reached men of letters, and soon English literature had surrendered itself to sentimentality.[34] Benevolence then moved from pulpit and novel into more mundane settings. Shortly after 1700, scattered but vocal complaints indicated that the harsh, even cruel, discipline traditionally the lot of English public-school boys had begun to shock tender sensibilities. One of the most popular "benevolences" of the eighteenth century, the charity school movement, combined religious impulses and concern for the stability of the social order with a surprising degree of compassion for the sufferings of the poor.[35]

A similar mixture of Christianity and compassion inspired the prison reformer John Howard. Appalled by the moral corruption and physical suffering that, as sheriff of Bedfordshire, he saw in prisons, Howard extended his investigations to other British and continental jails and became the driving force behind parliamentary legislation to improve prison conditions. The same religious and humanitarian enthusiasm fired "the Howard of America," Thomas Eddy. In 1773, the year Howard became high sheriff in Bedford, the founders of the Society for the Discharge and Relief of Prisoners Imprisoned for Small Debts, horrified by the "iniquitous treatment" and "ghastly conditions" that debtors faced, began the movement to abolish debtors' prison in England.[36]

Of all eighteenth-century flowerings of the new humanitarian sensibility, the most celebrated was antislavery. Already, around 1700, Quaker teachers on both sides of the Atlantic were coming to think that the Christian spirit of "love, compassion, mercy, and goodness" was incompatible with slavery. Pennsylvania Quakers formally denounced the institution in 1696; English Quakers followed suit in 1727; and in the 1760s and 1770s both moved to expel slave traders and slave holders. Lord Chief Justice Mansfield, in the Somerset case in 1772, found slavery "so odious that nothing can be suffered to support it but positive law" and outlawed it in England—a position the Scottish courts adopted six years later.[37] One by one, the northern states of America wiped out the institution in the years following the Revolution. Perhaps the greatest figure in English antislavery, William Wilberforce, deeply stirred by his sympathy for the slave's miseries and pricked by his Evangelical sense of duty, helped to launch the Abolition Society in 1787. He and his allies found their most effective weapon, even in Parliament, to be the appeal to compassion.[38] In the next century it would goad the English conscience to eradicate slavery from the empire.

These eruptions of compassion would scarcely have been conceivable a century earlier, and they were not the norm even in the late 1700s. The organizers of the Society of Universal Good Will (1784) were atypically sweeping in their benevolence. Compassion, strongest among the minority of actively religious folk, touched most Englishmen and Americans only fitfully, and it coexisted with a harsh daily experience of cruelty and misery that would appall us—but one to which contemporaries were mostly blind. Yet John Wesley, no Pollyanna, concluded toward the end of his life that "benevolence and compassion toward all forms of human woe have increased in a manner not known before, from the earliest ages of the world."[39]

More directly to the point was the extension of benevolence in another direction. This flood of sympathy, embracing all people, could hardly fail to overflow its original bounds and brush with pity the sufferings of other sentient beings. Particularly at a time when scientific discoveries suggested a closer kinship between men and beasts (and the Latitudinarian preachers of benevolence were notably sympathetic to the new science[40]), animals began to benefit from this exuberance of compassion.

Even before the Restoration an occasional eccentric, out of the many nourished by the Civil War and Interregnum, protested against the cruelty of baiting bulls and bears.[41] Early Quakers (as well as their descendants) seem to have been unusually sensitive to animal suffering.[42] Such concern became less rare after Latitudinarian benevolence filled the air. Both Sir Matthew Hale, chief justice under Charles II, and the diarist John Evelyn showed sympathy for animals. John Locke advised that children "be bred up in an abhorrence of killing and tormenting any living creature. . . . And indeed, I think people from their cradles should be tender to all sensible [i.e., sentient] creatures."[43] Sentiments like these were certainly spreading in the seventeenth century, especially among the educated classes—and reinforced there by the more fastidious ideal of the gentleman. Still, compassion for animals was far from general and appears to have mattered little even to those who displayed it.

A few journalists and an occasional poet broached the theme in the early eighteenth century. But for the most part, literary animals continued to be caricatured men in beasts' clothing.[44] The engines of benevolence, however, were building up steam, and at least a pose of sentimentality had by midcentury become *de rigueur* among the English elite.[45] The Scottish poet James Thomson explicitly adopted the theories of Shaftesbury and Hutcheson and, in *The Seasons* (1730), liberally meted out pity to animals and men alike. Thomson's beasts, significantly, were real, not the conventional poorly disguised people of his predecessors.[46] After *The Seasons,* attacks on blood sports or little poems lauding the fidelity of dogs began to appear from time to time in literary periodicals.[47] Along with such poetic sentiments went a strengthening of the affective ties that bound people to animals, especially pets, which figured largely in these literary effusions.

This growing literary intimacy with animals found a parallel in scientific thought. In his *Systema naturae* (1735), Linnaeus unabashedly grouped *Homo sapiens* with other mammalian species and, more precisely, with other primates in the order *Anthropomorpha.* This may have encouraged the many students of that influential work to think more readily of man as an animal.[48] But probably more important in fixing man securely among the beasts was the nominalistic assault, rooted in Locke and Leibnitz, on the whole concept of species. Some of the most renowned naturalists of the century, even for a while Buffon, questioned its validity. According to these scientists, Nature always proceeds up the chain of being by minute gradations; distinct "species" are no more than a biological convenience for organizing the study of what is actually a continuous, unbroken spectrum of natural forms.[49] Since humankind was woven into this seamless fabric, it followed that no clear line separated man from the brutes:

> . . . animal life arises from this low beginning in the shell-fish, thro' innumerable species of insects, fishes, birds, and beasts to the confines of reason, where, in the dog, the monkey, and the chimpanzè [sic], it unites so closely with the lowest degree of that quality in man, that they cannot easily be distinguished from each other. From this lowest degree in the brutal Hottentot, reason, with the assistance of learning and science, advances, thro' the various stages of human understanding, which rise above each other, 'till in a Bacon, or a Newton it attains the summit.[50]

Even those naturalists who insisted on the reality of species agreed that the boundary between the most manlike apes and the "brutal Hottentot," though impassable, was scarcely visible. A few finessed the whole problem by asserting that man and ape were, in fact, but different varieties of the *same* species.[51] In 1773 Lord Monboddo declared that orang-outangs were a primitive variety of the human species that had not yet learned language.[52] Indeed, all through the century writers tended to link together black Africans and apes. Nor was this peculiar speculation confined to the learned: "Little black men" were perenially popular exhibits in traveling animal shows. The impact of all this on racial attitudes has been much discussed, but there were correlative implications for animals. The very process of pushing blacks down toward the beasts tended to bring animals closer to humanity.[53]

Wide diffusion of such biological notions, wedded to the cult of benevolence, gave birth to a conventional, almost fashionable, mode of sentimental commiseration with the sufferings of animals:[54]

> . . . the patriot's soul
> Knows not self-centered for itself to roll,
> But warms, enlightens, animates the whole:
> Its mighty orb embraces first his friends,
> His country next, then man; nor here it ends,
> But to the meanest animal descends.[55]

Not only human sympathy had descended to the animals. A few writers suggested that animals shared that archetypically human attribute, an immortal soul. In 1722 the Spy Club at Harvard debated "Whether the Souls of Brutes are Immortal," and as orthodox a divine as Bishop Butler thought it probable that brutes would enjoy an afterlife. Soame Jenyns concurred, as did the Methodist theologian Augustus Toplady.[56] John Wesley, for once, publicly agreed with Toplady, while two lesser-known clergymen devoted entire books to demonstrating the immortality of animal souls. Admittedly, despite these impressive advocates, a good many people found it hard to take seriously the vision of horses and hounds among the heavenly choir.[57]

Even if sharing Paradise with animals still seemed bizarre, concern about cruelty to beasts had become pervasive enough by midcentury to provoke widespread and serious consideration. Belletrists lamented the sufferings of brutes regularly in verse and essays.[58] William Hogarth's series of engravings, *The Four Stages of Cruelty* (1751), depicted the degeneration of a youthful animal-tormentor into a hardened murderer. Hogarth hoped thereby to aid in "correcting that barbarous treatment of animals, the very sight of which renders the streets of our metropolis so distressing to every feeling mind."[59] A similar benevolent impulse inspired a few of the more earnest among the clergy to preach "on the duty of clemency to brutes." The presumably less earnest laity settled for Charles Dibdin's light opera "Liberty Hall; or, A Test of Good Fellowship" (1795), which included a musical account of the hard times of an aging racehorse.[60]

By no means confined to a coterie of litterateurs or a band of divines, kindly feelings toward animals were becoming increasingly common among the tolerably well-educated or actively religious.[61] Quakers had always avoided inflicting unnecessary suffering, and the American Friend John Woolman, while in England, refused to travel by stagecoach because of the maltreatment of stageboys and horses. Woolman's neighbor Joshua Evans carried his Quaker kindliness as far as vegetarianism.[62] But people without any unusual bias toward compassion also displayed a new degree of affection and concern for animals. John Adams confessed that:

> . . . a Fondness for Dogs, by no means depreciates any Character in my Estimation, because many of the greatest Men have been remarkable for it; and because I think it Evidence of an honest Mind and an Heart capable of Friendship, Fidelity and Strong Attachments being the Characteristicks of that Animal.

Adams had in mind Charles Lee's notoriously unbridled enthusiasm for dogs. Lee once promised Adams that he would "love Men as well as Dogs" when he discovered "in Men as much Fidelity, Honesty and Gratitude as he daily experienced in his Dogs."[63] Another revolutionary patriot, Samuel Dexter of Massachusetts, thought well enough of his horse to pension him off in a Sudbury meadow when the animal reached retirement age.[64] And it was in that revolutionary *annus mirabilis,* 1776, that the first book-length treatment of the duty of kindness to animals appeared.

In that year, in the exalted company of the *Wealth of Nations,* the *Fragment on Government, The Decline and Fall of the Roman Empire,* and the Declaration of Independence, there was published in London a work rather less well-remembered, *A Dissertation on the Duty of Mercy and Sin of Cruelty to Brute Animals,* by the Reverend Dr. Humphrey Primatt. In keeping with his clerical calling, Dr. Primatt devoted the bulk of his book (some 245 of its 326 pages) to a *tour de force* of biblical exegesis, showing forth the scriptural foundations of our duty to animals. But the first eighty pages "endeavor to plead the cause of the Dumb

Eighteenth-century compassion outraged
(William Hogarth, *The First Stage of Cruelty*, 1751)

Creatures on the Principles of Natural Religion, Justice, Honour, and Humanity." In those pages Primatt rang the changes on virtually every intellectual tendency that had worked in the past century and a half to reshape Anglo-American attitudes toward animals.[65]

Primatt began by reminding his readers that "Love is the great Hinge upon which universal Nature turns." Benevolence should shine upon man and beast alike, for, although our mental powers may place us ahead of all other "terrestrial animals" in the "great Scale of Being," all creatures are necessary cogs in the divine machinery of Nature. Moreover, "similar nerves and organs of sensation" in human beings and beasts, as well as similar cries and groans, prove that a brute is "no less sensible of pain than a Man." Superior mental prowess gives people no more right to abuse beasts than whites have to tyrannize over blacks because their skin is different. Religious sectarianism and theological quibbling should not obscure this great moral duty of kindness to all sentient beings.[66]

All this by 1776 was unexceptionable if not commonplace. But Primatt —perhaps just because he was first to contemplate these various themes together and at length—belabored two questions that were evidently becoming sore spots in the developing complex of attitudes toward animals.

One of these foci of special concern was the very problem of pain itself. The doctrine of benevolence had from its earliest appearance emphasized sympathy with suffering. The accent, however, tended to fall on the sympathy rather than the suffering. A pitying heart, tears of compassion, the "Self-approving Joy" of the merciful, and similar subjective feelings of the empathetic observer were stressed at the expense of the objective, observed plight of the distressed fellow creature. Eighteenth-century novels drowned in tears, not blood, as any reader of Laurence Sterne is aware. But Primatt shifted his gaze from the pitying subject to the pitiful object. Although not ignoring the delights of benevolence, he tended to play down the sympathetic emotions and concentrate on the pain and misery:

> Superiority of rank or station exempts no creature from the sensibility of pain, nor does inferiority render the feelings thereof the less exquisite. Pain is pain, whether it be inflicted on man or on beast; and the creature that suffers it, whether man or beast, being sensible of the misery of it while it lasts, suffers *Evil. . . .*[67]

If pain is so dreadful, then the pointless infliction of it is a terrible wrong. Primatt therefore turned away from the traditional, positive exhortations to benevolence and launched instead a furious denunciation of its opposite: "We may pretend to what RELIGION we please; but Cruelty is ATHEISM. We may make our boast of CHRISTIANITY; but Cruelty is INFIDELITY. We may trust to our ORTHODOXY; but Cruelty is the worst of HERESIES."[68] Primatt tried to redirect the century's compassion. He picked up the doctrine of benevolence and set it down facing the other way.

In less dramatic fashion, he also began to edge away from the close kinship of people and animals. Physical similarity provided an important argument for kindness to animals, and Primatt did not neglect it. But he rejected the by now widespread belief that animals possessed something like human reason; in fact, he stressed rationality as the dividing line between us and them. He preferred the word "brute," with its connotations of dumb insensate physicality, to the more neutral "animal" in describing the objects of his compassion. To put his mind completely at rest, he also called attention to the necessity of subordination "in the natural, as in the political world": Beasts must remain "subservient" to people. Apparently, animals were growing a bit too close for the comfort even of an animal lover.[69]

To do more than mention these shifts in emphasis overstates the novelty of Primatt's outlook. The tensions between his *Dissertation* and the benevolent tradition from within which he wrote were subtle, a matter of shading, of tone, of passing quickly over one topic while lingering over another. Still, the differences were real. In the next century they would loom larger.

Meanwhile, Primatt was nowhere more orthodox than in his concern over the abuse of animals by children. Presumably little boys have for centuries satisfied their curiosity and their sadistic impulses by tormenting unlucky dogs and cats.[70] Only in the eighteenth century—due partly to new attitudes toward animals, partly to the influence of Evangelicalism at the end of the century, and perhaps partly to increased interest in child rearing as such—did this juvenile barbarity begin to disturb many adults.[71] John Locke's prescient concern became more common in the mid-1700s and took concrete form in efforts to reclaim young miscreants by preaching to them in storybooks.[72] In *Goody Two-Shoes* (1765), the first book-length work of children's fiction in English, the heroine Margery Meanwell devotes prodigious energies to succoring maltreated beasts. Probably the most popular juvenile book of the era, Sarah Kirby Trimmer's *Fabulous Histories* (published in 1786, still in print a century later), was intended to "excite compassion and tenderness" for suffering brutes. But then, the same could be said about any storybook of the period.[73]

What primarily inspired these authors, however, was not the woes of animalkind. In fact, the pastime they most often railed against was "spinning the cockchafer," in which a kind of beetle was pinned to the end of a string. Spun around rapidly, the beetle emitted the sort of loud whirring noise that children notoriously love. This victimized only an insect, and, however soft Mrs. Trimmer's heart, her head was not soft enough to think it a major cause of animal suffering. But precisely because the mildest of children delighted in this seemingly innocent amusement, the spinning 'chafer veiled a more insidious moral danger than skinning cats or mutilating dogs. Our fallen nature, as "melancholy experience" proved, could actually derive pleasure from giving pain. Toying with a beetle's presumed anguish was the first brutalizing step on the road to callousness, sadism, and—who could say?—murder:

> For who'er to a fly can barbarity show
>   Will not scruple the worst deed to do.[74]

This concern, restated, modified, elaborated, would crop up again and again in nineteenth-century propaganda for kindness to animals.

Before the end of the eighteenth century, two fresh streams of thought, merging with the cult of benevolence, presaged a sharp change in the pattern of attitudes toward animals. First in time, though less dramatic in impact, was the Utilitarian morality usually linked with Bentham's name. Though Bentham certainly carried the doctrine to its *ultima ratio*, or perhaps *reductio ad absurdum*, belief in pain and pleasure as the springs of human action antedated him and its influence radiated far beyond his circle.[75] Once morality had been reduced to a calculus of pleasure and pain (formally, as in Bentham, or loosely, as was more generally the tendency), it was hard to exclude any sentient being from the charmed circle. If, inverting John Stuart Mill's critique of Bentham, it was better to be a pig satisfied than Socrates dissatisfied, then surely the pig deserved equivalent moral and political consideration. Bentham did not shrink from this startling conclusion: "The question is not, Can they *reason*? nor, Can they *talk*? but, Can they *suffer*?"[76] As if to give Mill his answer in advance, Bentham kept "a 'beautiful pig' which used to come to him and grunt contentedly as he scratched its back and ears."[77]

Bentham's pig had reason for contentment. Its master not only drew animals under the umbrella of moral law but formalized this protection by extending them rights akin to those of people—"rights which never could have been withholden from them but by the hand of tyranny."[78] In this he joined hands with the radical writers inspired by the French Revolution. Revolutionary ardor, especially when mixed with the pervasive ethos of benevolence or the philosophic radicalism of the advanced Utilitarians, tended to spill beyond the constraining limits of the political realm or even the human race. The Rights of Man soon expanded, for some, to the Rights of Animals. An improving farmer and stockbreeder named John Lawrence, powerfully moved by the Revolution, devoted a long chapter of his 1796 treatise on the care of horses to the "Rights of Beasts."[79] But this was tepid compared to John Oswald's *Cry of Nature* (1791). Oswald ultimately died fighting for the French Republic in the Vendeé, but not before publishing an impassioned plea to his countrymen to leave off slaughtering animals and return to their ancestral diet of vegetables. Even the archradical Thomas Paine fell short of Oswald's exacting culinary standards, but Paine did briefly urge kindness to animals in the radical bible, *The Age of Reason*.[80]

Relatively few people could easily conceive of sharing their unalienable rights with cattle, and fewer still gave up the roast beef of Old England. Nevertheless, by the end of the eighteenth century, most people of the middling and upper classes almost certainly believed that simple morality forbade cruelty to animals. But this belief, though widespread, was also spread thin. For Bentham, it meant a long footnote, for Paine, a sentence or two—and these men were advanced thinkers. Brutality toward animals drew disapproval from educated Englishmen and Americans—after all, do animals not suffer just as we do?—but it seriously upset hardly anyone. If it were possible to assign relative weightings to Anglo-American values in the late 1700s, kindness to animals would surely rank very low. Only for a handful of enthusiasts did concern for animals have any emotional force behind it. Others *believed* in kind treatment of animals but hardly *cared* about it.

Moreover, even the enthusiasts often seemed disturbed by cruelty to animals more because of what it implied about people than because of what it did to their victims: Witness the tone of much juvenile literature. To be sure, after paring away the indifferent and the impure, a small core remained of people deeply and genuinely distressed by suffering animals. Yet even these devoted animal lovers had not entirely shaken off the intellectual trappings of centuries. Rank and degree might be under attack in the political order, but in the natural order the proper subordination of brutes to human dominion went unquestioned—at least consciously. The new trends in biological science brought animals close enough for sympathy. Few wanted them closer.

In a sense, animals only nibbled at the leavings of eighteenth-century humanitarianism. Still, that was a much heartier diet than their traditional fare.

II
Cruelty in
a Factory Age

In the first weeks of 1800, several gentlemen journeyed up to London from the country to confer with William Wilberforce. Their names are lost, but they reportedly knew at first hand the "inconveniences" occasioned by the "savage custom of Bull-baiting" and had determined to apply to Parliament to suppress this outrage. Wilberforce, the parliamentary field general of the Evangelical movement, was involved in a bewildering variety of crusades and bore especially heavily the burden of antislavery. He declined to take on animals, too, but he did encourage his visitors and promised to introduce their bill if no one else would. That proved unnecessary. On April 2, 1800, Sir William Pulteney, the highly respected M.P. for Shrewsbury, moved a bill to outlaw the sport of bull baiting.[1]

In the debate two weeks later Wilberforce's earnest brigade, abetted by the handful of radicals in the House of Commons, led the attack on this "cruel and inhuman" practice. Despite their efforts, the measure failed even to interest most members. In an ill-attended sitting enlivened chiefly by Tory taunts, the bill went down to defeat.[2] Wilberforce blamed Pulteney, who "argued it like a parish officer, and never once mentioned the cruelty." However flawed Pulteney's performance, his bill probably failed for more substantial reasons, since a similar measure introduced two years later by John Dent suffered a somewhat more decisive rebuff.[3]

The defeat of the bull-baiting legislation called forth a certain amount of clerical fulmination.[4] But most Englishmen who bothered to consider the question probably agreed with the *Times* editorial writer who thought the whole thing beneath the dignity of Parliament. And, although Dent briefly threatened to bring in another bill in 1805, several years actually elapsed before cruelty to animals was again attacked in Parliament.[5]

Yet the assault, when it finally came, was far more formidable than its predecessors. It was launched, not by a suspect crew of "Jacobins and Methodists" clamoring from the back benches of the House of Commons, but by an individual closely identified with the august dignity of Parliament, a man who had sat on the woolsack and governed the debates of the Lords. It aimed not to abolish a single brutal pastime but to suppress "wilful and wanton" cruelty to *all* domestic animals. On May 15, 1809, Thomas, Baron Erskine, former Lord Chancellor, rose in the House of Lords "to propose to the humane consideration" of his peers "a subject which has long occupied my attention and which I own to your lordships is very near my heart." Erskine did not exaggerate his interest. Lord Ellenborough recalled that the unhappy plight of animals had disturbed Erskine for twenty years; Erskine himself claimed that his Cruelty to Animals Bill was the only alteration in the law that he had proposed in a parliamentary career spanning three decades.[6]

Putting forward such legislation was perhaps not unexpected from a man of Erskine's inclinations. He lavished affection on a menagerie of pets, including several dogs, a goose, and two leeches; his politics were leftish Whig, leaning to radicalism of the Paine stripe in the 1790s; and he befriended Bentham.[7] More surprising was the reaction to his bill. The *Times* enthusiastically endorsed it. The Lords, worried about the practicality of so far-reaching a measure, voted to limit its scope to beasts of draught and burden but then passed it unanimously. Only one peer out of more than a hundred present even ventured to intimate an objection. When the bill went down to Commons, its manager there, Sir Charles Bunbury, expected no real opposition. He got some, though not enough to prevent a large majority voting for the second reading. However, the session was drawing to a close; there were "scarcely enough members to form a House"; and the Solicitor General voiced doubt as to the wisdom of hastily approving so novel a measure without careful consideration. The few members present apparently agreed and voted it down by a margin of ten votes.[8]

Yet Erskine had reason to be cheered by the bill's reception. So, after oiling the engines of public opinion with a printed version of his speech on the bill, the next year Erskine introduced it again. To his consternation, a "revolution . . . had been effected in their lordships' minds." Several peers sniped at the proposal, and no one but Erskine spoke in favor of it. Shaken, Erskine agreed to postpone consideration of the measure for a week. At the end of that time, unable to dislodge the opposition, he withdrew his proposal. Although he promised to bring in a more acceptable measure, that promise was never redeemed. Nor did any other champion of the brute creation emerge at Westminster. For the next decade, aside from one or two feeble and speedily quashed efforts, the issue languished in Parliament.[9]

Yet the campaign to protect animals was never confined to Parliament. Voluntary associations for moral and humanitarian reform, which had enjoyed a brief vogue around 1700, revived toward the end of the eighteenth century under Evangelical auspices.[10] These groups were typically more concerned with the reform of manners than the relief of material distress; and, although widely despised as prying busybodies trafficking with slander-for-cash informers, they flourished nonetheless on the benefactions of "serious" Christians. At least one of these pious organizations, the Society for the Suppression of Vice, founded in 1802, included animal-baiting sports among the vices to be suppressed.[11]

In the fall of 1809, an attempt was made to establish a society at Liverpool solely for the protection of animals. But its members fell to bickering over the goals of the new society, and it crumbled before it had really got under way.[12] Its collapse, however, did nothing to dampen rising interest in animals and growing concern about their treatment. Clerical denunciations of brutality to beasts flowed on unabated in what had become a routine.[13] But alongside these now traditional pronouncements, novel manifestations of sympathy for animals began to appear. Of these, the most profoundly subversive of conventional values was vegetarianism.

Advocacy of a vegetable diet was not itself new. The seventeenth-century naturalist John Ray apparently believed that man was herbivorous by nature.[14] George Cheyne, a prominent eighteenth-century physician and member of the Royal Society, cured himself of extreme obesity by strict adherence to a milk and vegetable regimen. He then spent the rest of his life preaching the virtues of vegetarianism and temperance to the genteel gourmands of Bath. Another physician, William Lambe, carried the cause into the nineteenth century. One of Lambe's converts, John Frank Newton, presided over a sort of vegetarian salon in the early 1800s. It was there that Shelley, a frequent guest, became persuaded of the merits of the "natural" diet.[15]

This school of vegetarians eschewed meat for reasons of health; the morality of killing animals for food bothered them hardly at all. Toward the end of the eighteenth century, however, a few devout though somewhat eccentric Christians came to believe that Christ's teaching of mercy forbade inflicting death on beasts merely for human pleasure. The American Quaker Joshua Evans was one of these. Around 1790, a short-lived Vermont sect, the Dorrilites, prohibited not only eating meat but also wearing apparel made at the expense of animal life.[16]

A more enduring and influential vegetarian sect appeared in England some twenty years later. William Cowherd was a Swedenborgian minister at Salford, near Manchester, who mixed chemistry, astronomy, and radical politics with his pastoral duties. He broke with the orthodox Swedenborgians in 1808 and a year later founded his own Bible Christian Church. A few months after its birth, the new sect, on both humane and medical grounds, made vegetarianism and teetotalism compulsory. Reverence for animal life was not surprising in a disciple of Swedenborg; less predictable was the success of the new sect. It survived at least into the 1880s, sent one of its members to Parliament, and—most important for the future of vegetarianism—expanded to America. William Metcalfe, whom Cowherd had converted in 1809, migrated with other Bible Christians to Philadelphia in 1817. There they started an American branch of the church, with Metcalfe as pastor. While ministering to his congregation, Metcalfe also found time to write *Abstinence from the Flesh of Animals* (1827) and other vegetarian propaganda. Together with Sylvester Graham and William Alcott, whom he steered toward vegetarianism around 1830, Metcalfe helped to found the American health food and vegetarian tradition.[17]

It is significant that Metcalfe's influence worked through his secular contacts and not his church. A vegetarianism based primarily on peculiar religious doctrines obviously limited its appeal. Of broader and more lasting import was the development of a corresponding secular vegetarianism, drawing its power not from medical or nutritional theories but directly from revulsion against animal suffering.

The first published protest on nonreligious grounds against the "murder" of animals for food came in 1791 from the pen of the British soldier John Oswald. Oswald, a native of Edinburgh who served as an army officer in America and India, worked out his vegetarian ethics while studying Hinduism. Despite its source, his vegetarianism was not religious; Oswald indeed professed atheism. His motive for shunning meat was plainly horror at the shedding of animal blood. On returning from India to England in the mid-eighties, he turned to radical pamphleteering. Soon after the outbreak of the French Revolution, he hastened to Paris and joined the Jacobin Club. Oswald died for the Revolution in 1793, along with his two sons.[18]

If the oriental inspiration of Oswald's "natural diet" was unusual among vegetarians, his radical politicking was not. The solicitor and amateur literary historian Joseph Ritson shared both sympathies. Ritson, who began as a Jacobite in the 1770s and ended as a Jacobin in the 1790s, was more consistent in matters of diet. In 1772 he read Bernard Mandeville's *Fable of the Bees,* which belittled the supposed differences between men and animals and wondered (tongue in cheek?) whether people would continue to eat animals if they stopped to ponder what they were doing.[19] This awoke Ritson to the appalling injustice of slaying our fellow animals for food, and he remained a convinced vegetarian for the rest of his life. In 1802 he produced a vegetarian tract, the mainspring of which was empathy with the pain and death of slaughtered animals, although he also cited a host of other reasons for subsisting on vegetables, ranging from the danger of flesh eaters slipping into cannibalism to the claim that "mal-regimen of diet" is the sole cause of lunacy. The following year Ritson announced that he was at work on a pamphlet proving Christ an impostor, barricaded himself in his chambers, and threatened violence to all who approached him. His friends came and took him away, and he died two weeks later.[20]

Ritson's publisher, Richard Phillips, was founder of the *Monthly Magazine,* a radical republican in politics, a purveyor of advanced democratic literature, and also a vegetarian. George Nicholson, an early popular printer in the West Midlands and a vegetarian propagandist, fitted much the same pattern as Oswald, Ritson, and Phillips.[21] Radical politics and other unorthodox notions went hand-in-glove with their vegetarianism. Ritson was a spelling reformer of the most bizarre stripe; Phillips stoutly denied the validity of the theory of gravitation. Only Ritson slipped over the edge of madness, but all of these early vegetarians dwelt, intellectually, on the fringes of English life.[22] Yet they bear noting because they reflect—exaggerated and caricatured but for that very reason more easily visible—the roots, the rationale, and the growing power of sympathy for animals.

There is no doubt that concern for animals was swelling. Only a handful of eccentrics foreswore meat, and less than half of Parliament voted to bring beasts within the shield of law. But even these unsuccessful minorities were straws in the wind signaling one of those pervasive but virtually subliminal changes in the intellectual climate that filter in quietly and are almost as elusive as the ether of nineteenth-century physicists. People were simply growing more interested in animals, and not only in protecting them from abuse. For example, in 1800 there appeared a lavishly illustrated volume called *Cynographia Brittannica,* by a man with the equally portentous name of Sydenham Teak Edwards. Edwards's book was not only the first British book about dogs to be illustrated with accurate colored plates but the first in which "the dog is regarded as worthy of attention quite apart from its role in sport." Only four years later, another "friend of that *truly* generous animal" rehearsed its merits in "a volume of Canine Anecdotes" calculated to show the "sagacity and faithful attachment" of dogs. This maudlin tome, *The General Character of the Dog,* by Joseph Taylor, was the first of a long line of purely sentimental dog books. It evidently enjoyed enough success to provoke a sequel, *Canine Gratitude,* in 1806, and, after a lapse of twenty-two years, a third volume, *Four-footed Friends* (apparently the *locus classicus* of that familiar phrase).[23]

A rather different kind of interest in animals prompted the founding of the London Zoo in the Regent's Park. Although the zoo did not actually open its gates until 1828, the project began in 1817 when Sir Thomas Stamford Raffles, the founder of Singapore, conferred with Sir Joseph Banks, president of the Royal Society, about the possibility of assembling a collection of beasts to "interest and amuse the public."[24]

The whole pattern of English attitudes toward animals, its centuries-old traditional configuration shattered, was shifting during these decades into an unfamiliar new constellation, its outlines still blurred and obscure. In America, the same transformation was under way, though it moved more slowly. Storybooks preaching kindness to animals—which English children could avoid only by illiteracy—were also common in the United States, though they were often reprints of English juvenilia. Similarly, the adult Americans most concerned about the welfare of animals apparently were those most closely in touch with England. In 1817, for example, the House of Bishops of the Episcopal Church became the first ruling body of an American denomination to denounce specifically "cruelty to the brute creation."[25]

Whatever its sources, anticruelty sentiment was growing. In the 1790s, "the unlawful rage and cruel inclination" of a "depraved" Boston horse beater provoked a grand jury into indicting him, despite the inconvenient absence of any legal ground for the charge. American judges soon began to remedy that deficiency by stretching the ancient common-law offense of public nuisance to include wanton, open brutality to animals. A New York City court warned in 1818 that it would punish miscreants for cruelty to animals "with much more satisfaction than for cruelty towards one of our own species." An occasional clerical pronouncement reinforced the temporal arm. In this climate, bull baiting and cock fighting began to retreat into the darker corners of American life, away from the reproving gaze of respectable citizens. Perhaps the unlikeliest victim of this new sensibility was Thomas Jefferson, whom Federalists reviled in 1800 for having turned Monticello into "Dogs' Misery" by his painful experiments on animals.[26]

As the revulsion, even anger, stirred by the barbarities inflicted on animals deepened around the turn of the nineteenth century, it vented itself first in efforts to suppress bull baiting. That campaign is therefore the likeliest place to begin searching for clues to the growing intensity of anticruelty sentiment.

Bull baiting was just one variant among a host of traditional sports in which animals were set against one another. Bears and badgers were also commonly baited, and, while fanciers carefully bred and trained dogs and cocks, almost any sufficiently aggressive beast might be casually pitted against another. (The entrance into general use of the terms "cockpit" and "to pit against" suggests how well-entrenched these sports were.) The accompanying gambling, drinking, and rowdy high spirits probably contributed as much to the fun of these entertainments as the excitement of the fight itself. But these rollicking good times did not look like innocent fun to everyone. The baiting sports appealed so openly to blood lust and sadism that they had early become prime targets of outraged opponents of cruelty.[27]

Of all these popular amusements, bull baiting was the most violent and bloody. (Bear baiting was perhaps equally vicious but had become rare by 1800.) The rules were elementary. A bull, securely tethered to a stake in the ground by a rope long enough to allow him freedom of movement, was set upon by dogs, often specially bred for the sport. While the enraged bull defended himself—tossing, shaking, goring unlucky attackers—the dogs tried to slip in and clamp the bull's sensitive lips or nostrils in their vise-like jaws. The skill of the attackers, the tenacity of the bull, his bellows of anguish, dogs hurtling through the air with their bellies ripped open, gallons of beer, and the clink of silver all blended in a fever-heat of uproar and excitement. No wonder mill hands and rural laborers welcomed this spectacular break in their dreary routine.

Yet bull baiting was more than merely popular in England.[28] For centuries it had ranked as an institution—a customary, almost ritual part of the annual rhythm of life in scores of villages and towns, like dancing round the Maypole or beating the parish bounds. But with the gradual disintegration of the village community, many such time-honored customs slowly slipped into disuse.[29] Bull baiting, undercut also by a growing revulsion against cruelty, not only declined but declined under a cloud. Although it managed to survive in a number of communities, including parts of London, into the nineteenth century, its advocates found themselves increasingly on the defensive.[30]

When Wilberforce and his allies attacked the sport in 1800, they were laying the axe to rotten timber—and rotten in more senses than one. The moral stench given off by bull baiting offended them mightily. The Evangelicals suspected all worldly recreations as likely to distract the mind from higher things, but the rowdy atmosphere, the guzzling and gaming surrounding bull baits offered intolerably dangerous temptations to sensual indulgence. The fact that bull baits often profaned the Sabbath made them even worse. Wilberforce himself bemoaned the sport as one of the "multiplied plague spots" on England's moral complexion, "sure indicatives" of Albion's "falling state." Defenders of the pastime claimed that the Evangelicals were merely gratifying their "busy and anxious disposition to legislate" on petty matters, "a *pruritus leges ferendi*." But the Clapham saints insisted that bull baiting "fostered every bad and barbarous principle of our nature"; its degraded aficionados were most likely to be found "staggering out of a gin shop." When one unimpressed member thought he detected a disposition "to deprive the poor of their recreations, and force them to pass their time in chaunting at conventicles," Wilberforce retorted that:

> on the contrary he wished to rescue them from the ignominious reproach cast upon them, that they were so ignorant and debased as to be fit only to enjoy the cowardly amusement of tormenting an harmless and fettered animal to death.

In the Evangelical view, the abolition of bull baiting would clear away some of the moral rubble obstructing the godly reconstruction of England.[31]

Even those less ambitious for Zion's triumph often shared this moral outrage. The sport's chief defender, Burke's influential disciple William Windham, recognized this when he accused both "Jacobins" and "Methodists" of thirsting after a reformation of manners; reformers of all stripes wished the lower orders to display "a character of greater seriousness and gravity." Richard Sheridan, whom no one would mistake for an Evangelical, complained in Parliament with bitter irony of "the hopeful lessons of morality" taught by bull baiting. Particularly in places where it had lost its centuries-old status as a village celebration, bull baiting tended to attract the dregs of the community. Probably the last regular venue for the sport in London, Tothill Fields in Westminster ("Tuttle Downs"), a public dump roamed by pigs, was labeled the *"campus martius* of blackguardism." Bull baiting appeared to many Britons a running sore of moral degeneracy.[32]

It was not the only form of cruelty to animals reprehensible on this score. Even in America, cock fighting came under attack on the same grounds. Violence and tumult were seen as somehow natural concomitants of cruelty. Lord Erskine, when urging the adoption of his first Cruelty to Animals Bill, censured severely the moral level of abusers of animals:

> These unmanly and disgusting outrages are most frequently perpetrated by the basest and most worthless; incapable, for the most part, of any reproof which can reach the mind, and who know no more of the law, than that it suffers them to indulge their savage dispositions with impunity.

So, although Evangelicals condemned immorality more earnestly than others and although bull baiting came in for much the largest share of verbal abuse, concern about the moral dangers of brutality was neither peculiar to Evangelicals nor confined to any one cruel practice.[33] For the central moral issue, cruelty itself, was not monopolized by any sect or sport. Even the opponents of animal protection laws did not minimize the awfulness of cruelty. They mocked those who would make themselves "virtuous at others' expence"; they warned that the bills would give dangerous arbitrary powers to local magistrates; they explained that cruelty was only incidental to bull baiting, not intended by the participants at all; they insisted that deliberate, serious cruelty was "rare" and "hardly-heard-of"; and they declared that, at any rate, laws could not suppress an evil curable only by changes in popular opinion and habits. But they always viewed cruelty "with detestation" and agreed that its elimination "would be a most desirable object on the part of humanity."[34]

If the foes of animal protection merely detested cruelty, the friends of animals were appalled and horrified by it. Indeed, that was why bull baiting became the first object of their outrage. Beating a balky cow or overdriving a stagecoach horse certainly distressed the animals, but the infliction of suffering was only a dubious means to an acceptable goal; it reflected selfishness and lack of charity but not a delight in cruelty itself. Bull baiting was accounted the worst of offenses against animals, not because the beasts suffered intensely (though that was an evil), but because it "arose from a desire of cruelty."[35]

What was there about deliberate cruelty to animals that was not merely repulsive but almost terrifying? One constantly recurring theme in the arguments of animal protectors suggests at least a partial answer. The reforming jurist Samuel Romilly put it succinctly: "it was well known that cruelty to animals generally led the way to cruelty to our fellow creatures."

Few carried this notion as far as the vegetarian Joseph Ritson, who averred that "those accustom'd to eat the brute, should not long abstain from the man," especially since, "when toasted or broil'd," both would taste much the same. But in less extravagant form the belief was common that suppressing cruelty to beasts would "reflect back on our sympathies to one another."[36]

Yet this answer only moves the question back one step further along the chain of reasoning. Why should people have lumped men and beasts together in this way and inferred that cruelty to one meant cruelty to the other? The eighteenth-century tradition of benevolence had taught that benevolent sympathies embraced, though in decreasing degree, first one's friends, then one's countrymen, then other peoples, then the higher animals, and finally all sentient life. The link between kindness to people and mercy to brutes was weaker in the eighteenth century than later, but it was there. So the question must now be refined into two questions. Why did sympathetic people perceive the sufferings of human beings and of lower animals as fundamentally similar? Why did the tendency to do so grow more compelling around 1800?

The answers are a tangled skein, but one thread unknots fairly easily. Eighteenth-century natural history, for reasons discussed in the previous chapter, tended to bring man and beast closer together in the order of nature (though the roots of the developments discussed here go back earlier than that century). The influence of these biological ideas widened as what had originally been the property of devotees of natural history filtered down into the general educated consciousness. Moreover, the new intimacy of *Homo sapiens* and his mute relatives was reinforced around 1800 by the evolutionary theorizing of Erasmus Darwin and Jean Baptiste Lamarck. Darwin's effusive fantasies in particular enjoyed wide popularity, though probably more as poetry than as science.[37] No tolerably well-read Englishman or American in the decades after 1800 could escape the insinuation that he was uncomfortably close kin to his horse. Probably few people really believed that human beings were quite the same as animals. If nothing else, they had immortal souls. Still, this line of thinking was disquieting, and it subtly put the relations of people and beasts on a different footing.

One generally treats one's relatives better than total strangers, so naturally the recognition of human kinship with animals fostered the belief that, while recalcitrant brutes might properly be chastised like naughty children, wanton cruelty to beasts was hardly more acceptable than brutality in the nursery.[38] But behind this straightforward statement of moral principle lurked a more troubling, though only half-formulated, fear. It emerged most directly in the debate over that most vicious of cruelties, bull baiting.

The sport's opponents tended to perceive the crowds that flocked to bull baits not merely as rowdy laborers of easy morals and unquenchable thirsts but as a dark, barbaric, primitive horde. The adjectives used over and over again to characterize the sport and its participants reveal perhaps more than their speakers intended or even realized: "degraded," "barbarous," "savage," "ferocious," "brutal," "inhuman." It is no accident that these same words could easily be applied to wild beasts. For, like the "brutal Hottentots" that Soame Jenyns had barely been able to distinguish from apes, these scarcely human savages threatened to obliterate the thin line that set men apart from beasts. If animals shared our physical nature, organ for organ and sense for sense, if beasts even possessed a modicum of reason, then the only distinguishing trait of human beings was a spiritual nature; they, unlike the brutes, could control their animality by higher capacities. But giving way to passion, especially to animalistic blood lust, put this in question. In particular, when the ungoverned impulse involved cruelty to animals themselves, the threatening issue of human animality was highlighted intolerably. Who was the man, who was the beast, and where was the difference? To acquiesce in the continuance of bull baiting meant to confound the two, to put people on a level with "the bull-dogs [which] had an instinctive desire for this sport."[39]

Who, then, could defend a practice that so obviously tended to "brutalize" behavior and "to render the human character brutal and ferocious"? Clearly, no one who really understood the nature of this savage amusement and what it implied. Wilberforce, for one, was "certain" that if Windham, "or any other member, had inquired into the subject minutely, he would no longer defend a practice which degraded human nature to a level with the brutes." Indeed, as William Smith pointed out, one of the main goals of the campaign against bull baiting was to save the common people from becoming mired "in a degraded and brutal state." Abolition of bull baiting, by helping to polish the manners and elevate the morality of the lower orders, would actually "raise them in the scale of being."[40] This was one way of neutralizing fear of the animal in man.

The theorizing of natural historians thus had ramifications far beyond the classification of *Lepidoptera*. Yet the prevailing unease over the beast potentially growling inside every person only begins to explain the startling upsurge of animal welfare activity in the decade after 1800. Why should these biological notions have drawn such wide interest and provoked such a nervous response? To be sure, any questioning of human superiority touched a raw nerve, for people have never lacked a certain *amour propre*. But the reaction to similar doubts of man's uniqueness in seventeenth-century England—or for that matter in France around 1800—was markedly milder.[41] Even allowing for the greater potency of ideas that have had a century to ferment in the public consciousness, other influences must have helped to charge the concern for animals with higher emotional intensity, with the force that carried kindness to animals from pulpit and pamphlet into Parliament.

One obvious place to look for the affective taproots of anticruelty is amid the teeming cities and whirring mills beginning to blanket the English countryside with red brick and soot. Broadly speaking, England was moving from an overwhelmingly agrarian society, where animals, if not the entire economic backbone of life, were at least the lumbar vertebrae, to an urban and industrial society, in which animals played an increasingly peripheral role. One would expect this shifting of the social and economic bedrock to touch off a sort of psychic earthslide, a sharp reorientation of attitudes toward animals. It has therefore been suggested, though rather vaguely, that the "changing outlooks and values" associated with the "whole process of 'modernization'" worked in "subtle ways" to undermine popular recreations like bull baiting.[42]

Indeed, simple geographic evidence almost requires a link between militant kindness to animals and the new England of factories and cities. The first agitation against bull baiting centered in the industrial areas around Birmingham.[43] Although little is known of the extra-Parliamentary support for Erskine's bills, when animal protection legislation was revived in the early twenties, petitions backing it came in overwhelming proportion from London, other urban areas, and the factory districts.[44] To note that city folk take a livelier interest in kindness to animals than do farming populations is no novelty; indeed, it is almost a commonplace.[45] Clearly, urbanization and industrialization in some way helped to generate the new concern for beasts. But this is merely an observation, not an explanation. Why should abandoning the farm have inclined people to embrace animals?

The monotonous throbbing of pistons and clanking of looms in the new mills suggests one key to unscrambling this riddle. The regular but spacious rhythm of agricultural life, in which bone-wearying spurts of intense labor at times like the harvest alternated with days or even weeks when laborers found little to occupy their hands—or, for that matter, the intermittent cadence of the putting-out system of manufacturing, in which workers, such as cottage-based handloom weavers, set their own pace—contrasted sharply with the gait of factory life. Now the perpetual, repetitive motion of water wheels and steam engines set the beat. If the mill hand were not at his post at six every morning, six days a week, precious capital lay idle; unit costs of production climbed; and the manufacturer's competitive position slipped. A factory manager did not have to be a Gradgrind to insist on punctuality and regularity from his employees.[46]

Blood sports were an anachronism in this world. Since their conclusion depended on the endurance of the animals, they could go on for hours and could not be ended at the stroke of a clock. Since they went hand in hand with gambling and drinking, they promoted prodigality instead of thrift, irregularity instead of sobriety and orderliness. Absenteeism, inefficiency, and dyspeptic managers were their inevitable consequence. Hallooing after terrified animals might make for contented squires, but it produced lamentable mill hands. Of all blood sports, bull baiting was the worst offender: the longest drawn-out, the rowdiest, and the drunkenest. Those who petitioned Parliament to suppress the sport, although they also expressed shock at the inhumanity and immorality of bull baiting, made no secret of their worries about the effect of the practice on "the Industry and Labour of the Persons employed" in manufacturing. This "cruel and odious" amusement, carried on "for several Days together, occasion[ed] great Stagnation in the different Works and Manufactories, to the very great Injury of the Proprietors thereof."[47] The lament of the respectable inhabitants of the manufacturing town of Dudley, near Birmingham, could have come from any factory center in the Black Country:

> . . . the Practice of baiting of Bulls, which has long prevailed in that [i.e., this] Part of the Country, to the great Disgrace of Humanity, is now grown to such a Height, as not only to injure the Morals of the People, by leading them to Habits of Idleness and Drunkenness, but also essentially to affect the regular Progress of working and carrying on the Mines and Manufactures of the Country, and thereby to occasion great Loss and Inconvenience to the Persons immediately concerned therein, as well as to the Community at large.[48]

More than simply "Loss and Inconvenience" was involved. A person who had internalized such values as prudence, regularity, and orderliness, and who held these virtues in high esteem could not help being offended by the spectacle of idle, drunken workers gaming at a bull bait.

These considerations of work discipline figured prominently in the parliamentary debates on bull baiting—too prominently, a few thought. Looking back in 1809, Lord Erskine thought that the framers of the bull-baiting bills, although "actuated by motives of humanity," unfortunately "rather obscured the principle of protection to the animals" by mixing it with these "very laudable objects of human policy."[49] What Erskine meant is strikingly illustrated by the brief rationale Pulteney put forward when he introduced the first such bill:

> The reasons in favor of such a motion as this were obvious. The practice was cruel and inhuman; it drew together idle and disorderly persons; it drew also from their occupations many who ought to be earning subsistence for themselves and families; it created many disorderly and mischievous proceedings, and furnished examples of profligacy and cruelty. In short, it was a practice which ought to be put a stop to.

William Windham, the great advocate of bull baiting, thought this absurd. The "industrious labourers" of England needed their amusements. They worked harder and longer at other times to make up the time and money expended on relaxation. He accused the foes of bull baiting of worrying not lest improvident workers ruin their families, but lest their profligacy throw them on the poor rates and thus raise the taxes of the rich. And he reminded those distressed by the "excesses to which bull-baiting gave rise" of "all the confusion and riot which horse-racing produces"; was it not really a question of whose ox was gored? Pulteney insisted that Windham did not appreciate the magnitude of the evil. Workers did not merely absent themselves for an hour or two; they "often left their work to attend on this sport for days and even weeks together, and thus consumed the money which ought to go to the support of their families."[50]

Windham's arguments would not creep meekly away when faced with the corrosive effect of bull baiting on factory discipline. For Windham and his allies did not much like the new mills. In fact, two distinct social out-looks—almost two separate societies—confronted each other in this battle. Blood sports clashed not only with the specific demands of factory work but, more generally, with the whole emerging urban-industrial style of life.[51] For one thing, the increasing density of population and buildings devoured the large open spaces required for amusements like bull baiting. The growing efficiency of communications, transportation, manufacturing, and commerce tightened the work schedules of clerks and tradesmen as well as factory workers, thus depriving them of the flexible free time needed for sports involving animals. Simply living in a large city, where the basic demands of life (going to work, getting to the market) often consumed considerable time, had a similar effect. (It is no accident that the blood sports surviving today are either those of the rich and leisured, such as fox hunting, or those that require relatively little time and space, like cock fighting. Even these flourish only in rural areas.) Moreover, the fact that people no longer got much exercise at work contributed, somewhat later in the century, to a "self-conscious pursuit of physical exercise" and a consequent shift to sports in which people rather than animals exerted themselves.[52] Apart from racing, amusements dependent on nonrational beings had little place in a rationalizing society. (The keeping of pets is an important exception. But not only is it compatible with the demands of urban life, its increasing popularity also hinged on the new attitudes toward animals discussed later.)

For this very reason, the defenders of the old order clung all the more tenaciously to animal sports. Windham and his cohorts insisted, indeed, that the cruelty of bull baiting was not really what irritated its opponents. These sham humanitarians ignored a host of genteel and aristocratic cruelties: shooting, fishing, hunting, and more. Were not "the lower orders of the people entitled to their amusements, as well as the higher"? The wealthy could "gratify themselves by a thousand different ways," while even the "harmless pleasures" of the poor were often forbidden by the magistrates. "To dance at all out of season, was to draw on their heads the rigor of unrelenting justice." Even the benighted Catholic nations allowed their poor "many more amusements" than England. Now the last straw: Parliament was asked to snatch from the lower orders the few sports left them. Windham, "shocked and scandalized," could only conclude that the campaign against bull baiting was nothing more than a bare-faced attack on the amusements of the poor. What was behind this blatant class legislation?[53]

The answer was only too clear. The foes of bull baiting aimed at nothing less than "the destruction of the old English character, by the abolition of all rural sports." In vain did supporters of the bill protest that no one "was more unwilling" than they "to encroach upon the amusements of the lower orders." Richard Sheridan exclaimed that he was a prime mover of "a project to revive old English diversions in the country." All disclaimers were to no avail. "The national character was . . . implicated in the present question." The defenders of bull baiting conjured up a vision of an older, rural England, in which hardy village lads passed their time in "manly sports and invigorating exercises." This kind of life—and bull baiting, hallowed by "more than a thousand years" of tradition, was an integral part of it—was what "made us what we were." If so, the abolition of village sports and all that they stood for would turn England into something quite different. That was just what the defenders of bull baiting feared.

Underlying their rhetoric was a powerfully appealing yet fundamentally defensive image of what England ought to be. Drawing on real elements of rural life (which gave it persuasive power), the image exaggerated, mythologized, and projected those elements larger than life into a sort of bucolic Golden Age, an idyllic, harmonious rural society of happy villagers and hearty squires, where "athletic, manly" yeomen, sturdy and tenacious as the English bulldog, devoted themselves to "manly amusements." No one (least of all the canny Windham) really believed that England was the embodiment of this dream world, but they thought England was something like it and hoped it could be more so. This vision of the old England stood in sharp contrast to what England was coming to be; indeed, fear of the new was what evoked the glorification of the old. The traditional rural culture was slipping away, and the foes of bull baiting, Windham exclaimed, were scheming to destroy it! These reformers claimed that they only wished to change the "social habits" of the lower orders to make the poor more serious and more virtuous, but such projects for the reform of manners cloaked "so many steps of a departure from the old English character."[54]

The defenders of the "old English character" groped for an explanation. Who would set out to destroy a way of life older than the memory of man? And why? Windham pointed his finger at his favorite enemies, "the Methodists and Jacobins"; the attack on bull baiting was part of a plot to prepare the people to swallow their detestable doctrines.[55] Windham's lurid picture of conspiratorial goings-on was far-fetched, but he was right—perhaps more right than he and his opponents knew—to insist that the whole rural culture, the traditional agricultural way of life, was somehow at stake in the struggle over bull baiting. Bull baiting and the life it was part of could not survive in the coming world of railway schedules, time whistles, and red-brick respectability. Windham and his cohorts knew what they stood for but never fully realized what they fought against. It was futile for them to dig in their heels in defense of village England, for their real enemies were not Methodists and Jacobins but the burgeoning cities and proliferating mills.

So both the friends and foes of bull baiting half-wittingly emphasized that the death throes of that sport were a twinge of the birth pangs of urban-industrial England. But in this respect the bull-baiting controversy was merely one example (though the clearest) of a broader development. In America, too, a new concern for animal suffering and its implications for people was growing from the transforming experience of urbanization and industrialization. No acrimonious legislative battle, as in England, suddenly illumined starkly the tangle of fears and hopes that fired an issue like bull baiting. But the social and psychic turmoil behind the emergent new sensibility was the same on both sides of the Atlantic.

The United States had no London, but it had Boston, New York, Baltimore, Philadelphia, and other towns maturing into metropolises. It had no Black Country, but it had Lowell, Manchester, Providence, and whole river valleys burgeoning into factory centers. Urbanization and industrialization, in America as in Britain, marched hand in hand with intense concern for public morality and work discipline—both flouted by brutality to animals.[56] Like their English brethren, American Evangelicals now frowned on the "too free indulgence in worldly pleasures" represented by baiting sports. But not only Evangelicals reproached "the inhuman madmen" whose cruelty to animals, of a piece with their "swearing" and "coarse language," looked disconcertingly like the behavior of literal brutes. The new order had no place for the easygoing morals and erratic habits of an earlier era. Sports like bull baiting and cock fighting—"with all the vices attending in their train"—not only "occasioned idleness, fraud, gaming" but "tended much to paralyze every effort that could be made for the increase of morality and virtue among the people." Every American who had molded himself to the values of a modernizing society, from the pioneering mill owners of the Boston Associates to their clerks and mill hands, knew that such brutal pastimes "unfitted the onlookers to function in a well ordered society." In this, America mirrored England.[57]

America, nevertheless, was not England. English industrialization was well under way in the eighteenth century. The first factories appeared in America only at the end of that century, and sustained industrial growth, most scholars now agree, dates from the 1830s. Even in Massachusetts the factories did not absorb a majority of manufacturing workers until around 1850.[58] Moreover, whereas Britain's agricultural sector soon shrank to the point where the nation depended on foreign food, the United States retained huge, indeed growing, farming regions. The farms counterbalanced the new cities and factories, slowed the revolution in national self-conceptions, and perhaps cushioned the psychological blows of modernization. A looser class structure and more democratic political habits may also have made Americans less uncomfortable with the new industrial working classes. And after all, Britain had shown the way and survived more or less intact; modernization still had its terrors, but no longer the terrors of the unknown. For all of these reasons, the new concern about animals ought to have taken hold of the American imagination somewhat later and less powerfully than it captured the English mind—as it did.

Yet Americans and Englishmen were in the same boat, weathering the same stormy sea change. The entire developing ethos of kindness to animals reflected the worries and psychological stresses of a once-agrarian society suffering the trauma of modernization.[59] The essence of that trauma was the gradual tearing of man out of the fabric of the natural world. Men and women used to working in the open air under the light of the sun now labored within high brick walls lit by flickering gas jets. No longer the urgent lowing of the cows, each known by name and disposition, but the blasts of an anonymous factory whistle called one to work. The sounds of a rural village—the twitter of birds, the distant cries of field workers, the dull clump of horses' hooves on a dirt lane, all outlined and made distinct by the prevailing stillness—were drowned by the clatter of looms, the rumble of water wheels, the hiss of steam: whistles, bumps, and yells, all absorbed in a constant stream of noise, rising and ebbing but never ceasing. Care must be taken not to exaggerate the speed of this transition; after all, horses still pulled New York's and London's loads into the twentieth century. Nor should one romanticize the lost bucolic past; the rural folk who flocked to the higher pay and regular work in the new mills certainly did not.

The point is not that the new society was better or worse than the old. There may have been little to choose between the bumpy discomfort of a stagecoach and the sooty ride of an early railway carriage, but one was pulled by real horses and the other by iron horsepower. A people who had lived on intimate terms with the natural world not just for their own lifetimes or their grandfathers' but for the lifetime of the race were now pulling away from it at an accelerating pace. It was not merely that some farm-bred individuals found themselves in factories or cities. Even for the city-born and city-bred, the character of life was changing as machines, the machine-made, and the machine-paced intruded more and more frequently. More important, for people both rural and urban, the image, the conceptualization, the "feel" of their society's and their own relationship to nature was now fractured and twisted. To find a truly comparable change in human society, one probably must go back to the Neolithic invention of agriculture. To be sure, people had in many ways tried to free their lives from nature's control for centuries, if not millennia, and their increasing success at it in Western Europe dates at least to the late Middle Ages. But it was during what is conventionally called the Industrial Revolution—in England and roughly in the century between 1750 and 1850—that the bonds between the old world and the new really snapped for the first time for a whole people.

Eventually all this meant prosperity, longer lives, and comforts undreamed of. But it also meant—especially for those most directly caught up in the sweep of change, those who lived in the cities and industrial areas—confusion and sometimes alarm at the strange new order. Even those (apparently a majority) who welcomed Progress could not help sometimes feeling a twinge of uneasiness, a touch of longing for the familiar life fading away.[60] This appeared most vividly in the striving of artists to recreate man's intimacy with the natural world. Wordsworth put "man's relationship to the natural world in which he lives" at the center of his poetry. Thoreau put it at the center of his life. What Romantic writers expressed on paper, the new schools of landscape painting said on canvas. Constable's intensely lovely yet somehow indefinably remote vision of rural England dates from this period, as does the solitary, ungraspable wilderness of Thomas Cole. Cole's "extreme tenderness of heart" flowed, in private life, into "fondness for domestic animals." With George Stubbs, who transformed English animal painting from the business of memorializing successful racehorses into the art of re-creating nature, painting took a penetrating new look at beasts.[61]

Behind this "creative search to grasp nature" lay the psychological need to come to terms with the wrenching changes wrought by factory and city. Both need and response were shared by the not-so-creative. Romantic attitudes inevitably filtered into the conventional notions of the educated classes. In 1846 the gentleman farmer Sydney George Fisher, of Philadelphia and rural Maryland, sighed to his diary:

> There are few more beautiful sights than a herd of fine cattle in a field of rich grass. Such noble & stately animals are they & of such various colours. Some are feeding—some standing motionless under the cool shade of a spreading tree—some stretched at ease on the couch of full herbage with an air of voluptuous comfort, all evidently *enjoying* the bounties of nature & the sense of existence. Half the pleasure of the country would be lost to me without the presence of the domestic animals. They are so beautiful & their habits are so interesting. Their life and nature too are such a deep mystery.

Fisher's apotheosis of his cattle was neither original in expression nor, one suspects, very deeply felt. Yet it displayed a cast of mind, an approach to the world, that had the potential to dislocate many conventional attitudes.[62]

The very notion of nature had undergone a basic transformation. What in 1700 was a rational principle (Newton's nature) had become by 1800 largely an emotional principle (Wordsworth's nature). "Nature and Reason are normally associated in the earlier part of the [eighteenth] century,

The animal observed
(George Stubbs, *Green Monkey,* 1798;
reproduced by permission of Walker Art Gallery, Liverpool, England)

Nature and feeling in the latter."[63] Now that nature was serving more and more as an escape from or at least counterpoint to the rationalization of human society, it could hardly itself remain rationality incarnate on a universal scale.

Here is where animals came in. What was more "natural" than beasts? Their paucity of reasoning power only enhanced their symbolic role as emblems of feeling. Moreover, since they exhibited many of the same emotions as people, they served as a very direct way of linking man with nature through the ties of feeling:

> And, indeed, has not nature given, to almost every creature, the same spontaneous signs of the various affections? Admire we not in other animals whatever is most eloquent in man, the tremor of desire, the tear of distress, the piercing cry of anguish, the pity-pleading look, expressions that speak the soul with a feeling which words are feeble to convey?

Animal lovers were not ashamed to admit that their campaign to protect brutes from abuse was "more the result of sentiment than of reason." Significantly, the very conceptions of "justice" and "rights" that animal lovers used to indict maltreatment of beasts rested not on the traditional foundations of divine or natural law nor even on the newer contract theory, but on feeling, on the capacity of animals to suffer.[64] The defense of animals was, indirectly, a defense of nature and of man's emotional bonds with it.

Animals were a psychological bulwark against the onslaught of modernization in another, more direct way. Few things are so closely associated with the nonfarmer's notion of rural life as animals. They served as living, tangible relics of the old agricultural way of life that people, whether removed from the farm by generations or a few years, feared to let slip away completely:

> The boy comes to the city from his father's home, he has been familiar with animals on the old farm from his earliest days, and as he rises in wealth and position how eagerly he supplies himself either with his favorite horse or his pet dog; or he must have that cow in his stable, not that her milk is any better than any other cow's but he cannot resist the old association.[65]

It was hardly accidental that early animal protectors succored almost exclusively cattle, swine, sheep, and horses: archetypal farm animals. Other creatures (dogs, for example, many thousands of which lived in visible misery in large cities) were almost wholly neglected until the latter half of the century. It becomes clear why the rising concern for animals was largely a phenomenon of cities and factory districts, seldom shared by farmers and other rural folk. By standing up for the animals that they or their ancestors had left behind, city dwellers could ease the need to feel a sense of kinship with their rural past.

There was another, nearly accidental, yet fundamental reason why concern for animals blossomed in the nineteenth century. Industrialization and urbanization greatly augmented the sense of compassion for suffering that was becoming almost second nature to most educated English and Americans. These social changes inevitably shocked, and thus stimulated, the humane feelings already astir. Whether the Industrial Revolution actually increased the sum of suffering, even of visible suffering, is irrelevant. By dislocating and destroying the old forms of society, it made people more aware of the suffering it created and even of that it did not. In doing so, it strengthened the revulsion from suffering and kindled a much deeper and more widespread sympathy with it than had characterized the eighteenth century.

Much of this compassion naturally flowed directly into attacks on the evils spawned by industrialism and urban slums. English concern for juvenile mill hands, for example, issued in a series of Factory Acts—ineffectual ones in 1802 and 1819, laws with teeth in 1833 and 1844—and protection was extended to women in 1844. Massachusetts, earliest industrialized of the American states, enacted similar laws regulating child labor in 1842, 1866, and 1867 and female labor in 1874. The other states gradually fell into line.[66] English humanitarians trying to rescue slum children from the nearly animal existence of the desperately poor inaugurated the Ragged School movement. In America, where noisome slums did not become a severe problem until after midcentury and never equaled the appalling degradation of early Victorian Manchester, the impulse to educate the poor was, until century's end, subsumed in more broadly conceived campaigns for universal public education—again, earliest in the industrialized Northeast.[67] The temperance movement, which dramatically reduced alcohol consumption on both sides of the Atlantic, was partly a response to the miseries of factory work and slum life—and specifically the drink that temporarily eased and permanently aggravated those sufferings.[68]

Other expressions of the invigorated humanitarian sensibility were less obviously linked with industrial and urban problems. English public schools remained ostentatiously untainted by industrialism; yet the wave of compassion was a major force in the Victorian reform of these schools, especially of their discipline, led by Thomas Arnold of Rugby.[69] At the other end of the social scale, the same sort of spirit appeared in the movement to humanize the penal code. In England in 1832 and again in 1837, the number of capital crimes was drastically reduced, with a consequent decline in death sentences from 1,549 in 1831 to 116 in 1838 and in executions from 52 to 6. Similar action by American legislatures was less dramatic, since American penal law had never deployed the death penalty so enthusiastically, but it manifested the same impulse. These endeavors carried over into the humanizing of less drastic punishments: England abolished the pillory in 1837 and two years earlier had appointed the first prison inspectors; American experimentation with prisons that would actually rehabilitate their inmates became world famous.[70]

The list of humanitarian reforms goes on indefinitely: the education of the blind and deaf, treatment of the mentally ill, measures to improve public health, endowment of libraries, founding of hospitals, philanthropic housing for the poor. Perhaps most storied was the drive to abolish human slavery. The heroic efforts of Wilberforce, Sharp, Clarkson, and Fowell Buxton culminated in the abolition of the British slave trade in 1807 and of slavery itself throughout the empire in 1833. In the northern states of America, a growing uneasiness with slavery, encouraged by a dedicated abolitionist movement from the 1830s, ended in a political force powerful enough to capture the presidency in 1860, send a frightened South fleeing from the Union, and finally smash slavery itself on the anvil of civil war.[71]

To call these movements simply "humanitarian" is an oversimplification of a very large order. American hostility to slavery, for example, was nourished as much by racial prejudice and distrust of the South as by sympathy for the slaves—perhaps more. Likewise, prison reform owed as much to concern for the social order as to compassion for prisoners. The Factory Acts reflected an incredible jumble of motives: the agitation of working people for relief, Tory distaste for the factory system, Evangelical enthusiasm, middle-class fear of social disorder, the Victorian apotheosis of womanhood and family life, and sympathy for the sufferings of eight-year-old factory hands.[72]

Human motives are always mixed. The point is not that a newly aroused tenderheartedness was the mainspring of any of these reforms, but that compassion was part and parcel of the inseparable bundle of worries, ideals, and emotions that powered all of them. An overwhelming Evangelical sense of duty drove the Earl of Shaftesbury in his parliamentary campaigns for lunacy reform and the Ten Hours' Bill. But it was his sympathy for the sufferings of the insane and the factory children that, at least in large part, guided his religious energies into these channels. Mary Carpenter's worship of her father impelled her to a life of idealistic sacrifice, but her compassion for the pitifully deprived children of the slums focused her efforts in Ragged Schools and reformatories. Charles Finney's revival made Theodore Dwight Weld a warrior against sin, but pity for the slave's miseries convinced him that slavery was America's greatest sin and proved the most compelling lure to draw other devout souls to the cause of abolition.[73] A deepened humane sensibility by no means suffices to explain the nineteenth century's great crusades. But it was a necessary ingredient in many, perhaps most, of them.

Concern for the sufferings of animals must be understood in this wider context. Far from an aberration, animal protection embodied the temper of the age. Wilberforce helped to lead the fight to eradicate bull baiting and later to found the Royal Society for the Prevention of Cruelty to

Animals, a venture in which his antislavery successor Thomas Fowell Buxton joined him. Shaftesbury would become vice-president of the RSPCA and president of the Society for the Protection of Animals liable to Vivisection. Samuel Gridley Howe, educator of the blind and deaf and first head of the Massachusetts Board of Charities, would serve as a director of the Massachusetts SPCA. The antislavery writers Harriet Beecher Stowe and Lydia Maria Child later lent their pens to succor animals. The great clans of reforming Quakers—the Gurneys, the Peases—found themselves involved with animal protection as naturally as temperance and antislavery.

The links ran as regularly in the other direction. The dominant figures in animal protection typically emerged from the milieu of humanitarian reform. George Angell, founder of the Massachusetts SPCA, shared a law office for fourteen years with the abolitionist leader Samuel Sewall. Caroline White, his Philadelphia counterpart, was the daughter of Thomas Earle, abolitionist lawyer and reforming journalist, and the niece of Pliny Earle, the most influential American innovator in the medical care of the insane. Frances Power Cobbe, the *grande dame* of English antivivisectionism, worked with Mary Carpenter at Red Lodge. The Baroness Burdett Coutts, probably the most influential single voice in the RSPCA in the latter half of the century, was even more celebrated for her other philanthropies, especially the Ragged Schools.

Clearly, animal protection is misunderstood if torn out of the general urge toward compassion flowering amid the urban-industrial transformation of England and America. What is not so obvious is why much of this sympathy should have been invested in animals. After all, the suffering of human beings would seem to have a prior claim. Children endured appalling lives, victims of the factory system and, all too often, of their tortured parents. In America, blacks who ate the bitter bread of slavery mutely mocked the ringing affirmations of Fourth of July orators. In this light, at first, the needs of animals might seem to fade.

They did not. They loomed larger. True, efforts were made to ease the lot of the most pitiable human sufferers. But these attempts entangled themselves in a dilemma. Either they were too feeble to have much effect, in which case consciences still ached. Or they seemed to put the social order somehow at risk and frightened off most conventionally minded people. Even the efforts to relieve children's distress violated accepted canons of family government and threatened to replace the family with the state. "So sacred was the home and family life to Victorians, that Lord Shaftesbury, archpriest of humanitarians, considered cruelty or neglect there 'of so private, internal and domestic a character, as to be beyond the reach of legislation.'"[74] Similarly, American abolitionists challenged the Union itself, and ministering effectively to the anguish of the millions sunk in the slums of the big cities and factory districts might have toppled the whole structure of society and economy. The risk was simply unthinkable.

Compassion was dammed up behind a wall of convention, ideology, and interest. A radical few breached that wall entirely. Larger but still daring minorities—sometimes swelling to narrow majorities—chipped away at it in behalf of slaves or factory children. Yet even they dared not contemplate a wholesale assault, in the teeth of the prevailing economic and moral wisdom, on the sufferings of the masses of poor. More cautious men and women would not even take the first step. But no one could turn a stopcock to shut off the now copiously flowing humane feelings, so a great many people remained trapped between sympathy and social caution. In this distressing situation, one wholly acceptable object of benevolence presented itself: the suffering beast. Kindness to animals profaned no social taboos and upset no economic applecarts, either in the theoretical systems of political economists or in the harsh daily encounter of capital and labor. When other channels were blocked, the rising tide of sympathy almost inevitably flowed to animals, especially now that they had drawn concern for other reasons. Though hardly the only unthreatening outlet for humanitarian impulses, animal protection did provide an attractive one at a time when few were available. Thus, by force of circumstance, the movement for protection of animals nourished and shaped a humane sensibility of much broader import.

Dissecting the motives of animal protectors in this analytic way violates both the integrity and confusion of their ideas. All the notions discussed so far (and presumably others as well)—some wholly explicit, some barely conscious, some even inconsistent with others—swirled inseparably in people's minds, weaving different patterns, colliding with beliefs about other matters, reshaping and reinforcing each other. The rowdiness of mill hands at a bull bait perhaps awoke fears, not only of a breakdown of factory discipline but of wider disorder following from the collapse of traditional rural society. And were such scenes not a frontal assault by the industrial world upon the animal world, putting in still greater jeopardy man's increasingly tenuous bond with nature? Likewise, the nostalgic longing for a continued close relationship with animals may have disposed people to treat less skeptically the scientific suggestions of a physical basis for the relationship. The interplay of ideas works subtly. Only speculation can now try to reweave a fabric long since torn.

Whatever the variations in design, some of the basic motifs are clear enough: a drive to reform the manners of the lower orders; a wider recognition of the kinship of people and animals, which both inspired more considerate treatment of these dumb relatives and stirred more deeply the fears of the animal element in human nature; a specific, practical concern that brutal sports threatened work discipline in the new mills; a more general psychological reaction to modernization that engendered a desire for closer intimacy with the natural world so long taken for granted; and the simple fact that humane feelings often had nowhere else to go. All of these sources, and probably others more elusive, fed the broadening and deepening concern for animals in the decades after 1800.

This concern was not, strictly speaking, new. Sympathy for the sufferings even of animals had evoked an occasional sigh in the previous century, and naturalists had gravely debated the relationship of Englishman and orang-outang. But the sympathy was little more than a sentimental attitude, and the order *Anthropomorpha* a natural philosopher's conversation piece. The twin revolutions of factory and city changed that. A once shallow compassion and a once casual interest in animals were infused with new urgency, given new resonance and relevance, and broadcast among a wider and more receptive audience. Modernization had stood midwife to a new sensibility. But no one stopped to realize it, and the infant's future, as yet, was clouded and uncertain.

III

"... This Humane and Civilizing Charity"

Attitudes are airy things, likely to be dissipated by the breezes of fashion, unless quickly embodied in the solidity of institutions. The new attitudes toward animals, so fundamental in their implications for people, could hardly remain disembodied long. Statutory protection of animals began in England in the 1820s, followed in short order by societies to ensure it. But it soon became apparent that the primary role of these organizations was less prosecutory than prophetic. Protecting beasts came second to preaching the gospel of kindness, and these societies became the most direct sounding boards of the new sensibility. Their leaders, however, made strange prophets, for we think of revolutionary ideas as borne by revolutionaries, and these prosperous merchants and aristocrats were far from that. Yet this incongruity also reveals part of the meaning behind the habits of kindness developing a century and more ago.

Before the 1820s, all efforts in England to outlaw cruelty to animals foundered on the still prevalent indifference,[1] and in America apathy forestalled even effort. In 1821, a bill was introduced in Commons "to prevent cruel and improper treatment of Cattle." Its sponsors included the Evangelical leaders William Wilberforce and Thomas Fowell Buxton, but at their head was Richard Martin, M.P. for Galway, a high-living, hard-drinking Irishman hitherto more distinguished in dueling than debate. Petitions supporting Martin's bill flooded in, mostly from London and other urban areas, and it easily passed Commons. But before Lords could act, Parliament was prorogued.[2] Undeterred, Martin submitted his bill again in 1822. With wide support from the clergy and magistracy of London, the bill sailed through both houses and on July 22 received the Royal Assent. At last the law recognized the rights of beasts.[3]

Their rights, however, were minimal. The Act extended only to "Horses, Mares, Geldings, Mules, Asses, Cows, Heifers, Steers, Oxen, Sheep, and other Cattle." Dogs and cats were left helpless. Moreover, the courts contrived to exclude the bull ("an animal of higher degree") from the meaning of the term "Cattle"; so, despite twenty years of effort, bull baiting remained legal. Nevertheless, Martin's Act was a milestone. Cruelty now incurred not merely the odium of the humane but a substantial fine and up to three months in jail. Martin undertook with relish the role of chief prosecutor, but he would soon have to share his satisfactions.[4]

Martin's Act seems to have stoked the hopes of animal lovers. In the fall of 1822, a group of Londoners, under the guiding hand of an obscure Anglican clergyman named Arthur Broome, gathered at a coffeehouse (called, inaptly enough, Old Slaughter's) to organize a society for the prevention of cruelty to animals. It lasted only long enough to call another meeting.[5]

Broome did not despair. On June 16, 1824, he assembled at Old Slaughter's another, and a remarkably diverse, collection of gentlemen to try again. Richard Martin was there, together with Wilberforce and Fowell Buxton. The Old Squire and the Evangelicals mingled with the utilitarian philosopher Sir James Mackintosh, the Tory editor William Mudford, the energetic reformer Basil Montagu, the elderly antiquarian Edmund Lodge, representatives of Commons and the Church, and—looming over all—one C. Carus Wilson, seven feet four inches tall, who used to amuse Londoners by lighting his cigar at street lamps.[6] Broome had at least demonstrated that concern for animals cut across all the usual divisions of political party, social outlook, age, and attitude.

The new Society for the Prevention of Cruelty to Animals was only a few minutes old when its parents began to quarrel about the infant's future. Some insisted that only a vigorous campaign of policework and prosecution would rid London's streets of the appalling brutality that daily assaulted the sensibilities of passersby. Others, probably a majority, feared that their SPCA *redivivus* would dig its grave again if it appeared before a dubious public as a "confederacy of prosecutors." At this time the establishment of even a government police force was still widely suspect as meddlesome, un-English, and a threat to liberty. These more cautious men preferred that prosecutions, admittedly necessary, be subordinated to propaganda. The spirit of compromise prevailed, and the meeting decided to pursue both. To Arthur Broome, elected honorary secretary, fell the task of translating this ambitious program into action.[7]

For a time the SPCA flourished in a modest way. Magistrates generally welcomed its prosecutions; its few tracts were widely circulated; several noblemen lent their prestige to its membership rolls. The optimistic Broome resigned his living to devote full time to the work. This was not to be the last exhibition of his financial ineptitude; by early 1826 the Society was hopelessly in debt. In May the governing Committee eased Broome out and named as honorary secretary *pro tem.* another of the Society's founders, Lewis Gompertz, a quondam inventor, fortunately of independent means. The SPCA had to suspend operations for two years but, under Gompertz's adroit management, it survived. By 1828 it had recovered; Broome had virtually disappeared from the scene, and Gompertz had emerged as the new leader of the Society.[8]

The SPCA now began to attract wider and more prestigious support. William A. Mackinnon, author of the recently published treatise *On Public Opinion in Great Britain and other parts of the World* and soon to be elected Tory M.P. for Dunwich, joined the governing Committee in 1828.[9] Throughout the rest of his long life, he was an untiring advocate in the lobbies of Parliament and the drawing rooms of the wealthy and influential. Perhaps it was his efforts that now helped to lure to the Society's list of patrons and patronesses the several noble names added in 1828, among which glittered that of His Royal Highness the Duke of Gloucester.[10]

The social luster and widening appeal of the SPCA were not unmixed blessings. They brought to a crisis a hitherto submerged conflict, inherent in the group since its founding. The controversy involved, in the widest sense, the policies, the tone, the very nature of the Society as a reforming organization. But the storm actually broke over the unsuspecting head of Lewis Gompertz.

Gompertz had proved an active and efficient honorary secretary. Not only had he rescued the SPCA from its financial disasters, but during his tenure the Society opened a new City office off Lombard Street and considerably expanded its activities in several directions.[11] Despite his zealous and successful stewardship, Gompertz's contemporaries could hardly have thought him the ideal man to fill a position so sensitive, so central in the public image by which the SPCA would be judged. Partly, his liabilities were social—not that his family was insignificant. His father and grandfather had been prosperous London diamond merchants; his elder brother Benjamin was a distinguished mathematician and actuary, member of the Councils of the Royal Society and the Astronomical Society. But Gompertz was a practicing Jew, and even a socially prominent Jew (Benjamin was brother-in-law to Sir Moses Montefiore) was an outsider in early nineteenth-century England, distinctly not an asset to a group trying to appeal to the men and women who set the tone of London society. But not only his Jewishness made people uneasy.

Though not exactly unbalanced, Gompertz was a little extreme in everything he did. This tinge of fanaticism showed in his two great passions, inventing and animals. Gompertz's enthusiasm for mechanical inventions (and here, perhaps, he was his brother *manqué*) resulted in an astonishing flood of devices, which his biographer tactfully describes as "ingenious rather than practical." Gompertz did invent the expanding chuck, but most of his creations were of a character more like his reflecting fortress, which was supposed to bounce attackers' cannon balls back at them. His zeal for animals likewise showed little concern for practicality. He held it wrong to put an animal to any use not directly beneficial to the beast itself and, in keeping with this tenet, refused to eat animal food (including eggs and milk) or to ride in a carriage. Such high-minded consistency was doubtless laudable, but it may have made prospective SPCA members wonder what they were getting into. Perhaps his colleagues may be forgiven for sometimes doubting whether Gompertz's dedication and hard work were worth the price.[12]

These doubts erupted with sudden violence in 1831. The obvious question is Why not earlier? However, existing records are too sparse to yield an answer. At any rate, a physician named John Ludd Fenner had joined the SPCA shortly after its founding. But a year or two later he resigned to form his own animal protection society. This soon collapsed, and Fenner returned to the SPCA, where he eventually became a member of the governing committee.[13] A clergyman named Thomas Greenwood now entered the picture. Perhaps owing to his influence, Fenner fell out with Gompertz; in June 1831 Fenner and Greenwood left the SPCA and founded their own Association for Promoting Rational Humanity toward the Animal Creation (the title a jibe at the seeming irrationalities of Gompertz).[14]

The dissidents concentrated their fire against the SPCA and Gompertz personally along two main lines. First, they resurrected the hoary but still powerful arguments against extensive use of "informers" (salaried inspectors) to prosecute offenders against Martin's Act. The Rational Humanity group had no objection to occasional condign punishment of "notorious offenders." But the SPCA, they claimed, "vindictively" persecuted unfortunates whose poverty and ignorance led them willy-nilly into cruelty. Humane education, not jail, was the cure for brutality of this stamp. "Mr. Martin's Club for the patronizing of informers" did little good for the suffering beasts and only succeeded in bringing the law into disrepute. In fact, some evidence does suggest that magistrates were growing uneasy with the SPCA's prosecutorial policy.[15]

Most of Fenner and Greenwood's slings and arrows, however, aimed at an easier target: the peculiarities of Lewis Gompertz. Although that gentleman had not used his office to thrust his personal views on the SPCA, his *Moral Inquiries* (1824) had laid his eccentric opinions open for all to marvel at. Greenwood lambasted Gompertz for adhering to "the strange and long-exploded doctrines of Pythagoras, which prohibited the eating of flesh" and did his best to make his unhappy victim an object of ridicule. Nor did he stop there. He questioned whether the SPCA ought to be led by "an individual who is not a christian." Gompertz was furious. He insisted that he had kept his personal opinions to himself; that, even though a Jew, he had zealously enlisted the cooperation of the Christian clergy; and that, far from "persecuting" the poor and ignorant, the SPCA brought to book "rich as well as poor delinquents" with impartial rigor.[16]

The SPCA Committee tactfully ignored the abuse hurled its own way and tried to smooth over the "misunderstanding" between Gompertz and the Fenner-Greenwood faction. After private efforts at reconciliation failed, the Committee arranged a public meeting at which the warring parties could air their views "and also to consider how far it may be advisable to remodel the Society." This stormy meeting ended with a resolution that managed, at one and the same time, to express confidence in Gompertz, declare neutrality in his quarrel with Fenner, and offer union to Fenner's Association.[17]

The attempt at merger came to nothing, at least formally. The Association for Promoting Rational Humanity simply faded away after a year or two, and the SPCA absorbed most of its active members. But Lewis Gompertz had won a Pyrrhic victory. A scant few months after the SPCA had voted confidence in him, control of the Society's financial affairs and at least partial management of its propaganda were turned over to a newcomer, Robert Batson. Gompertz remained honorary secretary but became more and more a figurehead. In the summer of 1832 he resigned his office. Although he remained on the Committee, he grew increasingly disillusioned with the SPCA.[18]

He had reason for dissatisfaction. In June 1832 the SPCA adopted a declaration that "the proceedings of this Society are entirely based on the Christian Faith, and on Christian Principles."[19] In September the Committee dealt with Fenner and Greenwood's other chief complaint. To obviate the "danger . . . that prosecution should be more attended to than prevention of Cruelty," the SPCA inspectorate was suspended, and the Committee pledged to bring charges only against "flagrant" offenders and to concentrate instead on educational measures. Gompertz was beaten.[20]

His defeat meant schism. Gompertz did not even wait for the SPCA formally to abolish its inspectorate. In August 1832, with his dissatisfied supporters, Gompertz founded the Animals' Friend Society. The new organization took over the SPCA's old offices, its inspectors, and apparently a substantial minority of its paying members. It even claimed the allegiance of Richard Martin, now in refuge at Boulogne from financial embarrassments. The Animals' Friend Society insisted that it alone adhered faithfully to the original SPCA program. But purity was not enough. After a few solvent years, the AFS found that it could no longer compete successfully with the more respectable SPCA for the largesse of monied animal lovers. The financially weakened society was then racked with dissension, and the last printed AFS report confessed moribundity. Gompertz himself died in 1861. The scattered remnants of his group finally rejoined his old enemies in 1864.[21]

The SPCA's tactful, roundabout purge of Gompertz and his supporters proved a huge success. Freed of the incubus of a vegetarian Jew as its chief—and blandly refusing even to notice his attacks—the SPCA flourished. Between 1832 and 1834 a host of new faces appeared on the Committee, most of whom would serve extended terms, nearly half more than twenty years each. A galaxy of noble patrons and patronesses glittered in the annual reports. In 1835 this list was crowned by the Princess Victoria and her mother, the Duchess of Kent. The enormously wealthy Quaker banker Samuel Gurney accepted the office of treasurer in 1832 (and held it until 1856, when his son succeeded him).[22]

Along with the Society's prestige, its income began to rise steadily in the early thirties; by 1838 the Society had an endowment of more than 1800 pounds. A move into new offices in Exeter Hall, the London capitol of the benevolent empire, marked in another way the SPCA's rising status. By 1837 the Society had grown so active that it had to hire an assistant secretary to cope with "the increase of business." The final seal of its eminence came in 1840: henceforth, by Queen Victoria's command, the SPCA was to be styled the Royal Society for the Prevention of Cruelty to Animals.[23]

How can this meteoric success and wide appeal be accounted for? More precisely, why did the Society's 1832 revolution in policy reap such remarkable rewards? The welter of accusations and countercharges that swirled around the unfortunate head of Lewis Gompertz holds the answer to that question. The fundamental issue at stake in that battle was the still plastic character of the SPCA. Was it to be a radical ginger group, a little clique of dissidents and critics? Or a well-mannered, well-tailored organization making a quiet conservative appeal to the wealthy and high-born and, through them, to the respectable middle classes? In short, would it campaign for animals by shouting itself hoarse from the sidelines or by insinuating itself into the drawing rooms of the Establishment?

The controversial issue of prosecution centered on this same question. An organization striving for social acceptance could ill afford the opprobrium heaped on "spies" and "informers." Moreover, if the Society intended to woo the allegiance of the elite, spending money to prosecute the poor (or, even worse, the rich) was simply a misallocation of resources —much better to channel funds into more visible and less controversial activities.

Finally, since the SPCA strategy envisioned kindness slowly trickling down to the lower orders from their increasingly humane superiors, the obvious tactic was some sort of educative process, not fines and jail terms. The well-mannered purge of Gompertz and the ensuing exodus of his followers put the organization on just this road. Although prosecutions soon resumed as paid police became familiar and respectable, the Society continued to concentrate on various programs of education. Hundreds of thousands of tracts descended on British workingmen, and in 1860 the RSPCA assembled 3,000 cab and omnibus drivers to watch a demonstration by the American horse trainer Rarey. A special school fund subsidized from 1837 a similar assault on the rising generation through essay contests, children's books, hortatory engravings, and revised editions of standard schoolbooks. By adopting such methods, the SPCA had chosen to make its appeal to the "respectable," to the conventionally minded members of the middle and upper classes. To judge from the Society's success, the respectable were ready to listen.[24]

By the time that royal approbation had certified the prestige of the new sensibility in England, wider interest in animals was also astir across the Atlantic. In the most widely used American textbook of ethics, *The Elements of Moral Science* (1837), Francis Wayland decreed that "We are forbidden to treat [animals] unkindly on any pretense, or for any reason." The New York legislature had anticipated him in 1828 by making cruelty to horses, sheep, and cattle a misdemeanor. Massachusetts enacted a similar law in 1835, followed by Connecticut and Wisconsin in 1838. Before the Civil War, eighteen states and territories had adopted anticruelty statutes, though one should not make too much of these laws. Clearly in the first two states, perhaps in others, the statutes resulted from general revisions of the state code, not from any outcry against cruelty, and they drew on British example. Moreover, they were seldom enforced. Still, legislators now believed that cruelty ought to be illegal, and that alone evidenced shifting values.[25]

More significantly, a growing number of animal lovers began to speak out openly and vigorously. In 1835 an Albany publisher brought out a stout, pocket-sized anthology of exhortations to kindness called *The Spirit of Humanity*. The book was dedicated to "the LONDON SOCIETIES FOR PREVENTING CRUELTY TO ANIMALS," and most of the extracts came from British sources. But many were culled from native newspapers and magazines. Clearly, the sufferings of animals had begun to disturb more and more Americans.[26] In Boston in 1837 the Rev. Charles Lowell preached an entire sermon against cruelty to brutes. Nine years later a minor tempest boiled in the Boston *Transcript* over truckmen abusing their horses. One outraged citizen exploded that "such scenes . . . have made me shudder and my blood run cold" and promised "to spend my time and money in any feasible way" to bring the perpetrators of "such outrages to punishment." The next year the eminent Boston physician John Collins Warren addressed the Legislative Agricultural Society urging kinder treatment of horses. His efforts were seconded that same year by John H. Dexter's pamphlet, *A Plea for the Horse*. In 1855 the Secretary of the Massachusetts Board of Agriculture, Charles Flint, issued a circular encouraging protection of small birds, not merely in the farmer's own interest but in the bird's interest, too.[27] All of these scattered advocates were still only unorganized individuals, but their swelling numbers were approaching a critical mass.

In the summer of 1860, the RSPCA received a letter from the United States. S. Morris Waln, a wealthy Philadelphian, had read in the *Times* an account of the Society's annual meeting and wrote "asking to be supplied with some information in order to facilitate the good example of the Society being followed" in America. The Civil War interrupted Waln's plans. A few months after the war's end another Philadelphian, a newspaper executive named M. Richards Mucklé, tried to interest his friends in organizing an animal protection society. In the aftermath of the war he could stir up little enthusiasm, so he temporarily shelved the idea.[28] But in New York similar efforts by a man named Henry Bergh moved forward.

The son of Christian Bergh, a rich New York shipbuilder and active Jackson Democrat, Henry Bergh was born in 1813.[29] Tall, gaunt, erect, with a long, cadaverous, equine face, Bergh struck even his friends as extraordinarily peculiar in appearance. Yet his unostentatious good taste, minute attention to dress, total conventionality of habit, and quiet gentlemanly manner somehow managed to transform his striking ugliness into a sort of compelling dignity, reinforced by an utter absence of humor. By his middle years, Bergh's powerful sense of his own dignity had ossified into sheer autocratic hardness. Yet this chill aloofness was nothing more than a carapace to shield from the blows of an uncaring world a personality easily bruised. Sometimes, on returning home at the end of the day, he locked himself in his bedroom and *"enjoyed a jolly good cry."*[30]

After leaving Columbia College without a degree and dabbling in the family shipbuilding business for a few years, Bergh finally settled down to a life of uninterrupted leisure. A legacy of several hundred thousand dollars enabled him to travel extensively in Europe. In 1863, finally weary of doing nothing, he obtained appointment as Secretary of the American legation in St. Petersburg. Neither the climate nor the American minister agreed with him, and in October 1864 he resigned. The Russian interlude was not, however, without significance: Bergh was "horrified" at the Russians' barbarous treatment of beasts. By November he was back in the more congenial atmosphere of London, and the following months were played out in a round of social engagements. During the spring of 1865 Bergh attended the RSPCA's annual meeting and chatted with Lord Harrowby, the Society's president. At the time Bergh thought little of it; the occasion found no place in his journal. In early June he embarked for home.[31]

Now the wheels began to turn in his idle mind. The itch to do something, which he had vainly tried to appease in the diplomatic service, had not faded. At some point in the summer or fall of 1865, his memories of abused brutes in St. Petersburg aligned with that spring afternoon at the RSPCA, and Bergh's future fell into place. He would bring the SPCA idea to

America; he would rid New York of the human brutes who daily bruised his tender sensibilities by their cruelty to animals.

Oddly, Bergh's softer feelings had never before extended to animals. He had no use for dogs, hated cats, and (contrary to a legend concocted apparently by desperate hagiographers) rarely laid his hand on a horse "in caress however slight." However, his personal distaste for animals did not mean that he liked to see them abused, and his "quivering self-consciousness" made him sensitive to the sight of any suffering.[32]

The social *éclat* of the RSPCA also appealed to Bergh. Like many Americans of his background, he was something of a snob and a thoroughgoing Anglophile. The Society, patronized by a dazzling array of English peers, was positively "smart," which undoubtedly tickled Bergh's sense of *noblesse.* Importing the idea demanded no unseemly trafficking with the *ignobile vulgus;* he could transcend his useless past and make his mark without having to stoop to conquer.

A series of anticruelty exposés in *Leslie's Illustrated Newspaper* perhaps steeled Bergh's resolve. He made the rounds of New York's elite soliciting promises of support for his proposed society. A hundred people enlisted, including the mayor, the president of the Board of Police, Peter Cooper, August Belmont, John Jacob Astor, Jr., Hamilton Fish, George Bancroft, Horace Greeley, and dozens of their sort. In early February, at a crowded Clinton Hall meeting of the American Geographical and Statistical Society, Bergh delivered a paper on "Statistics Relating to the Cruelties Practiced on Animals," with "a view to founding a society for their protection." After denouncing a mass of everyday cruelties, Bergh explained the workings of the RSPCA and urged New Yorkers to follow its example.[33]

He next set his influential allies to work. Mayor John T. Hoffman (soon to be governor), the iron magnate Peter Cooper, and the Rev. Henry Bellows (the Unitarian "pope") petitioned the legislature for an act of incorporation. Bergh himself went to Albany, armed with his list of wealthy backers. On April 10, 1866, the legislature passed the necessary act of incorporation, and on April 19 added a new anticruelty statute, drafted by Bergh himself with the aid of Ezra Cornell and Gideon Tucker. Three days later the American Society for the Prevention of Cruelty to Animals (ASPCA) was formally organized at another meeting in Clinton Hall. By-laws drawn up by its directors in early May set dues high at ten dollars per year (women could become "patronesses" for five): President Bergh and his cohorts did not welcome the common man.[34]

Exclusivity did no harm among those whose support Bergh courted. As early as May 1866, he exulted that "already it is *fashionable to defend the friendless dumb brute.*" New York's newspapers almost unanimously supported the passage of Bergh's anticruelty law, and, though sometimes critical of his zeal, the press generally continued to support him.[35] Backing came in more tangible ways as well. The ASPCA spent the impressive sum of $5,047 during its first year, yet its income still exceeded expenses by almost $2,500. In May 1867 a delighted Bergh reported that "unlimited sympathy and substantial aid are being showered on this humane and civilizing charity by every degree of respectable Society."[36]

Despite its name, the ASPCA was only a New York City organization, but success in New York could hardly fail to find imitators elsewhere. Still, the reaction to the new society was extraordinary: Bergh had unwittingly touched a match to a trail of kerosene. Word of his work gave the final push to others already on the brink of action elsewhere. Less than a week after the organization of the new group, M. Richards Mucklé resurrected his plans for a Philadelphia animal protection society and inserted in the *Evening Bulletin* a call to like-minded Philadelphians. That same day, April 27, the Philadelphia *Ledger* announced an offer by S. Morris Waln to subscribe $10,000 to such a society. Within a matter of days Mucklé was in touch with Bergh. For months the ASPCA spouted advice on organization, tactics, public relations; more important, it passed along the name of another Philadelphian interested in the cause, Caroline Earle White.[37]

The daughter of Thomas Earle, an eminent Quaker lawyer and abolitionist politician, Caroline Earle grew up accustomed to wealth and social position, if also to a certain degree of unorthodoxy in opinion. In 1856, at the age of twenty-three, she married Richard P. White, scion of "one of the most respected Catholic Tory families of Ireland." The next year she converted to her husband's faith and to a career as a bustling Catholic laywoman. An active clubwoman, she also found time to write romantic fiction and travel books. From her husband she learned of the RSPCA, and she had apparently given thought to extending its work to America when the Civil War called a halt to less urgent endeavors. But in 1866, having heard of Bergh, she made a point of stopping off to see him on her way to her summerhouse in Nantucket.[38]

That fall, armed with Bergh's advice, White returned home to enlist other wealthy Philadelphians in the cause. As Bergh had done in New York, she canvassed the city's elite, collecting pledges of support. Somehow she missed both Mucklé's and Waln's newspaper advertisements and knew nothing of their work until the ASPCA brought them together in early 1867. After a preliminary meeting in May and an infusion of $6,000 from Waln, the Pennsylvania Society for the Prevention of Cruelty to Animals (PSPCA) was formally organized on June 21. Business left Mucklé and Waln too little time to run the new society, so Dr. Wilson C. Swann became president. Caroline Earle White had probably done more than anyone else to launch the enterprise, but her cautious and proper colleagues blanched at the thought of a female on the Board of Managers; her husband was elected as a surrogate.[39]

The heat of summer, when those who could afford it fled the city, retarded recruiting; however, by early September the PSPCA had enrolled

231 members. That number grew, despite the postwar recession, to 384 by December. In April of 1868 the Pennsylvania legislature granted a charter. In January 1869 the Society sponsored a lecture by Henry Bergh and turned out 2,000 people to hear him. That year the PSPCA's income approached $6,000, and by 1870 membership exceeded 600. The Pennsylvania Society had not mushroomed as rapidly as the ASPCA, but if success came less spectacularly than Bergh's, it was equally solid.[40]

Boston eclipsed both. As early as December 1866 the ASPCA had encouraged the temperance reformer Dio Lewis to organize a society there.[41] But in the summer of 1867 Bergh enlisted a more promising recruit: Emily Appleton. The daughter of the Dr. Warren who had preached kindness to horses twenty years earlier and the wife of William Appleton, son of one of the wealthiest merchants in Boston, she brought to the task both a deep concern for animals and the social position that Bergh thought essential. He urged her on, and soon teacups were tinkling on Beacon Hill. By late October she had amassed an "array of illustrious names" willing to underwrite a Boston SPCA. Early in 1868, with ninety influential supporters, she filed with the legislature an act of incorporation. At that point chance took a hand.[42]

On February 24 the Boston *Daily Advertiser* reported the death of two horses in an exhausting cross-country race. The story caught the eye of a prosperous middle-aged lawyer named George Angell. Cruelty to animals had disturbed him for years, and he had heard of Bergh's work; this latest atrocity finally moved him to action. The next day's *Advertiser* printed a letter from Angell pleading for allies to fight cruelty. Within hours Mrs. Appleton came to his office, and Angell immediately took charge. He had already written Bergh for advice; now he redrafted the act of incorporation and appealed for funds in the Boston papers. On March 23, the legislature acted, and Angell promptly called an organizational meeting. On March 31, in a hall above his law office, some forty persons founded the Massachusetts Society for the Prevention of Cruelty to Animals (MSPCA). To serve with the energetic President Angell (whom Bergh, much impressed, thought "raised by inspiration" for the job), the members elected "some of the best-known and most distinguished names of Boston" as directors. But, as in Philadelphia, the female co-founder was not among them; she, too, was honored *in absentia* by giving her husband a seat on the board. Indeed Angell reported that "Mrs. Appleton did not think it proper to even attend the meeting at which our society was organized . . ."[43]

Immediately Angell, aided by Massachusetts Chief Justice George Tyler Bigelow, an MSPCA director, drafted a new anticruelty law. The legislature, perhaps intimidated by this herd of Brahmins, added it to the statute book before mid-May. Meanwhile, Angell's influence had enabled him to borrow seventeen Boston policemen for three weeks in order to canvass the entire city; they raised $13,000 and enlisted more than 1,500 members.

Angell also recruited a hundred prominent honorary vice-presidents, including the governor and lieutenant governor, Saltonstalls, Choates, Peabodies, and Ralph Waldo Emerson. The state's best-known reformer, Samuel Gridley Howe, then head of the Board of State Charities, escaped a vice-presidency only because he was already a director. All of this left Bergh agape: Angell's whirlwind campaign "is a veritable prodigy."[44]

Angell did not hoard the Society's infant riches. On June 2, 1868, the MSPCA published two hundred thousand copies of a new monthly magazine, *Our Dumb Animals*. Although two or three animal protection periodicals had limped through brief careers earlier in the century, the scale and sheer audacity of Angell's venture marked a new departure in humane propaganda.[45] The city police, again pressed into service, delivered a copy to almost every house in Boston. Bergh thought *Our Dumb Animals* "glorious" and told Angell that the New York papers were now calling him "an Angell of mercy." Soon the new journal claimed—without undue exaggeration—a monthly readership of fifty to a hundred thousand. The MSPCA did not have to rely solely on its own publicity. Angell reported that the Massachusetts newspapers from the beginning had stood "ready to commend our general purposes and our paper, and to call special attention to any special effort we were making." And if its excellent press relations ever failed it, by mid-1869 the Society had its own agents in seventy cities and towns in all parts of the Commonwealth. During 1871-72 the MSPCA raised the stunning sum of almost $40,000; still more impressive, the Society needed every penny.[46]

The hero of this rise to riches was George Angell, whose own life read like a Horatio Alger tale. Born in 1823, the son of a small-town Baptist pastor in central Massachusetts, Angell was not yet four when his father died, leaving widow and child nearly destitute. His mother, an intensely religious woman, taught school to provide for George, who was farmed out to various friends and relatives in rural New England for most of his childhood. After an apprenticeship in a Boston dry goods emporium in his early teens, George finally entered Dartmouth and, by scrimping and part-time work, got his degree in 1846. Thereupon he took the stage to Boston where, aided by a lawyer uncle and a schoolteaching job, he studied law. Admitted to the bar at the end of 1851, he went into partnership with Samuel Sewall, the abolitionist politician. Their association lasted fourteen years, after which Angell struck off on his own. Success came quickly: Angell's single-minded devotion to business made him rich before he reached fifty. By 1875 he could afford to abandon his practice to devote full time to his work for animals.[47]

The contrast between Angell's career and those of the other two leading pioneers of American animal protection could hardly be more striking. Henry Bergh and Caroline White knew only wealth, luxury, and privilege from cradle to grave. Angell spent his youth clinging to the tattered fringes of respectability, hanging on only by a precarious fingertip grip above the pit wherein the Victorian Age confined the ruined once-bourgeois to live out their shameful lives. His hard-earned wealth never erased the memory of his poverty or of his steel-willed struggle to escape it. Yet, in his attitudes toward wealth and class, he emerged almost a caricature of his two co-founders born to the purple. Bergh and White, because their lives had shown them nothing else, presumed without self-consciousness that the monied aristocracy should rightfully dominate. But Angell's hardscrabble ascent had pounded into him an almost religious awe of wealth, especially of unearned riches handed down from father to son. That awe may help to account for his fawning on the English upper classes, a tendency that immediately strikes the reader of Angell's accounts of visits to England. Even more, his climb had engendered a ravenous sense of insecurity, constantly demanding to be fed with public attention. Hence perhaps grew the roots of his insatiable hunger for work, for achievement, for self-advertisement.[48]

In another man, in another post, these traits might have proved crippling. But they were key to Angell's triumphant captaincy of the MSPCA. His itch to move among the rich and well-born impelled him to pack the Society's leadership with people of wealth and position—and thus of power and influence. His need to prove himself, coupled with his habits of untiring industry, drove him restlessly to pile success upon success. His compulsion and genius for self-advertisement made him one of the most versatile publicists of his age and kept not only himself but his cause in the forefront of public attention.

Caroline White did not find the same satisfactions in the PSPCA. Her sex barred her from active leadership, a role she deserved on every ground. Morris Waln, elected PSPCA president in 1869, sympathized but apparently felt—or thought the community did—that women had no business running an organization that included males. He proposed instead the creation of a Women's Branch of the PSPCA. Mrs. White leapt at the idea, and on April 14, 1869, at a meeting in Waln's home, the Women's Branch was organized. The thirty women there elected Mrs. White president (a post she was to hold for almost half a century) and then chose a slate of officers who would have been welcome in the most elite Philadelphia drawing room and whose collective assets would have warmed a banker's heart.[49]

Those attributes did the Women's SPCA no harm.[50] Barely a month after its founding, the WSPCA had already persuaded the mayor of Philadelphia to erect more merciful facilities for killing stray dogs; before its second birthday it had its own animal shelter, which had entirely taken over from the city the collection and disposal of strays.[51] Even before the shelter was begun, the women had hired a full-time agent to patrol the streets and had published 2,500 "little books" for children, as well as thousands of picture cards to distribute in schools. Nearly four hundred women joined before the Society was a year old, and its income approached $10,000 in its second year. It was typical of the Society's shrewd management that $2,000 of that $10,000 was invested. In fact, one of the WSPCA's first decisions was to invest all donations over five dollars in a permanent endowment.[52] Caroline White had proved she could match the Philadelphia men in members and dollars. In drive and enthusiasm—and probably in concrete achievements—the genteel ladies had outclassed them.

New York, Philadelphia, and Boston gave birth to the American animal protection movement, and they remained its strongholds and guiding lights. But other cities quickly joined in; here was an idea whose time had come. A Buffalo "branch" of the ASPCA (actually wholly independent) was organized as early as 1867. Efforts in San Francisco resulted in 1868 in the first Society outside the Northeast. In 1869 SPCAs appeared in Albany, Baltimore, Bangor, Davenport, Newark, and—curiously—Fishkill, New York. In the next two years eighteen more societies were organized, and by 1874 scarcely a major city outside the South lacked one.[53]

The high hopes that launched these groups did not always carry them through more than a year or two, but most survived. As in England, the societies helped to enforce the anticruelty laws by prosecuting blatant violators—sometimes spectacularly, as in Henry Bergh's assault on "Kit" Burns, New York's impresario of blood sports. But most of their efforts, like the RSPCA's, went toward education in one form or another. Angell lectured to audiences ranging from the Philadelphia police to the school-teachers, "white and colored," of the District of Columbia. The Philadelphia ladies handed out children's books and organized juvenile humane societies. And Boston's young filled the Music Hall to hear the governor admire their literary efforts in behalf of animals. In 1881 the RSPCA's *Animal World* observed half-enviously that "our cause has made more progress in the United States during fifteen years, than in England during fifty years."[54]

The *Animal World's* estimate was perhaps exaggerated. But it was certainly true that "our cause" had progressed among the same sort of people in the United States as in England. The wealthy and influential supplied its leaders, the solidly middle-class its followers. The spread of mass education, the increase in working-class standards of living, and the absorption of an ever higher proportion of the labor force in white-collar jobs since the nineteenth century have by no means obliterated class distinctions. But these changes have enormously reduced the self-consciousness typical of the middle classes of the Victorian era. It was these people—status conscious, sober and respectable, deferential to wealth and success, and many fewer in number than the masses of poor and near-poor who surrounded them—who were the anonymous force behind the animal protection movement.[55] There is no evidence of a significant presence of manual workers or artisans in any SPCA activity during the nineteenth century, with the exception of a few public meetings specially drummed up to enlighten-while-entertaining teamsters, cab drivers, and the like. Even the SPCA leaders, often distinctly upper-class, typically embodied the virtues of middle-class respectability—with the possible exception of Henry Bergh who, if he himself singularly failed to exhibit the Protestant Ethic, at least insisted that Irish immigrants should.

Kindness to animals must have carried an important message to the Victorian middle classes. Moreover, it obviously conveyed this in a peculiarly palatable way. Another road had been open to animal protectors: the radicalism embraced by some other reformers, abolitionists in America and Chartists in England. But SPCA's had deliberately chosen to appeal to the conventional and respectable. The RSPCA early expelled the unconventional; its American counterparts simply avoided them. The societies' swelling membership rolls and fat treasuries vindicated the prudence of their choice but did not explain the secret of their appeal. To understand this, one must examine the special needs of their constituency.

The anxieties stirred up by the kinship of people and brutes, given an added edge by the industrial transformation of England and America, disturbed a great many people. But not all who were slightly troubled by these semi-conscious worries were bothered enough to embrace the radical answers of vegetarians or even to associate themselves with an organization of dubious social standing. In short, most people were not ready for Lewis Gompertz. Still, their concern, though mild, was real. To them the SPCA's—obviously safe; offensive to almost no one; even bearing (second-hand from their prominent supporters) a certain social *ton;* and genuinely effective in a slow, careful way—offered a soothing anodyne. Animal protection served as a sort of intellectual pacifier for the thousands of literate individuals who now had to learn to live with the idea of the cousinhood of man and brute and, though not deeply disturbed by that notion, needed a little reassurance. To meet this need, SPCAs had to have a respectable image and wide appeal.

This image, together with the emphasis on education in kindness, enabled the societies to soothe other fears as well. Industrialization and urbanization raised a troop of worries to haunt the men and women who lived through the process.[56] Most of these anxieties really had nothing to do with animals. Yet even for some of these, the animal protection movement provided a kind of therapy.

Not only workers, for example, were disturbed by the conditions of life in the factory districts and urban slums. But people near the top of the economic pyramid were often barred by ideology and self-interest from protesting the grinding hours and squalid homes that industrialism imposed on those at the bottom. The laissez-faire teachings of political economy inhibited all but the most flexible and imaginative members of the commercial-industrial middle and upper classes from questioning the justice (or at least necessity) of the factory system. And, ideology aside, people who lived relatively well on the sweat of factory workers could hardly be expected to denounce the very system that profited them. Yet not even the iron laws of Manchester ideology and the survival of the fittest, reassuring though they were, could wholly quell an occasional upsurge of guilt. Was it right, was it Christian, to live so handsomely off those who lived so poorly? Still, it was not merely wrong but futile to transgress the natural laws by which the economy reliably yielded the comforts of life.

This was a distressing psychological dilemma, and one cannot help wondering whether animals offered one way out. Might not some of these uneasy Victorians have subconsciously transferred their charitable impulses from the forbidden ground of the working-class slums to a more acceptable object of benevolence? And what more acceptable than suffering animalkind? Succoring beasts helped, without social risk, to relieve the obligation, as Lewis Gompertz expressed it, of those who lived on the labor of the poor to return the benefit to the world.[57] This sort of displacement of guilt from exploited workers to maltreated brutes would be impossible to document; no animal lover would confess such motives, even if conscious of them. But the rhetoric of animal protection, regarded in this light, suggests a great deal more than its makers intended.

Animal lovers insisted that beasts—"faithful" and "hardworking servants" —merited fairer treatment from their "masters." References to the "working classes" or to "labouring classes of domesticated brutes" were fairly common. One of the most perceptive of later humanitarian writers, Henry Salt, shrewdly observed that animal lovers had traditionally viewed the "lower orders" and "lower animals" in much the same way.[58] Moreover, SPCA supporters justified their campaign for kindness by a line of argument based on a transparent analogy to the relations of employers and workers: "We are bound to reciprocate duties: brutes give us their labour, and in return, we are bound to provide them food and tender treatment." This argument was repeated so often that it became virtually a reflex.[59]

A few animal lovers went so far as to suggest that, by some form of social faith healing, eradicating cruelty to brutes would actually raise the standard of living of the lower orders.[60] This took wishful thinking to an extreme. But even among the more realistic, alleviation of animal suffering may possibly have provided a cathartic outlet for consciences uneasy about the sufferings of their own species.

Guilt was not the only feeling evoked by the bleak spectacle of the industrial masses. An even more urgent response was fear: of impending revolution; of a society increasingly swayed by a "barbarous and brutal" mob; in brief, fear of anarchy.[61] The abuse showered on animals by the lower orders was both proof and reminder of their frightening savagery. SPCA members saw in the tormentors of animals the brutality of the lowest classes, "accustomed daily to intemperance" and resorting to "blows on every trifling occasion." Worst of all, their violent impulses would not long expend themselves on beasts alone, for "habitual cruelty to animals predisposes us to acts of cruelty towards our own species."[62]

Americans had special reason for worry. The "misgoverned nations of the earth are pouring their discontented hordes into this . . . Utopia of the dreams," bringing with them "their dreadful doctrines of cruelty." Henry Bergh glared down upon the Irish in particular as an inferior race, whose abuse of animals evidenced a natural inclination to crime. Yet one need not have been inflamed by immigration in order to harbor fears of social unrest. "Crimes of violence and a spirit of lawlessness have grown wonderfully," warned George Angell, portending "great and dangerous conflicts between capital and labor." A troubled member of Parliament explicitly linked brutality to beasts with revolutionary political violence.[63] But the RSPCA had an answer for these social problems:

> . . . by the discouragement of cruelty and insensibility of heart, in the treatment of inferior creatures, human beings will be rendered more susceptible of kind impressions towards each other, their moral temper will be improved, and consequently, social happiness and genuine philanthropy must, infallibly, be strengthened and enlarged.[64]

Training in kindness might yet root out the hatred, cruelty, and anarchy thought to flourish in the lower classes. "When the rights of dumb animals shall be protected," Angell assured, "the rights of human beings will be safe." Thomas Fowell Buxton, years earlier, had put it more baldly: The RSPCA must "spread amongst the lower orders of the people" at large—not just among those who had care of animals—"a degree of moral feeling which would compel them to think and act like those of a superior class." Public safety demanded that the people, wild animals in the nation's midst, be tamed.[65]

However alarming, the situation was far from hopeless. Actually, those concerned sometimes found very humane people among the poor. They believed that only deficiencies of education (understood as the inculcation of a proper sense of duty and the repression of socially disruptive tendencies) prevented the lower orders from outshining the rich in humaneness. The duty of their betters was therefore clear. The working classes, especially their still malleable children, must "be drilled and disciplined to virtue; to practise the duties if not to feel the sentiments of mercy and compassion." The poor "will be brought up with their spirits more humbled, and will more faithfully fulfill their duties with [*sic*] their fellow-men."[66]

Middle- and upper-class Britons and Americans, afraid of social upheaval (and, to give them their due, distressed that their fellow men should wallow, as they saw it, in ignorance and barbarism), clutched almost frantically at the panacea of education. "Simply as a question of dollars and cents for the protection of property and life, can there possibly be any better way of preventing railroad wrecks, incendiary fires and the explosion of dynamite bombs than by carrying . . . into all the schools of our country an education that will make our youth and children more humane?" Humane education, to which SPCAs devoted more and more of their resources as the years passed, might tame the savage dispositions of the working classes. At least it would soothe their masters.[67]

Guilt and fear did not dominate the lives of prosperous Victorians. An occasional twinge of conscience or shiver up the spine, however uncomfortable momentarily, drove only the most sensitive souls into rebellion against the system. Yet people trapped even occasionally between shame and terror could not remain blind to the moral ambiguities of industrialism and the capitalist spirit. The condition of workers was an irritating, risky topic, threatening to dislodge the underpinnings of Victorian bourgeois society—both its intellectual scaffolding in political economy and its sense of moral justification. Some other release was needed for minor qualms of conscience, and the status of animals under industrial capitalism provided a safe outlet for some mild carping at an economic system otherwise warmly embraced by its grateful beneficiaries.

The plight of overworked animals provided much of the grist for their mills. "Avarice," one critic grimly noted, "is the chief impelling motive to cruelties of this denomination." He was not alone in lamenting "the sordid love of gain," which "leads men to regard beasts of draught and burden as mere machines." This comparison itself suggests certain doubts as to the direction of industrialism. Indeed, the mainspring of the market economy, the competitive spirit, drew the most fire. Economic competition provoked much of the notorious brutality of the lower orders. But it affected not only the poor; too often it drove their social superiors to maltreat their own animals. Even the chief beneficiaries of the progress of material civilization had to face up to its harsher effects. "It strengthens every principle of selfishness; under its influence calculation supersedes humanity . . ."[68] In this respect, animals had much to teach their masters:

> Compare a crowded street; each individual panting and striving to outdo his fellow, looking as if they struggled to hold their self-importance fast, lest they should lose one atom of the rare and precious commodity; a spirit of repulsion and contest, the ruling feature of the mass: compare this, we say, with a troop of oxen grazing in a meadow. Behold the noble placid sedateness, the firm elastic step, void of timidity or fear, with which they crop their sustenance, all seeming to breathe a spirit of peace and harmony with nature around them, and with nature's God.[69]

Here was an antidote for the poisonous spirit of competition and greed that had crept over the land like an evil fog. The prophets of political economy insisted that competition was the lifeblood of industry and trade. So be it. But this sordid necessity must be held in check, kept in its proper sphere and under close control. "The instructors of youth should first try to excite the feelings of humanity" before "ventur[ing] to place in their hands the powerful engine of ambition." Let men learn from the beasts—or, more precisely, from the idealized, anthropomorphized virtues of such mythical brutes as the foregoing troop of noble cattle. Animal protection not only eased middle-class consciences by allowing a few complaints about capitalism; through its emphasis on the softening influence of education in humaneness, it actually held out the hope of smoothing the rougher features of laissez-faire.[70]

This hope was an obvious phantasm. But that was precisely its attraction. The harmless, unoffending, cheerfully hopeless character of SPCA reform was a main reason for its wide appeal. This is not to say that efforts to improve the lot of animals were unrealistic, only the dream that this would alter the face of industrialism. For the people who flocked to SPCA meetings and there basked in the reflected glory of the wealthy and titled were not malcontents, not rebels, not fundamentally reformers at all.[71] They were conformists, comfortable, at heart happy with their up-to-date industrial world. Yet they were also neither blind nor wholly self-satisfied. They sometimes saw the ambiguities, felt at the back of the mind the guilt and fear that were the price of affluence. They wanted to wipe out the shame and fright, but not the prosperity that came with it. They wanted to protest the sordid acquisitiveness of Victorian capitalism, but not too loudly. The animal protection movement opened for them a path toward peace of mind.

Seen in this light, the attack on Gompertz and the revolution in RSPCA policy become easier to understand, as does the courting of the prosperous by American SPCAs. These societies eased troubled but conventional minds by providing a harmless release for widespread anxiety over the kinship of people and beasts, for guilt spurred by working-class poverty, for fear of anarchy and rebellion, and for disgust at the greedy excesses of competition. If they were to function effectively as this sort of safety valve, they could not begin by alienating the self-consciously respectable middle classes. Likewise, the priority on prosecution naturally gave way to an emphasis on education, which was uncontroversial and confronted more directly the specific concerns that disturbed their members. The RSPCA abandoned whatever pretensions to radical reform it once cherished, pretensions that its American counterparts never entertained; both settled down comfortably to work hand-in-glove with the Victorian Establishment. Arguably, that was the most practical long-term strategy for easing the sufferings of brutes.[72] It was certainly the most effective way to bring psychological relief to their masters.

Through the rest of the century, the major SPCAs never deviated from the path marked out by the RSPCA in the 1830s. Sensitivity to their basically conservative, middle-class constituency conditioned their every move. Even though women composed probably a majority of SPCA members from the beginning, no society admitted them to its official leadership until the 1870s, by which time such things had become respectable. Only after cooperation with Jews had lost all taint of disreputability did the RSPCA once again publicly associate with them—and then only with the safest and most eminent Jews, men like Baron Rothschild and Rabbi Marks. To have behaved otherwise would have jeopardized the SPCA mission to the middle classes.[73]

The societies' programs reflected this mission. All the anxieties that drew the well-off to animal protection cried out for the elevation of the working classes. So SPCAs encouraged "humbler" folk to attend their public meetings (though not to mingle there with the fashionable). They distributed hundreds of thousands of tracts to working men. They staged elaborate mass entertainments calculated to soften lower-class hearts. Above all, they struggled for years to nip cruelty in the bud by making kindness to animals a regular part of school curricula.[74]

It is hard to judge what impact all of this had on its targets, but its appeal to the upper ranges of Victorian society cannot be doubted. The campaign for humane education of the masses alleviated just those concerns that had drawn respectable people to animal protection in the first place. Moreover, the prudence and propriety of SPCA leaders satisfied even the most conservative that here was no club of tinkering fanatics but a force for stability and order in an uncertain age. Armed with policies perfectly attuned to the intellectual and psychological needs of Victorian England and America, the SPCAs could only prosper. In the latter decades of the nineteenth century, the major societies were among the largest and most influential voluntary organizations in the Anglo-American world.

The new attitudes toward animals had become solidly entrenched not only in thousands of minds, but in powerful institutions that would ensure their continuance. This happened in part because humane feelings had few other socially acceptable outlets. But, at a deeper level, this entrenchment reflected the ambivalence of respectable, conventional people toward their rapidly changing society. The new middle classes could live at peace with the new ideas, the new factories, the new masses of the Victorian Age only by insisting that kindness also become part of the new way of life.

Any radical renovation of attitudes—any fundamentally new sensibility —must be tamed and sanitized before it can permeate a culture. Otherwise, it almost invariably threatens the stability of important social institutions or mores and is hastily rejected by the instinctive prudence of most human beings. The new concern for animals was successfully domesticated in the SPCA movement—so thoroughly gentled that it even became a safe release for sympathetic impulses and guilty worries that would have endangered the status quo if allowed to play back upon their real sources. This sounds like a loss of virtue, and perhaps it was. But it also helped to enshrine sympathy for suffering, and not only for suffering animals, among the dominant values of Anglo-American culture.

IV
Man Becomes an Animal

Kindness to animals was incontrovertibly part of the "social question"; it provided relief for the internal discomforts involved in digesting fundamental social change. But after the middle of the century other more personal and perhaps more troubling problems helped even more to focus on animals the era's deepening concern for suffering. Novel ideas about the nature of beasts meshed with new perspectives on human nature to force a reassessment of humanity's relationship with animals. This offered obvious new reasons for sympathy with animals; more important, it raised profoundly disturbing questions about people's own animality. Compassion helped to quiet them.

The biological affinity of people and animals had grown increasingly evident since the end of the eighteenth century. Advances in comparative anatomy and physiology had brought animals a great deal closer to people. The enormous vogue of Sir Edwin Landseer's animal paintings, with their "serious allocation to animals of distinctly human attributes," demonstrated the spreading belief in the kinship of people and beasts.[1] But the idea broke through to a new level of influence around the middle of the nineteenth century. It reached more people and affected them more deeply; the rhetoric of animal protection recorded the shock like a seismograph. The natural slow seepage of ideas into the public consciousness partly accounted for the change. But only in small part: Much more powerful forces were at work.

One force was unleashed by Charles Darwin. It was not surprising that the *Origin of Species* and later the *Descent of Man* stirred scientists and the many amateurs of science. But Darwin affected other literate people almost as profoundly—in some cases more deeply. For months after its publication, the *Origin* dominated conversation at sophisticated dinner parties. While the impact in London came more immediately, ultimately Boston was no less impressed. The rapid acceptance among the well-

60

educated of the evolutionary theory, at least as a tenable hypothesis, seemed amazing. By 1870 it had vanquished all but die-hard opposition, though many remained dubious about the full Darwinian creed of natural selection and the evolutionary origin of man.[2] Yet even the latter proposition rapidly won many converts. Perhaps there was really nothing remarkable about this. As the intellectual history of animal protection demonstrated, the past hundred years had severely corroded belief in the majestic isolation of human beings from the animal kingdom and the natural world generally. If the walls came tumbling down at the sound of Darwin's trumpet, it was because the humble termites had nibbled for years.

Animal protectors naturally followed the progress of Darwinism with keener than ordinary interest. Opinions differed widely and vociferously within the movement. The Rev. Francis Orpen Morris, a pioneer of bird protection and later a vocal antivivisectionist, penned a series of vitriolic tracts denouncing the infidel doctrine in terms that finally prodded the *Animal World* to urge him to restrain himself. Others joined the attack with equal vigor if greater tact.[3] Probably more animal lovers, however, came down enthusiastically on Darwin's side. They made less noise, perhaps because, confident of eventual vindication, they felt less need to storm and strut. For them evolution had become a simple matter of fact—no longer an issue for debate but an assumed starting point for further discussion of the relations of people and animals.[4]

Most animal protectors, probably in common with most other interested readers, looked on Darwinism as neither blasphemy nor revelation. No one had to commit himself, and only a minority did. Many indeed began to use Darwin's theory, though at first rather gingerly, long before they completely accepted it. Belief settled in slowly over decades of increasingly comfortable cohabitation with the ideas; familiarity bred confidence. The revealing circumstance is not *when* Darwinism became an article of faith but *how* it was employed.[5]

Typical was the sermon preached by the Rev. Richard Metcalf at Winchester, Massachusetts, in May of 1878. He held the Darwinian hypothesis at arm's length, like some exotic, possibly poisonous, species of reptile. If the theory is correct, he argued, then we owe beasts the consideration due to relatives. If, on the other hand, the biblical version of creation holds true, then men and animals still share the same Almighty Father, and we owe our spiritual brethren a duty of kindness. In his 1865 annual sermon to the RSPCA, the Dean of Westminster cut through the whole tangle of scientific argument with one stroke. Darwinism, regardless of its scientific validity, taught an "unquestionable" moral truth "in its description of the common origin of man and of the brute creation." Another animal lover insisted that: ". . . any who believe apes to be our cousins not so very far removed, should surely give some practical recognition of this kinship, and also extend a helping hand to other animals, their possibly more remote ancestors, or poor relations." A book about animals appeared in 1872 with exactly this title: *Our Poor Relations.*[6] Thus Darwinism was put to work for animals long before most animal lovers fully embraced it.

What principally bothered those reluctant to confess the full Darwinian gospel was its uncompromising materialism. Darwin himself had left only the narrowest crevice through which the supernatural might creep back into his evolutionary world. The *Descent of Man* filled the antivivisectionist Frances Power Cobbe "with the deadliest alarm" for exactly this reason. She and Cardinal Manning, prophesying woe together at an antivivisection meeting, "augured immeasurable evils from the general adoption" of the theory "that Conscience was merely an hereditary instinct fixed in the brain by the interests of the tribe, and in no sense the voice of God in the heart." At first it may seem strange that Darwin alarmed so heterodox a theist as Miss Cobbe, who had strayed far beyond any recognizably Christian position decades before. But her rejection of most received religious beliefs only impelled her to cling the more desperately to the few she had left. Darwin had the same unnerving effect on her theological sympathizer, the Rev. James Freeman Clarke, one of the surviving monuments of New England Transcendentalism. He found the Darwinian hypothesis distressingly "unspiritual." However much these animal lovers appreciated evidence of their close ties with animalkind, they did not want to be related to godless brutes.[7]

The difficulty was not insuperable, for the concept of evolution was marvelously malleable. Darwin's writings, like any other scripture, were subject to exegesis. One could interpret sympathetically the more appealing passages, while quietly ignoring the unfortunate absence of the Deity. Thus Clarke balanced against the "unspiritual" character of Darwinism its "profound faith in perpetual improvement"—"the most startling optimism that has ever been taught, for it makes the law of the whole universe to be perpetual progress." This outweighed the theory's unspirituality by implying the "continued advance" of animals' souls as well as people's. A more orthodox but equally humane clergyman, Professor Mattoon M. Curtis of Western Reserve University, refused, like Clarke, to base the claims of the lower animals on the "might makes right" philosophy of Darwin's own writings. The "altruistic" versions of Darwinism preached by Fiske, Drummond, and Spencer he found much more congenial.[8]

Animal lovers contrived for themselves a much altered "Darwinism," softened, sterilized, and injected with a healthy dose of godliness. It fitted their purpose nicely. Not only did it stress the blood kinship of human beings and beasts, but it mitigated the bestiality of the latter. Instead of degrading people, it elevated animals.[9] It provided simultaneously a powerful argument for kindness to animals and an antidote to the threat of man's own animality, as posed by Darwin.

Darwin had played a large part in sharpening the sense of kinship with animals, but he was by no means solely responsible. Perhaps equally though more quietly influential was the rapid development of ethnology, anthropology, and prehistory. Both the American Ethnological Society and the Ethnological Society of London date from the early 1840s. The more broadly conceived field of anthropology began to take shape in the early sixties.[10] Sir John Lubbock's *Prehistoric Times* appeared in 1865. Even people who took no interest in these new studies could scarcely avoid the avalanche of explorers' and travelers' accounts of primitive folk. Henry Stanley and Richard Burton were merely the most famous of these by-products of imperialism.

What did the daily lives of Fuegians have to do with attitudes toward animals in London and New York? The answer lies in the extreme primitiveness of some of the peoples encountered by Europeans during scientific and imperialistic adventures. The Australian aborigines and the Bushmen of southwest Africa, for example, lived in not merely Stone Age but Paleolithic cultures. This posed a worrisome question: "Were all the colonized peoples human as their colonizers were human?"[11] The question, with all its implications for animals, was not new, but never before had it confronted so many people so directly. The answer, with little delay, was usually yes. But the very need to ask shook the prevailing belief in a sharp demarcation between the human and the bestial. Many Victorians perceived little difference between the family dog—clever, affectionate, sensitive, and capable of rather complex learning—and what they saw as some naked savage who knew nothing of agriculture, scarcely more of rudimentary tools, and whose vocabulary consisted of a few rude grunts. Darwin himself confessed to "some difficulty in conceiving how [the] inhabitant of Tierra del Fuego is to be connected with civilized man."[12] If one had to accept a Fuegian as cousin and a Neanderthal as great-grandfather, how could one avoid admitting at least the higher animals into the family?

The impact of all this on the public consciousness is difficult to measure but not hard to see. One curious straw in the wind: In the 1860s, English and American cartoonists began to depict Irishmen as creatures with gorilla-like bodies and simian faces. The Irish had suffered obloquy before, but never this.[13] The barriers between men and beasts had never before broken down so utterly. Quadruped, ape, savage, and civilized man now followed close upon one another in a biological continuum where distinctions had become all but invisible.

The language of animal lovers reflected this confusion. Angell called himself "the advocate of the lower races," by which he meant dogs and cats, not the heathen Chinee. On the other side of the Atlantic, Canon Basil Wilberforce described the objects of his concern as the "animals other than man (I do not call them the lower animals)."[14] The Canon's careful phrasing was understandable: The close study of man had revealed how much like a "lower" animal he could be.

Other studies were showing how much like people animals could be. Scientific work in animal psychology gave the *coup de grâce* to any lingering hope of human distinctiveness. Do animals reason? If so, how is their kind of rationality related to human intelligence? Questions like these had been canvassed sporadically since Aristotle. The upwelling of interest in animals after 1800, coupled with scientific advances (particularly in the physiology of the nervous system), fired the subject with new and more urgent interest. Long before 1859, even nonscientific journals sometimes grappled with the problem, usually contributing more confusion than illumination. An occasional early writer even asserted that the so-called instinct of animals differed only in degree from the vaunted reason of man.[15]

Darwin gave new arguments and a new burst of energy to the advocates of animal intelligence. His own work, especially the *Descent of Man,* undermined the foundations of human mental uniqueness. Disciples like George John Romanes and Sir John Lubbock, as well as lesser lights, thrust the new views of the animal mind into the forefront of scientific and popular interest. At Dublin in 1878 and Sheffield in 1879, the question of animal intelligence "specially occupied the attention" of meetings of the British Association for the Advancement of Science, the great annual conclaves of British science. Under this barrage, few knowledgeable people were prepared to deny the essential similarity of mental functions in human beings and beasts. It was only natural for a thinker like Charles Peirce, who kept abreast of scientific developments, to argue for a continuity between animal and human minds not only in perception and reasoning but in musicality and humor.[16]

Such ideas did not remain confined to scientific circles. Articles crammed with anecdotes to answer "The Question of Animal Reason" became standard fare in magazines like *Harper's* or the *Westminster Review.* The popularizers—and, in fairness, some of their scientific counterparts—handled these complex issues so loosely that what started as a debate in the 1860s had become by the turn of the century a quagmire.[17] More careful investigators, particularly Edward L. Thorndike in America and C. Lloyd Morgan in Britain, finally protested. Both insisted on subjecting conclusions to the test of experiment rather than anecdote. In 1894 Lloyd Morgan enunciated his famous canon of parsimony: "In no case may we interpret an action as the outcome of the exercise of a higher psychical faculty, if it can be interpreted as the outcome of one which stands lower in the psychological scale." Ultimately, views such as Morgan's undercut the belief that animals think just like people.[18] But this new fastidiousness took years to penetrate the lay mind. Out of all the confusion a great many literate people had formed the opinion (one still flourishing after 1900) that at least the higher mammals shared human reasoning powers, human sentiments like affection and shame, and perhaps even human religious and aesthetic impulses. An "intelligent dog" was capable, at a minimum, of the "same thoughts" as "a Bushman or a Digger Indian." Perhaps the dog could even outthink the savage. Only "an arbitrary and conventional line . . . separates the intellect of animals from that of men."[19]

In this climate of opinion, the stock-in-trade of popular natural history writing became the assimilation of animals to people. Storytelling of this sort, propagating the most generous assessment of the animal mind, enjoyed extraordinary popularity in both England and America during the late nineteenth and early twentieth century. Its detritus remains in the countless dog and horse stories still a staple of the prepubescent reader's diet. The chief of this tribe of literary outdoorsmen, Ernest Thompson Seton, fabricated "animal heroes" from scattered fantastic anecdotes of many individual animals. His beasts easily "proved" how human animals were. But even the more scrupulous popularizers, like the American John Burroughs or the English clergyman J. G. Wood, fell into the same trap of picturing animals as just like people—though perhaps a shade nobler.[20] The sales of their books suggested that people agreed.

Taken literally, these beliefs could produce striking behavior. On one occasion the patrons of a little restaurant in Versailles observed George Angell dining at a table with two dogs and a cat.[21] But the new views of the animal mind had more sweeping ethical implications:

> The most important deduction in a moral point of view from the doctrine of evolution . . . is the essential oneness of the mental faculties of man and the higher animals. . . . We are reminded that not only are the lower animals capable of experiencing the same physical pain and suffering with ourselves, but also that they are in possession of the same kind of reasoning faculties.

Perhaps, it was suggested, cruelly treated animals suffer as much from a sense of injustice as from physical pain. Since animals share our mental faculties, their "claims" on us "rest not upon the considerations of mere passing sentiment" but upon "the eternal laws of justice, as well as of sympathy, with our fellow-beings and fellow-creatures."[22] Animals, after all, were now members of the family:

> Amid all this life man stands as elder brother,—the youngest, yet the oldest, —the last born of all, perhaps, and for that reason having most antiquity organized within him. . . . An elder brother's place! That suggests the thought of one who helps, and pities, and protects, who leads the younger brother up-wards. . . .
>
> Christianity has waited long to preach its gospel to *these* poor. But now science comes, and its prophet face revealing truths is ever heralding good news to all things.[23]

Here was a new gospel indeed. So thoroughly was man assimilated to animals that he could be urged to assume leadership within the animal kingdom. This pushed even science's prophecies rather far. Yet it was hard to deny that the suffering beast had now to be acknowledged as kin. That conceded, surely one owed even the poorest of relations kindness and sympathy.

All was not well, however, between human beings and their beastly cousins. The revolution in thought that had struck down the barriers between the two also loosed new demons to torment anxious Victorians. These fears were bound up with attitudes toward nature. The Victorian Age had inherited a view of nature already transformed from the divinely ordered, clockwork, rational universe of Laplace and Pope into the sublime, if sometimes terrible, Nature of Romantics like Wordsworth and Thomas Cole. Now fossil discoveries and uniformitarian geology pushed the age of the earth far back into an inconceivably distant past. Nature grew ever vaster, more impersonal, and more potent, human beings ever more diminished and insignificant. "How fleeting are the wishes and efforts of man!" wrote Charles Darwin, "how short his time! and consequently how poor will his products be, compared with those accumulated by Nature during whole geological periods!"[24]

Darwin's theory of natural selection added the final gruesome touches: death and wastage on an enormous scale, whole species formed and then blindly squandered, and the only virtue a talent for killing before being killed. Yet even before Darwin the word "nature" had often come to evoke the vision of a dark jungle, a glimpse of fangs dripping blood. Darwin himself had imbibed, from the pages of Charles Lyell's *Principles of Geology* (1830-33), the view of nature as an arena of ceaseless strife, where whole species fell victim; it was the reading of Lyell that inspired Tennyson's "Nature, red in tooth and claw with ravine."[25] What religious doubt and the endless ages of geology had begun, Darwin finished with a view of the world rendered still more chilling by his matter-of-fact depiction of it. For some, the picture soured the taste of beauty, tore down God from the heavens, and left a hollow sense of duty and the ties of personal affection the only purpose in living. Others held on to their faith in the goodness of God and the meaningfulness of life, but often only by rejecting Darwin or by averting their eyes from his more troublesome conclusions. Even for disbelievers in natural selection, Darwin and his disciples had cast a pall of brutality over the cheery, comforting nature of Paley and the Bridgewater Treatises.[26]

Even those distressed by inhumanity to animals had to confess that "Nature [is] often no less harsh than man in dealing with her inarticulate offspring." Moreover, relatively few animals died of such neutral causes as falling trees, lightning, or even old age and disease. "Nature" in its cruelest aspect meant specifically beast eating beast:

> Life riots on life—tooth and talon, beak and paw. It is a sickening contempla-
> tion, but life everywhere, in its aspect of activity, is largely made up of the
> struggle by one being against another for existence. . . .[27]

These bloodthirsty creatures were the same animals that physiology, anthropology, psychology, and Darwinian evolution all certified as the near relatives of men and, worse, women. Darwinism struck a particularly troubling note because human descent from such brutes implied that even Victorians could literally have inherited their ferocious nature. Did the thin veneer of civilization cloak a ravening beast raging at its flimsy chains? Many anxious souls feared that it might. This worry was not new, but the explosion in scientific knowledge and the revolution in scientific belief during the middle years of the century had intensified the fear painfully.[28] Man, stripped of his uniqueness, had been plunged naked into the jungle world of nature, and it frightened him.

This semi-conscious terror crept into novels like Robert Louis Stevenson's *Strange Case of Dr. Jekyll and Mr. Hyde* and H. G. Wells's *The Island of Dr. Moreau.* Stevenson's "hardly human" Hyde—"ape-like," "insensate," "troglodytic"—represented the primal beast repressed within the cultivated Dr. Jekyll, while Dr. Moreau was a scientist who transformed literal animals into half-human monsters. Never one to veil his message in subtlety, Wells made his hero declaim: "I look about me at my fellow-men . . . I feel as though the animal was surging up through them." This was enough to give any post-Darwinian the shivers. *The Times* brewed its nightmares straight from the original flagon. Its review of the *Descent of Man* hinted broadly that if people thought they were beasts, they would act accordingly: "Morality," if Darwin's theories prevailed, "would lose all elements of stable authority."[29]

Victorians as readily saw the animal lurking in real people as in the Jekylls and Moreaus. The popularity in England and America of the ideas of the pioneer criminologist Cesare Lombroso testified to the depth of their anxiety. Influenced by both anthropology and Darwinism, Lombroso developed during the 1860s his theory of the criminal type. The "natural" criminal strikingly resembled, especially in brain and facial structure, the great apes. These physical atavisms accompanied a savage, profoundly atavistic personality, for the "criminal man" was literally a throwback to his bestial forebears, a living fossil of stunted evolution. Lombroso's native Italy greeted his theories more enthusiastically than England or America, but the respect accorded them by Anglo-American criminologists showed that Lombroso had struck a responsive chord.[30] By translating the ever-present fear of the "dangerous classes" into unease over the animal in human beings, he had married two of the Victorians' greatest concerns and used each to justify and reinforce the other. We must resist the temptation to write these off as hysterical obsessions of the insecure, guilt-ridden new middle classes. Whether in the insensate brutality of much of slum life, in the throat-slashing lawlessness of districts like New York's Five Points, or in the ruthless exploitation of children by mine owners and white slavers, violence always lurked around the corner in the Victorian's unlovely world.

Criminality constituted for the middle-class Victorian a problem of, so to speak, external defense. But a still graver threat to internal security also menaced. Tom Brown confronted it at Oxford:

> We have most of us walked the like marches at one time or another of our lives. . . . Times they were of blinding and driving storm, and howling winds, out of which voices as of evil spirits spoke close in our ears—tauntingly, temptingly whispering to the mischievous wild beast which lurks in the bottom of all our hearts. . . .

The wild beast burrowing in the darkness of Tom's heart was sex.[31] Middle-class anxieties about sex during this period, nurtured if not sown by Evangelical morality, are too well known (and echo too loudly in our own day) to require amplification here. Their association with animals is not now so obvious, but contemporaries understood it. Fornication, adultery, impure thoughts, and that whispered uncleanness, masturbation, meant the escape of the animal caged in the human breast. The universality of the sexual impulse heightened the fear. Crime stained principally the souls of the "dangerous classes," but sex blighted everyone—except possibly the untouched maiden.

Women were often believed to have been spared the bestial desires of sex. Perhaps their relative freedom from animality rendered them, in the subliminal mind, especially fit for the kindness-to-animals movement, in which they exercised unusually powerful influence despite the social conventions of the age: Witness Caroline Earle White and Emily Appleton. For similar reasons, the perceived sexlessness of children may have helped to foster the nineteenth-century cult of childhood. In Victorian art, as Ronald Pearsall notes:

> The nude adolescent girl was considered less heinous than the nude woman, if only for the absence of voluptuousness and pubic hair, which was a constant cause of affront to the respectable; a thesis could be written on the effect of pubic hair on Victorian sexual thinking. Pubic hair was the omnipresent reminder of the animal in man, the hairy beast brought to the knowledge of the shocked middle classes by Darwin.[32]

Sex and animality: those two fears (if indeed they could be wholly separated) reinforced one another. Sexual impulses reminded one of the beast inside. Mention of human animality brought to mind the banked fires of sex, threatening always to flame up out of control. It took no psychologist to understand the American antivivisectionist Ross Perry's slightly oblique warning: "Does not every man here know that this civilization of today is a veneering; that it is a crust; that underneath all this film there are these passions, these fires? There is this brute animal nature from which we emerged, and which is still so strong in us." Sitting atop an active volcano was nerve wracking.[33]

The animal trapped within—whether it sought escape in sex, in crime, or simply in the unspecified barbarity of bloodstained, untamed nature —posed a frightening threat. As William James cautioned:

> The water-tight compartment in which the carnivore within us is confined is artificial and not organic. It never will be organic. The slightest diminution of external pressure, the slightest loophole of licensed exception, will make the whole system leaky, and murder will again grow rampant.[34]

For some, this threat assumed its rawest, most bestial form in cruelty to animals. In that situation human beings put themselves back in the jungle, unleashing brute passions in bloody battle with their primordial kin. Eating animals was arguably the most extreme case of this, and some radical animal protectors did not hesitate to say so. But the practice, after all, was hallowed by immemorial custom, and most animal lovers made no protest. The more common worry that, in abusing beasts, humanity nakedly exposed its own animality, had bothered people earlier in the century, but the animal within had then been only glimpsed behind the veil of human uniqueness. By the sixties and seventies that veil hung in tatters, and the beast snarled in full daylight. The issue thus grew much more sensitive and explicit:

> Nowhere are the brutish passions of man more displayed than in cruelty. Just so far as a man is cruel does he show less of the human nature and more of the animal nature which exist together in him—just so far does he show that he has forgotten that it is the glory of the human to control the animal nature.[35]

Science—biological, psychological, and social—had forced people to confront their own animality and its haunting implications. Now somehow the spectre of the human beast must be laid to rest. But how? Part of the answer was self-control: "It is the glory of the human to control the animal nature." The SPCA movement helped not only by suppressing outbreaks of brutish ferocity but by teaching from the cradle onward the importance of kindness, mildness, and self-restraint. Humane education acquired tremendous significance, not merely for animals, but for the future of the human race. In the end, as Henry Bergh insisted: ". . . the man is even a greater gainer than the animal, by being made to realize the possibility of self-control; and society are greater gainers still, by the subjugation of the demons of passion and violence in their midst."[36] Many also tried to shore up the tottering wreck of man's "higher" nature by wishful thinking about his "lower" nature. Refurbishing beasts created a counterweight to the dog-eat-dog ferocity of raw nature; a sweetened animal meant a less bestial human being. In 1863 an author in the *Christian Examiner* naively gave away the game. After the *Origin of Species* appeared, he said, the traditionally low estimate of animals' "faculties and attainments" rapidly gave

The animal in man
(An Irishman as ape, from *Punch,* October 29, 1881)

Human animality unleashed
(From *Our Dumb Animals,* October 1892)

The animal humanized
(From *Our Dumb Animals,* January 1875)

"place to a desire to advocate the cause of our silent companions." If Darwinism proved true, insisted another animal lover, "we shall not degrade man, but only elevate the brute."[37]

This remodeling of animals included a purge, mostly unconscious, of the English language itself. By the twentieth century, the word "brute" as a synonym for animal had virtually disappeared from common usage. "Beast" seldom referred to any beasts but the inexcusably bloodthirsty ones who inhabited jungles and other unhealthy places. The neutral "animal" became the standard term for everything else with four legs. One could feel tolerably comfortable with "the lower animals," but "the lower brutes" suggested too many unpleasant things about the higher ones.[38]

Brutes no longer, "our poor relations" grew recognizably more human. The attitudes, the personalities, the characters, the virtues attributed to animals all conspired to cloak them in quasi-humanity.[39] A humorous variant of this anthropomorphizing became a popular pictorial device: thus the innumerable Victorian prints of dogs playing cards and smoking cigars. Landseer's paintings in this genre remain fairly well-known, but a host of others—mostly forgotten now—like the English cattle painter T. Sidney Cooper, shared his success. People who could not afford oil paintings for their parlors could choose among hundreds of hand-colored lithographs in the same vein, such as Currier and Ives's *The Dairy Farm,* in which a pair of cattle, by all appearances kissing, mirror the courting of a dairymaid and her swain. To our taste this work is ludicrous, but it had significance in its own day. It quietly let animals into the human family through the back door.[40]

The natural history doted upon by animal lovers served the same purpose. Granted that the readers of *Our Dumb Animals* were not Darwins or even Lubbocks. Even for amateurs, they showed a curious proclivity for stories that illustrated not merely the intelligence of animals, but qualities like "generosity," "bravery," "faithfulness," and "gratitude." One SPCA leader wrote of a rescued stray:

> I have heard it said that animals weep, and I know that in the little creature's large brown, hunted-looking eyes I saw a glistening moisture that seemed like tears when I stooped down to give her the warm drink and food and spoke tenderly to her.[41]

Most popular of all were tales of loyal dogs who, at risk of their own lives, rescued masters lost in some trackless mountain waste—or else stood faithful guard over the frozen bodies of less fortunate masters. The latter animals seemed almost more appealing, perhaps because the dog, having nothing to gain, evinced a more nearly human sentiment. The February 1888 *Animal World,* which told of "the lamented death of the Rev. A. H. MacKonochie, and the faithful watching over his body by the two dogs," achieved an "unprecedented sale." In fact, it sold out and had to be reprinted to meet the demand.[42]

A few extraordinarily humane beasts did not satisfy everyone. Some writers embarked on a campaign to purge nature wholesale of its horrors. E. B. Hamley asked his readers to envision a world devoid of animals:

> What a dismal hush in creation! What a multitudinous charm and delight wanting to the woods, the fields, the shallows, and the deeps! What glory lost to the grass with the spotted lady-birds, the mail-clad beetles, and the slender grasshoppers! What splendor gone from the flower with the bronzed and fire-tipped bee that fed on its heart, and the painted butterfly that hovered above its petals!

Nary a man-eating tiger—nay, nary a drop of blood, only a little stolen nectar—lurked within Hamley's paradisiacal dream. Another animal lover, Myron Benton, painted the "animal tribes" in even milder tones. These "shy friends" dreaded mostly man, the real terror of the forests, who must win back "the forfeited trust," find "some clew to their subtle language," and "make pacific overtures to them toward the establishment of a better understanding."[43]

Not only had these writers turned ravening beasts into "shy friends," fellow-people in fur and feathers, but, like fairy godmothers, they had transformed nature itself, only lately "red in tooth and claw," into a garden of delights. Human beings no longer needed to fear nature; indeed, they had to measure up to its moral standards, a test they had to date failed lamentably.

This is not to say that this golden vision completely exorcised the haunting terrors of vast and impersonal nature or the fears of the wild beast beneath the veneer of civilization. These anxieties had burrowed too deeply to be eradicated by hopeful rhetoric; they continued to lurk beneath the optimism laid over them and to gnaw at its foundations. But usually the floorboards held firm enough for people to walk about without undue concern. This was especially true for the many people who never ceased to believe in a universe infused with divine goodness and purpose yet could never wholly banish from the backs of their minds the terrifying vision of a blank, purposeless world entangled in a bloody, meaningless struggle of beast against beast. A little whistling in the dark about noble beasts and Edenic nature helped to dissolve this nightmare.

One proof of this strategy's success was that nature became the standard by which to judge the proper treatment of animals. A bloody, amoral, threatening nature could never have assumed this role. Thus it was a triumph of hopefulness, though perhaps in a minor key, when Henry C. Merwin asserted that "the only way of utilizing the inferior animals which can with certainty be pronounced right is the natural way." People could rightfully take advantage of "the strength of a horse, the predatory instinct of a cat, the watchfulness of a dog," and so forth. But to drive an animal beyond its capacities or to employ it in a way unsuited to its native abilities was unnatural and therefore wrong. On much the same grounds, William Thomas Thornton had earlier attacked British high farming for its use of factory-farming techniques—criticisms picked up and rebroadcast in America. Keeping cattle permanently penned up in barns, no matter how comfortable, violated the dictates of nature. Nature intended cattle to graze the open meadows, not to live in houses.[44] Animals ought to live by nature's laws, not man's.

A corollary followed: They existed not to satisfy man's needs but to fulfill their own natures. "Modern philosophy teaches us [that] although we are at the head and infinitely higher than any animal, still, in the first place, animals exist for themselves; they enjoy their lives, and are happy merely because they live." This was revolutionary, a momentous reversal of two millennia of the traditional Christian attitude toward animals: that they exist to serve people. Only a radical handful of animal lovers drew the logical though awkward conclusion; most continued to enjoy their lamb chops with a clear conscience. Still, a new ethos had emerged, not replacing older beliefs but superadded to them: the autonomy of animals and of all nature, the "sacredness of life for itself." This new sensibility would in time flower with important consequences.[45]

Granting autonomous significance to animals—freeing them from total moral subordination to people—also had more immediate results. Coupled with the refurbished view of nature as a model of right living, it enabled animals to serve as exemplars of human behavior, something a mere slave of human whims could hardly have done. This seemed paradoxical. Animals had been remodeled precisely so as to resemble people; now, confusingly, people were told to model themselves on animals. The confusion was more apparent than real. These exemplary animals did not display all human traits, only the most admirable. Victorians wanted from animals reinforcement of their own moral and ethical standards. They therefore projected these onto the animal kingdom; in turn, the animals served fallible people as mirrors, reflecting back their own better selves under the guise of the moral teachings of nature.

The notion of learning from animals was not new. In one sense it was as old as Aesop, though the animals of traditional fables were really people in sheep's clothing. By the eighteenth century it had become commonplace, particularly in children's books, to exhibit real animals as models of virtue: "How doth the busy little bee . . ." But in this context animals could as easily warn against vice as encourage virtue: The tiger stood for cruelty as much as the dog for fidelity. A writer in 1847 went so far as to suggest that exemplifying good and evil "may be one purpose of their actual being."[46] This man's naive anthropocentrism could not easily survive in the post-Darwinian epoch, but his use of animals could and did. Children still learned of "the Dog, as an Example of Fidelity," "the Ass, as an Example of Patience," and "the Ant, as an Example of Prudence." True, those "who inhabit the human hive" sometimes rebelled:

> I object on principle, as a two-footed creature, to being constantly referred to insects and four-footed creatures. I object to being required to model my proceedings according to the proceedings of the bee, or the dog, or the spider, or the camel.

Frankly, however, the speaker of these lines, Eugene Wrayburn in *Our Mutual Friend,* was something of a wastrel.[47] Anyway, he need not have got upset. Had he analyzed Mr. Boffin's injunction ("Look at the bees"), he would have realized that Boffin had not asked him to pattern his character after a bee's. The bees served only as a reminder of one virtue (industry) sadly lacking in Eugene. One was not supposed actually to imitate the animal, only the virtue. In fact, in this older tradition, the traits exemplified by animals were not virtues at all *in the animal,* merely more or less mechanical instincts. An animal taught bravery only in the sense that a heroic painting did. An animal's character in itself had no moral value; strictly speaking, an animal did not even have a character.

Here the later-Victorian attitude broke sharply with the older view. Animals became role models for people in a much fuller way. The old school told children to imitate Fido's faithfulness, but the child would never have heard that the "dog possesses incontestably all the qualities of a sensible man," while the "man has not in general the noble qualities of the dog." Yet many Victorians now began to promulgate precisely this sort of thing. Animals showed, according to Caroline Bray, "intelligence, industry, docility, self-denial, fidelity, and affection"; few people could claim as much. Philip Hamerton made a virtue of the beast's intellectual failings, saying that these strong, silent types taught one not to fret about business anxieties or literary ambitions. Moreover, their "abounding vitality" acted as a stimulant to mopish sorts, and "the study of animals inclines man to a steady cheerfulness." Sometimes model animals served obviously ulterior motives. How comforting if the working classes would only copy "the faithful, intelligent horse or dog who has been trained to observance of his duties, and who manifests by every action his desire to learn from his superiors and his affection for those who teach him." But animals had something more fundamental and more universal to teach. Hamerton had hinted at it, and that early "positive thinker," Ralph Waldo Trine, put it squarely: "Heart-Training through the Animal World."[48]

The question of the head versus the heart—the demands of intellect as against the claims of emotion and sensibility—engrossed both Englishmen and Americans in the Victorian Age. Their fathers and grandfathers had begun the crusade for the heart, and the children carried it on. Secular Romanticism came close to making the heart a religion, and its sacred analogue, Evangelicalism, preached a "religion of the heart." Reformers of many stripes "yearned for an emotional and pietistic brotherhood, for an all-inclusive love which would embrace the wayward murderer as well as the suffering slave and degraded drunkard." In 1858 a Salem lady founded at Harvard the Plummer Chair of Christian Morals as a "Professorship of the heart." The sculptor Hiram Powers struck a common note when he told George Angell in 1870: *"Educate the hearts of the people, and the heads will take care of themselves."*[49]

Training of the intellect alone was not sufficient. It could not teach the thing most needful, the "instinct of pity," the "only safe judge of right and wrong." But animals could fill the gap, if people would attend to their lessons, and the immense success of Anna Sewell's consciously didactic *Black Beauty* (1877) testified to the market for such instruction. Untouched by quibbling reason and unchanged by education, animals possessed a natural wisdom of their own, a *"knowledge which did not depend on reason, and which was much more prompt and perfect in its way."* They exemplified those virtues sadly wanting in the realm of intellect: sympathy, compassion, love. In Dickens' *Hard Times* (1854), the circus animals embodied the instinctual love and loyalty of Sissy Jupe's world, as opposed to the coldly calculating intellect that turned the wheels of Gradgrind's universe. One animal lover insisted that the four legs and the "silky or shaggy coat of the dog" disguised an "inner nature of Thought and Love; limited Thought, it is true; but quite unlimited Love." This was why those who felt that the value of intellectual advancement had been grossly overestimated put so much confidence in animals as a corrective: " . . . *even in the homes of crime,* hearts may be made more tender by kind acts and words for the dumb creatures *that always return love for love."*[50]

Animal lovers found these virtues most easily in pets. Pets were nothing new, but their widespread presence in middle-class homes coincided roughly —and the efflorescence of sentimental enthusiasm for pets coincided more precisely—with the changing intellectual climate around the middle of the nineteenth century. When nature presented a terrifying image of beasts with fangs dripping blood, the kitten toying with its ball of yarn made a more cheering picture. When animal savagery threatened to burst forth in man himself, the lazy family dog curled on the hearth, symbol of civilization, soothed these anxieties. More than other beasts, pets displayed "a generosity, gratitude, fidelity and affection worthy of imitation." The pet encapsulated the virtues of the heart, unsullied by skeptical calculating intellect. In Harriet Beecher Stowe's eyes, a dog was "nothing but organized love—love on four feet encased in fur and looking piteously out at the eyes —love that would die for you yet cannot speak." A creature so splendidly endowed with heart could not fail "to win out philanthropy in our boys and girls."[51] By creating the modern pet—the cuddly puppy, the cute kitten —animal lovers manufactured an animal designed to quell savage nature with the balm of love.

Working hand-in-paw with pets in spreading the gospel of the heart were women. Unusually prominent in the animal protection movement from the beginning, by the 1880s women had achieved parity with (in many American societies, supremacy over) their male colleagues. They virtually dominated the work of humane education; only one man, George Angell, showed equal flair for it. This was only natural. The Victorian ideology of womanhood portrayed the gentler sex as having a special aptitude for such civilizing tasks. Woman represented "gentleness and sympathy," as opposed specifically to the harsh competitiveness of the business world. Like the heartful animals with whom she seemed to have a special affinity, her intellectual weakness was more than compensated by moral and emotional strength. "If my sex has a 'mission' of any kind," wrote one woman, "it is surely to soften this hard old world . . . on a question of mercy a woman is likely to have a truer, sounder judgement, *qua* woman, than a man." Woman's role was to bring the gifts of the heart to a heartless world.[52] This job she now shared with her spiritual soulmate, the remodeled, idealized animal.

Ironically, these selfsame animals, when they showed their bloody fangs, symbolized also the terrors of savage, uncaring nature. Perhaps this was contradictory; certainly consistency was not the great strength of

Victorian animal lovers. But this was less a conflict between two images of the animal than a transformation of one into the other—not a chronological progression from the first to the second, but a shifting back and forth as circumstances dictated. When scientists and social scientists decided that animals were close kin to people, animal lovers delightedly seized on their theories and themselves even emphasized the rationality of beasts, in order to strengthen the case for kindness to animals. But this left animal lovers and their contemporaries in a dilemma. For rationality was compatible with viciousness, and nature—in which human beings were now immersed with the animals—often appeared mere purposeless savagery, especially after Darwin. In response, animal lovers shifted from lauding the rationality of animals to glorifying their affective nature, their capacity for love, loyalty, gratitude, and sympathy. These qualities certainly precluded any disconcerting snarls.

The task of obliterating the image of nature as "red in tooth and claw" came to preoccupy many animal lovers and compelled them to undertake the extraordinary cosmetic surgery that they performed on the image of the beast. Forget the dog's taste for warm, raw meat; cherish instead his faithful affection. How could one fear a bright, friendly, sympathetic beast? More to the point, how could one fear the animal in one's own breast when the brute was no longer a primordial savage but a sort of high-minded curate in fur? Setting animals up as models of compassion and sympathy, then, served two ends. It reassured those anxious over the implications of man's new kinship with animals. And it taught how to tame the beast that still prowled at the back of the mind despite all efforts to disguise it.

Undoubtedly this flimsy, jury-rigged mental construction teetered uncertainly and was likely to topple over at any moment. But perplexed Victorians greeted even a patchwork solution with relief, for few problems boded more for good or ill:

> When we think of what earth might become were the tiger passions within our race to be bred out at last, and the divine faculty of love and sympathy to attain its obviously intended development, it would seem as if efforts for the improvement of our physical or sanitary conditions, or for the advance of arts, science or laws, were scarcely worth making, in comparison . . .

Indeed, the urgency of nourishing the "tender and humane passion in the human heart" argued as strongly as anything against cruelty to animals. Kindness (for that became the animal lovers' favorite synonym for sympathy, compassion, pity) "is too precious a quality to allow it to be hardened or effaced by practices such as we often indulge in."[53] Kindness to animals —and compassion for every living creature—was the surest refutation of the human being's bestial savagery.

The beast had come full circle. Darwin, the early anthropologists, the pioneering psychologists had forced the Victorians to look their animal cousins full in the face. The image that stared back—savage, vicious, bloodthirsty—more than terrified them; it threatened to drag them down into the same pit. So animal lovers set about reclaiming the beast, painting over its horrors. They gave it a mind and, more important, a heart. They ended with a new picture: no longer the beast but the animal, an image so appealing that it not only quelled the fears of man's bestial past but served as an emblem of the heart and an example to the human race.

This transfigured saint of the animal kingdom surely convinced few. Who could believe in so patently incredible a creation? But no one needed to. The point was not to manufacture a plausible animal that might tread the earth and crop the grass but to set up a series of counter-impressions of animal nature, to drain off some of the tension induced by man's kinship with animals. The strategy seemed to work. Slowly, sometimes awkwardly and painfully, people were learning to live with the idea that they were animals, too, and nothing animal was alien from them. In kindness to animals, people declared what they were, what the basic character of their world was. Compassion for animals meant that nature was not devoid of sympathy and love, that human beings were not beasts, and that human compassion—even for other human beings—was not a superficial and fleeting impulse but a basic direction of nature. No wonder kindness to animals had become for many a *sine qua non* of civilization.

V

"Revolting to the Cultivated Mind..."

Compassion for animals depended on a deepening sense of physical and emotional kinship with them. This was necessary but not sufficient. The growth of kindness also required—and we tend now to forget this, because it has become second nature for us—a revulsion from suffering, a horror of physical pain. The dread of pain forms one of the most basic bonds uniting us with our ancestors of a century ago, a bond overlooked only because so obvious. William James observed in 1901 that a "moral transformation" had "within the past century swept over our Western world. We no longer think that we are called on to face physical pain with equanimity. . . . to listen to the recital of cases of it makes our flesh creep morally as well as physically." Among the devils haunting the Victorians, as in our own hells, pain was an archdemon.

The very thought of pain called up a wave of disgust. "The infliction of pain is a thing naturally so revolting to the cultivated mind, that any description of it inevitably arouses strong sentiments of dislike, if not of horror. . . ." This dread of pain, not merely of pain in oneself but of pain wherever found, underlay the growing humane sensibility. What did people sympathize with in animals? Pain. What, in the traditional view, gave animals a right to human consideration? Their ability to feel pain. How indeed was cruelty defined if not as the deliberate infliction of unnecessary pain? And cruelty stank as the vilest of sins, blasphemy in the face of a merciful God. The "main doctrine of devil-worship" was "that it is delightful to inflict or to witness agony." So intensely did animal protectors abhor pain that they paradoxically ended by killing each year thousands of perfectly healthy animals in animal "shelters," in order to spare them the cold, hunger, and possible starvation that befell the stray. Nor did the horror of pain evoke only sympathy for animals. It also reinforced the dark underside of that sympathetic impulse, the fear of the animal within. More than any other act, the infliction of pain on animals turned man himself into a beast.[1]

Pain had not always inspired such loathing. In earlier centuries, people doubtless feared pain for themselves or their families, but it seems to have been endured as an unavoidable misfortune, perhaps a punishment for sin. Inflicting pain on animals certainly raised few qualms, as the common delight in blood sports testified. This traditional attitude faded very slowly. The eighteenth-century cult of benevolence gave the first clear sign of its passing, but only in the next century did the growing distaste for pain in the abstract or in others rise to the level of horror.

This transformation of commonplace attitudes, of one's reaction to everyday experience, bore momentous import for the structure of values and beliefs. Modulated by religious and humanitarian currents, the revulsion from pain played a major role, far transcending the narrow question of kindness to animals, in reshaping prevailing visions of the "good life" and the good society. The modern sensibility—in politics, in religion, in the arts—draws heavily on our response to suffering. When we can, we avert our eyes from pain; when we cannot, we approach it in fear and trembling. The pervasiveness of the so-called pornography of violence, now a common substitute for creativity in films and television, might seem to undercut this argument. But in fact it is precisely our reaction to pain that makes violence titillating. Pain in its full modern sense, externally perceived as evil, is not a biological reaction but a mental construction, a human invention, however unintentional. All this we owe largely to the Victorians.[2]

The origins of this obsession with pain remain even today little investigated and vexingly obscure. Perhaps it had something to do with man's magnified technological powers. So long as only God could change the world fundamentally, so long as human beings lived obviously at the whim of nature, people could only expect to bear pain as stoically as possible. There was simply no point in dwelling upon it. But perhaps the advent of the Industrial Revolution—and before it, to a lesser extent, that side of the scientific revolution epitomized in the Baconian ideal of mastery over nature—changed this attitude. If people could harness the forces of nature, if they could accomplish almost anything they set their minds on, could they not find a way to control pain? Under these altered circumstances, there was a reason to rage against pain, and the louder the better.

Possibly, too, the weakening of traditional religion focused greater attention on pain. When one's hope and true home lay in heaven, earthly sufferings paled into insignificance. Indeed, God sometimes even sent pain as a test, and patient endurance of it stored up treasures in heaven. With the decline of faith and especially with the growing uncertainty about immortality, worldly enjoyments loomed larger. If human beings had to find their only secure reward in this life, then pain became something not to be endured with resignation but to be got rid of as quickly as possible. Indeed, for wavering believers, pain insinuated that a loving God was a pious myth, and the ancient answers to that problem carried less assurance in an age of doubt. Faith, as well as self-interest, demanded the diminution of suffering. Perhaps all of this helps to explain why the theodicy problem apparently preoccupied theologians, both professional and amateur, more during the eighteenth and nineteenth centuries than ever before.

Yet heightened sensitivity about pain was only one ingredient in the Victorian revulsion from suffering. Equally necessary, and equally obscure in origin, was a deeper, readier empathy with the pain of others. In an urbanizing and industrializing society, communication among people became more frequent and more varied; perhaps this made it easier for an individual to imagine himself enduring another's anguish. But empathy may also have burgeoned as an antidote to the growing competitiveness and increased individual autonomy of a modernizing world. The old external social ties of village or clan, of master and servant, of landlord and tenant, which had bound people together since before the memory of man, were breaking down under the pressure of factory and metropolis. Perhaps empathy emerged as a psychological substitute for these crumbling social bonds, as a new, internalized way of linking people together when the older, external ties were weakening. This was arguably a specific case of a broader phenomenon: a shift from reliance upon external controls over human behavior to internalized controls. If so, it was part of the same process that made possible democratic rather than authoritarian governance, religious tolerance and pluralism rather than monolithic, coercive religions, and similar developments.

If empathy was a new social bond, then history had again indulged her taste for irony. Far from promoting callous neglect of suffering, the rise of a competitive, individualistic society had actually encouraged people to notice it. At any rate, notice it they did. The alleviation of pain seemed now among the noblest, most urgent of human endeavors. Here Philistines closed ranks with philosophers. In 1891 an advertisement for a laxative inquired liltingly: "What higher aim can man attain than conquest over human pain?"[3] This attitude would have seemed very nearly blasphemous two centuries earlier.

Yet that view summed up the feelings of many Victorians. Nowhere did this appear more vividly than in attitudes toward the practice of medicine. Medicine, at least at its higher levels, was an attractive career, prestigious and well-remunerated. But pain was the doctor's daily companion, and for many this reality blighted the prospect of a life in medicine. Darwin turned away from a physician's career for this reason; he especially could not bear the agony of surgery in the days before anesthetics. Henry Jacob Bigelow overcame the same aversion and ended a famous surgeon. But he could never stand "the needless fingering of a sensitive region" and therefore taught his students "the art of diagnosis by sight alone." No wonder he greeted anesthesia as "the greatest boon ever accorded to the physical welfare of mankind." Its discovery "forever silenced the dreadful shriek of agony" that made the surgical amphitheatre an arena of horror.[4]

Doctors indeed seized upon ether and chloroform with extraordinary haste, born of indescribable relief. Despite debates over its appropriateness in various applications, anesthesia may have passed into common use more rapidly than any previous medical discovery. Ether and chloroform were only the most spectacular of the pharmacological weapons against pain developed during the nineteenth century. The century opened with the isolation of morphine in 1806 (in common use by the 1820s); it closed with the introduction of aspirin in 1899. And the use of anesthetics and analgesics, by making pain avoidable, probably only intensified the fear and hatred of pain. William Lawrence, Episcopal bishop of Massachusetts at the turn of the century, thought his generation more intolerant of suffering than any other in history. "The blessing of anesthetics has so released humanity from the awful terrors of pain that we cannot endure even the thought of what our fathers passed through."[5]

The horror of pain showed itself most nakedly in concern for animals. As early as 1772, the Rev. James Granger had based his arguments for kindness to animals on their "acute sense of pain," and eighty years later the Rev. Richard Burgess offered exactly the same rationale for the work of the RSPCA. The suffering animal was the avatar of pure, simple, unmitigated pain. People could feign sickness and injury, but each tremble and cry of a brute evinced certain, sharply felt agony. People enjoyed mental pleasures that offset their physical pain, and they could also sublimate their suffering in higher moral purposes. But a suffering animal endured unalloyed, unrelieved, unredeemed agony.[6] Animal lovers therefore welcomed anesthetics with unusual enthusiasm. Ether had scarcely come into common use before the RSPCA began urging its application in veterinary surgery. The distinguished physician, sanitarian, and pioneer in anesthetics, Sir Benjamin Ward Richardson, who would later invent the "lethal chamber" for painlessly killing small animals, received a special award from the RSPCA for his work on ether spray as a local anesthetic. George Angell urged slaughterhouses to anesthetize livestock before killing, a suggestion seconded by Richardson, among others, in the *Animal World.*[7]

This enthusiasm for anesthetics underlined the animal lovers' extraordinary sensitiveness about pain. The sight of pain evoked disgust and even nausea. For centuries, bull baiting had delighted crowds of Englishmen, yet Richard Martin reported in 1824 that the sight of a bull bait had left a friend, notable for strong nerves, sick to his stomach. The cruelties of a nearby knacker's yard (a slaughterhouse for horses) forced another of Martin's friends to move his family four miles into the country. The Bishop of St. David's twenty years later endured "deep and acute pain" as "an involuntary spectator" of cruelty to animals.[8]

Caroline White also "suffered acutely from seeing, almost daily, animals subjected to cruelty and abuse" in Philadelphia. Even second-hand reports of cruelties depressed the more sensitive. A correspondent wrote to Angell: "From childhood, the sufferings of animals have weighed so heavily on my mind that at times I could scarcely rise above the despondency caused by the recital of the cruelties perpetrated around me." Angell himself felt ill at the sight of a slaughterhouse. Indeed, slaughterhouses were one of the first targets of the public health movement, perhaps not wholly for medical reasons. But it was hardly surprising that animal lovers reacted so strongly to pain, when even a scientific observer could maintain—in the face of centuries of gladiatorial contests, torture, bull baiting, and other blood-thirsty pleasures—that people *instinctively* shrank from the infliction of pain: "one of the most depressing sights to the human eye."[9]

Nowhere did the Victorian revulsion from pain surface so openly as in the public outrage stirred up by scientific experiments on living animals: vivisection, as the practice was then called.[10] Hostility to vivisection was graven onto the conscience of the SPCA movement by its founders. Richard Martin attacked it in the House of Commons in 1825, and a few years later he wrote to Lewis Gompertz: "As to the dissection of living animals it is in my mind too revolting to be palliated by any excuse that science may be enlarged or improved by so detestable a means." Martin's was a layman's reaction, but many scientists and medical practitioners shared his revulsion.[11]

Yet vivisection had a long and distinguished history. Many of the towering figures in medicine had employed it, as far back as Galen and beyond, including, for example, among Englishmen the great anatomist William Harvey and the pathbreaking surgeon John Hunter. The few English experimental physiologists active in the first half of the nineteenth century, men like Charles Bell and Marshall Hall, continued the practice.[12] Their work did not go unopposed. Occasionally in the eighteenth century, men of letters had raised their voices against vivisection, and the tempo of protest accelerated in the nineteenth century as sympathy for animals grew.[13]

Hostility to animal experimentation by no means branded an individual as antiscientific or obscurantist. Auguste Comte, though a self-consciously "advanced" thinker and an ideologist of science, held vivisection in contempt. Even within the medical sciences, experimental physiology was suspect throughout the first half of the century. Despite its contributions, vivisection seemed morally insensitive and technically crude. Most scientists of the era preferred to explore physiology through the supposedly more accurate and certainly more compassionate methods of comparative anatomy and clinical observation. In particular, the latter approach, revolutionized in the 1820s by P.C.A. Louis's introduction of statistical methods, appeared more precise, more scientific, and more up-to-date than vivisection. True, the brilliant Frenchman François Magendie was an expert and prolific vivisector. But his posthumous reputation as the father of modern experimental physiology has obscured the fact that he was in his own lifetime a rather lonely figure, overshadowed by his younger German contemporary, Johannes Müller. Müller's vitalism led him to a scornful rejection of vivisection, and it was Müller who dominated European physiology until his death in 1858.[14]

What scientists doubted, others detested. Even physicians sometimes organized "to prevent and discourage this 'physiological butchery.'" During the 1820s—probably in response to Magendie's notorious demonstrations in London in 1824—twenty-nine doctors at Newcastle and another thirty-eight at Bath signed protests against vivisection.[15]

Nearly all animal lovers who set pen to paper in behalf of animals felt obliged to denounce vivisection, at least in passing.[16] They complained not of the animals' deaths, but of "the protracted and intense agony to which they are subjected before they expire." This was not polemical excess; experimenters had no effective anesthetic before the late forties. To make matters worse, the uselessness attributed to such experiments by their critics implied that vivisection contributed only to the gratification of curiosity, not to the advancement of practical medicine. Even so, few urged abolition of vivisection. In rare instances, most conceded, its legitimacy had been established by its benefits to mankind. But in most cases, vivisection was deemed a pointless barbarity.[17]

From time to time, the anticruelty societies lashed out at vivisection. The RSPCA attacked it in its first publication and thrice over the next two decades skirmished with experimental physiologists. Lewis Gompertz's Animals' Friend Society offered rewards for information leading to the conviction of vivisectors for cruelty. Nothing much came of all this, but speakers at RSPCA annual meetings regularly cheered on the campaign against "the scarifying knife of [the] heartless and calculating tormentor" of "the poor dumb animal."[18]

The meager result of their indignation was hardly a surprise, considering the size of its target. Even in France, the birthplace of modern physiology, François Magendie and his pupil Claude Bernard were lonely pioneers before the middle of the century. In England and America, physiological experiment remained little more than the hobby of a scant handful of practicing physicians. After 1850 the situation on the Continent began to change. The rising generation of physiologists discarded Müller's vitalism in favor of a reductionist mechanistic materialism more congenial to experimental methods. In consequence, Magendie's methods triumphed even among Müller's students. Comparative anatomy sank into torpor, and experimental physiology now commanded the attention of the best minds in medical science. The makeshift laboratory of Magendie at the Collège de France multiplied into a number of established research centers. Claude

Bernard superbly carried on Magendie's tradition in France and, unlike his master, attracted a flock of students to expand his work. But leadership shifted to Germany, where three brilliant pupils of Müller—Hermann von Helmholtz, Emil du Bois-Reymond, and Carl Ludwig—did more than anyone else to make that country the center of physiological research.[19]

From across the *cordon sanitaire* of the Channel, British animal lovers watched the spread of experimental physiology with growing alarm. As early as 1846, the Rev. David Davis petitioned the French king to suppress the practice of vivisection at the veterinary school at Alfort, near Paris. Evidently Louis Philippe ignored his plea, for in 1857 the "detestable cruelties" at Alfort and other French veterinary schools came to the attention of a shocked RSPCA. The case quickly became a *cause célèbre*. Deputations went back and forth. The Society and *The Times* pressed for, and won, a full-scale investigation by the French government. The dispute smoldered through the sixties, and as late as 1878 the RSPCA was still importuning the French authorities.[20]

In 1863 a smaller storm blew up over the Florentine laboratory of the physiologist Moritz Schiff, a student of Claude Bernard. The English journalist Frances Power Cobbe, then a temporary resident of Florence, led the attack and prodded the English community there into action. British newspapers and the RSPCA joined in from afar. Like the French controversy, this one also persisted for over a decade. Neither affray brought any relief to the vivisected animals, though Schiff's exasperation may have hastened his departure for Geneva in 1876.[21] But both episodes made animal lovers touchier than ever about experimental medicine.

Actual vivisection was even rarer in America than in England, but, if anything, Americans reacted more violently. In the late sixties two investigators pioneered experimental medicine in New York: the younger Austin Flint at Bellevue Hospital and, at the College of Physicians and Surgeons, John Call Dalton, another of Claude Bernard's students and reputedly the first professor of physiology in America to demonstrate with living material. Henry Bergh heard of their work with horror. After a year of increasingly hostile correspondence with the enemy—culminating in an ASPCA spy's venture into Bellevue disguised as a reporter—Bergh tried in 1867 to smuggle a ban on vivisection into an anticruelty bill then before the legislature. Dalton and the state medical society foiled this maneuver, but battle was joined several more times in the seventies.[22] Similar, though less dramatic, skirmishes jarred medical researchers in Boston in 1869 and Philadelphia in 1870. The upsurge of antivivisection sentiment provoked fervent rebuttals from medical men.[23] On both sides of the battle, most of the arguments and evidence were borrowed from England—as was only natural, since the controversy had first erupted there. But Americans were not merely half-heartedly echoing English outrage. Vivisection touched raw nerves on both sides of the Atlantic.

All animal suffering distressed animal lovers. But nowhere did it stand out more starkly and dreadfully than in the laboratory. Pain headed the counts in the bill of indictment against experimental medicine.[24] Antivivisectionists opposed not the killing but the alleged torture of animals. They conjured up a hellish vision of millions of animals writhing in "incessant and excruciating torture," of "barbarities the mere mention of which makes the blood curdle in the veins," and of "the infliction of the most prolonged and the most intense anguish that living beings can be made to endure by any means known to us in the world. Nothing in either ancient or modern times can be compared to it." Vivisection earned the odious title of "the worst existing form of the worst thing in the world": cruelty. Henry Bigelow of the Harvard Medical School claimed that he would rather die "than protract existence through accumulated years of inflicted torture upon animals."[25]

Not the thoughtlessness of an ignorant drover, but the deliberate calculation of a rational scientist inflicted this agony. Was this not pure, refined heartlessness? In 1875 the physiologist Emanuel Klein calmly admitted to the Royal Commission on vivisection that he used anesthetics only as a convenience, for he had "no regard at all" for the suffering of his experimental animals. The commissioners recoiled in disgust. One of them, Thomas Huxley, no friend of antivivisection, privately denounced Klein as "an unmitigated cynical brute" and volunteered to support "any law which would send him to the treadmill." For decades afterwards the *bête noire* of antivivisection, Klein was equally execrated on both sides of the Atlantic. He epitomized scientific cruelty; intense pain, almost too dreadful to gaze on, he seemed ready to inflict with neither qualm nor shudder. Physiologists hastened to repudiate him, but too late. He had provided the classic example of what antivivisectionists saw in vivisection. Not torture per se, but calm, calculating torture made vivisection the most heinous of crimes.[26]

Even some of vivisection's staunchest defenders—Huxley, the anatomist Richard Owen—could not bring themselves personally to practice it. The very thought left Darwin "sick with horror." The suffering of animals had distressed Darwin as a boy, and his mature scientific investigations of the painful struggle for existence only reinforced this sensitivity. He accepted vivisection as a necessary tool of scientific research and actively battled antivivisectionism. But he did so with heavy heart, always hoped to minimize the use of vivisection, and never employed it himself.[27]

Darwin had likewise shrunk from the vision of universal suffering that he saw as the mainspring of his own theory of natural selection. Rather than believe in a God capable of creating a world in which evolution depended on "the sufferings of millions of the lower animals throughout almost endless time," he rejected God altogether. Such a deity, he wrote, "revolts our understanding."[28] Vivisection presented a similar dilemma. The many scientists who increasingly sealed off their professional pursuits from their religious beliefs perhaps evaded it. But many opponents of vivisection could not.[29] Pain loomed for them as the climax and symbol of physical evil. This horror not only pervaded the practice of vivisection, but man himself inflicted it—supposedly as the only road to a greater good. Had God so contrived the world? Did He require the human race to inflict this dreadful evil as the price of bodily health? An earlier age, less obsessed with pain, could have accepted such a God. But many Victorians refused. To them, this blasphemously mocked the divine goodness. Darwin's abhorrence of pain would not permit him to accept the kind of God who would create through natural selection; he followed his science and denied God.

The antivivisectionists made the opposite choice. They clung to a benevolent God and denied a world that operated on the principle of pain. They rejected the *"impious* doctrine—I say it deliberately, an *impious* doctrine—that God has made it any man's duty to commit the great sin of cruelty by way of obtaining a benefit for suffering humanity."[30] To believe otherwise would strain intolerably a faith already near the breaking point. Thus was forged another link in the chain within which pain, and vivisection, were quarantined and condemned.

Most Victorians chose neither Darwin's road nor that of the thoroughgoing antivivisectionists. The revulsion against pain, though powerful, did not drive them to reject all vivisection, at the cost of human life and suffering. Balancing with difficulty their faith in God and their dread of pain, their faith in science and their sympathy with animals, most animal lovers sought to compromise their conflicting principles, to restrict scientists but not hamstring them. Yet even moderates could not believe that much good could come of vivisection. The extremists, abolitionists like Henry Bergh and Frances Power Cobbe, insisted that no good could conceivably result from the devil's work. Pain only bred more pain. Manipulating the quivering, disrupted organs of agonized animals of course yielded contradictory and confusing conclusions and actually impeded medical progress.[31] Far from easing human suffering, vivisection would prolong it, and would add the animals' anguish to the sum of suffering.

Yet "human moral interests" required abolition or restriction of vivisection even more urgently than "the physical interests of the poor brutes." However "sickening" the pain of its animal victims, vivisection allegedly afflicted its practitioners with a far more serious curse. Even painless experimentation was deemed "exceedingly hazardous" because the "practice of vivisection hardens the sensibility of the operator and begets indifference to the infliction of pain."[32]

The effects of this calm, considered infliction of torture were thought to be as ineluctable as frightening. Mere witnesses of cruelty "first shudder, then enjoy, then imitate." How much more perniciously did it deprave actual practitioners! Cruelty usually "is an acquired vice; and it often happens that medical students, corrupted by hospital teaching, imbibe such a love of it that when they visit their homes they practise it for its own sake." True, vivisectors wrapped themselves in the mantle of science, but their opponents suspected them of indulging a depraved taste under the sanction of duty. Consider the routine of:

> a practical physiologist, rising every day and going to the same hideous employment with the morning light, keeping the tortured and mutilated creatures beside him week after week, month after month, refusing them even the comfort of a drop of water, if thirst will increase the "interest" of his experiment; think of him, eating and drinking, jesting and love-making, filling his belly and indulging his desires, then returning to his laboratory to devise and execute fresh tortures, his hands steeped in blood, his eyes greedily watching the throes he stimulates; think of what his daily and yearly existence is, and then judge if he be fit to consort with men of gentle temper and decent habitudes. . . .

What sort of men and women would the next generation be if people accepted without murmur the notion that such practices were right, nay, a duty? Vivisection polluted all decency, destroyed all kindness, hardened all the finest impulses of the heart.[33]

So it came back to pain once more. Pain constituted so great an evil that deliberate, cool infliction of it made one a moral leper. For many Victorians, no claim of utility, not even ultimate alleviation of human pain, palliated the wickedness of vivisection: "Be the physical benefits to man what they may—they would be far outbalanced by the moral evils which its practice would entail." The revulsion aroused by the pain of vivisection, the response of the tender, loving, uncorrupted heart, offered "the best possible proof of its immorality."[34]

Animal experimentation became the principal focus for the anxiety and dread stirred in Victorian minds by the thought of pain. The common use of dogs as experimental animals only made matters worse. One could all too readily imagine oneself in the place of the pet who shared hearth and home.[35] Even easier was to picture oneself in the shoes of the fellow human being doing the vivisecting, knife in hand poised over the trembling pet. One could see the knife plunging down, could feel it slice the flesh. Among people who shuddered at the idea of pain, that image sent chills up the spine. An era newly alive to the awfulness of pain needed to concentrate its anxieties on a tangible target, so that they could be attacked. By assailing pain, one publicly denied complicity in its infliction and washed away the guilt of membership in a society that tolerated such things. Lending a hand to defeat pain eased one's own fear of it. All the varieties of animal protection work helped, but antivivisection met these compelling needs directly.

For most of the century, however, experimental physiology remained a continental specialty, and there were limits to how angry one could become over the misdeeds of foreigners, who were suspect anyhow. What elevated antivivisectionism from a mostly latent sense of outrage into a ferocious public agitation was the large-scale importation of experimental physiology into Britain and the United States after 1870.

The experimental method penetrated English medicine more rapidly than American, if only because England lay three thousand miles closer to France and Germany. The new approach took hold gradually, but 1870 marked a watershed. In that year, Michael Foster became Praelector of Physiology at Trinity College, Cambridge—the first full-time teacher of the subject at either Oxford or Cambridge. John Scott Burdon Sanderson, yet another of Claude Bernard's students, filled Foster's place at University College, London, with E. A. Schäfer (later Sharpey-Schafer) as assistant professor under him. But it was in 1873 that the sudden leap forward in experimental medicine came most strikingly and alarmingly to the attention of the lay public. Burdon Sanderson and three of his colleagues published their *Handbook for the Physiological Laboratory,* the first manual of experimental physiology to appear in English.[36]

The book did not arouse an immediate furor as the vivisections at Alfort had done. But it profoundly disturbed many of those who monitored Britain's mind and morals for the newspapers and reviews. This was a manual for *British* students, not French or German. Moreover, Burdon Sanderson's unguarded language gave nonscientists the impression that rank beginners routinely performed scores of vivisections in English laboratories, and usually without anesthesia. To make matters worse, the Schiff controversy now flared up in the press once again.[37] In August 1874, against this background, a French physiologist named Valentin Magnan conducted in Norwich a demonstration experiment before a meeting of the British Medical Association. Even some of the doctors present found his experiment pointlessly cruel. The meeting was disrupted, and RSPCA Secretary John Colam got wind of it. The Society prosecuted Magnan and his sponsors under Martin's Act. Magnan fled the country, and his hosts were acquitted on more or less technical grounds. But the RSPCA had stoked to white-hot intensity the public outrage against vivisection.[38]

For one Englishwoman this was the last straw. Frances Power Cobbe had led the fight against vivisection in Florence, and she had no intention of letting it take root in her own land. In her the physiologists acquired a formidable enemy. She did not look the part: "round and fat as a Turkish sultana, with yellow hair, and face mature and pulpy," she could have passed more easily as a jovial grandmother than as a saboteur of science. But her hearty plumpness belied a keen mind and one of the deftest polemical pens in Victorian England.[39]

Born in 1822 of a moderately distinguished Anglo-Irish family, young Fanny lived a lonely life, though not, she later maintained, an unhappy one. She had no sisters, her brothers were substantially older, and her mother was an invalid. Her chief comfort she found in the strict but cheerful Evangelicalism of her parents. But science, in the form of the nebular hypothesis and *Vestiges of Creation* among other things, gradually eroded her childhood faith. Around her twentieth year she plunged into a despairing agnosticism. After wandering in the deserts of doubt for a year or two, she slowly pulled herself back to a nondogmatic faith in God and his perfect goodness. Theodore Parker's *Discourse on Religion* confirmed and completed her rescue. To Parker's doctrine of (in her words) "a Divine inflowing of mental light" as the source of faith in "God's holiness and love," Miss Cobbe soon added, as the foundation of morality, an intuitive ethical sense mainly derived from her reading of Parker's intellectual grand-father, Kant. The linchpin holding the whole structure together was the absolute goodness of God.

Miss Cobbe had painfully reconstructed a faith to give meaning to her life, but her crisis left two ineradicable marks on her world view. She now firmly subordinated science to faith as a source of final knowledge and as a guide to conduct; for the rest of her life she remained suspicious of the claims of science and scientists. And she refused to contemplate the possibility of any blemish on the perfect goodness of God and his world; any intimation that God might prove good to some of his creatures and cruel to others put too serious a strain on her hard-won faith. She had surmounted her crisis by grinding down science and its supposedly cruel, godless version of nature. In this she resembled many of her contemporaries.

In other respects she led an unusual life. She never married and indeed averred that she had never met a man whom she would have wished to marry. After a stint toward the end of the fifties working at Mary Carpenter's Ragged School in Bristol, she settled in London with her "beloved friend" Mary C. Lloyd, with whom she lived for thirty-seven years. About this time a four-year stretch of semi-invalidism resulted from a badly sprained ankle, maltreated, Miss Cobbe believed, by a succession of surgeons. This experi-ence, coupled with her conviction that medical incompetence had also caused her mother's invalidism, permanently soured her on the whole tribe of physicians. More urgently, it required her to find a more sedentary occupation than schoolteaching. She had written for the press in Bristol and now turned naturally to journalism as her life's work.

Her prolific pen argued for feminist causes, sketched her frequent travels in Italy, and addressed the religious and moral questions of the day in the grand tradition of Victorian high journalism. She soon built an impressive reputation and circle of friends. By the seventies she counted among her acquaintances Mill, Darwin, Jowett, Lyell, Spencer, Froude, Arnold, Kingsley, and many another pillar of Victorian culture, as well as a host of socially prominent people now forgotten. Wary of science, hostile to the pretensions of medicine, and clinging to a faith that required God to damn pain, Miss Cobbe easily caught the antivivisectionist fever. Her skilled pen and contacts among the influential inevitably made her a prime agent for its spread.

To these influential acquaintances she now turned for allies. In January 1875, Miss Cobbe organized a deputation to urge the RSPCA to press for legislation restricting vivisection. The petition presented to the Society bore the signatures of a sizable fraction of the bench of bishops, some twoscore peers and a flock of baronets and knights, eighteen admirals and generals, two dozen members of Parliament, the Lord Chief Justice, Lord Chief Baron, Lord Mayor of London, and Lord Provost of Edinburgh. And it was liberally garnished with the names of such other luminaries as Tennyson, Browning, Ruskin, Carlyle, and Manning. But the Society's leadership squirmed uneasily, caught between its zeal for animal welfare and its ingrained sense of caution. An extraordinary committee was named to investigate the question thoroughly and recommend a course of action.[40]

Miss Cobbe was in no mood to wait. Through her friend William Hart Dyke, the Tory whip, she arranged for a bill regulating vivisection to be introduced into Lords in early May with the government's sanction. But the scientists had a surprise in store for her. A group of them led by Charles Darwin and Burdon Sanderson had prepared their own bill to forestall her. Disraeli's government was in a quandary. Somehow vivisection had fired the emotions of a large and distinguished portion of the British social and intellectual elites. The periodical press grew obsessed with vivisection, feelings ran high on all sides, and the government could not much longer avoid taking a position. Prudently, the Cabinet felt the need for expert advice. On May 24 the Home Secretary, R. A. Cross, announced a Royal Commission to investigate vivisection.[41]

Miss Cobbe had no more confidence in the Royal Commission than in the RSPCA. She found an improbable ally in a former student of Claude Bernard, George Hoggan, who had recoiled in disgust from vivisection. Together they set out to organize the opposition. As titular leaders, Miss Cobbe recruited two of the most respected men in England: William Thomson, Archbishop of York, and, still more impressive, the seventh Earl of Shaftesbury, the great Evangelical statesman (or, in Huxley's view, "that pietistic old malefactor"). Then, on December 2, 1875, the Society for the Protection of Animals liable to Vivisection (soon less cumbrously nick-named the Victoria Street Society) held its first meeting.[42]

The Royal Commission reported on January 8, 1876. It recommended, vaguely, some form of state regulation of vivisection. After months of political infighting, deputations to the Home Office from medical men and animal lovers, and pressure on Disraeli's government from the kingdom's most prominent antivivisectionist, Queen Victoria, the Cruelty to Animals Act of 1876 at last received the Royal Assent on August 15, 1876. The Act protected all vertebrate animals. It required individual experimenters to be licensed by the Home Secretary, on the recommendation of specified medical authorities, and provided for the registration and inspection of places where experiments were performed. Experiments without anesthesia, experiments to illustrate teaching or to test former discoveries, and those in which the animal recovered consciousness required a special certificate.[43]

Miss Cobbe was outraged. The bill as passed, she claimed, did not protect "vivisected animals from torture, but vivisectors from prosecution under Martin's Act." She had tried to cooperate with the scientists, but they had "twisted" her concessions into a law worse than no law. No more compromise! Henceforth the Victoria Street Society demanded no less than the total abolition of vivisection, the position adopted from the outset by most English antivivisection societies. The physiologists, after an initial sigh of relief, were scarcely happier. They had evaded severe restrictions on the range of their experiments, but now, unexpectedly, it turned out that the Home Secretary intended to use his power to deny licenses. True, relatively few applications were rejected. But even those few hurt, especially when the decision flew in the face of the medical recommendations to the Home Secretary.[44] The law was settled, but the controversy was far from over.

In America it had scarcely begun. Aside from Bergh's continuing harassment of scientists in New York, American animal lovers launched no sustained campaigns against experimental physiology during the sixties and seventies. The relative immaturity of American experimental physiology, which lagged about a decade behind British work, accounted for this. Although presaged by the activity of men like Dalton and Flint, the opening of Henry Bowditch's laboratory at Harvard in 1871 marked the real beginning of experimental medicine in the United States. The succeeding steps came slowly. As late as 1880, only about a dozen scientists in perhaps five places carried on physiological investigations. By the middle eighties, they were reinforced by some six or eight bacteriologists, who also experimented on animals. But only after 1890 did the United States become a major center of animal experimentation.[45] Before then there was simply not much of an enemy for antivivisectionists to battle. Although SPCA leaders kept close watch on the English agitation and occasionally vented their wrath against an unwary American scientist, not even George Angell succeeded in organizing an antivivisection society.[46]

Frances Power Cobbe thought this "a disgrace to the country." Under her prodding, Caroline White organized at Philadelphia in 1883 the American Anti-Vivisection Society. The title expressed hope more than reality, since all of the officers were Pennsylvanians. At first the local medical profession regarded the whole enterprise as little more than a joke. But several prominent newspapers and magazines unexpectedly lent their support, and a handful of defectors from the medical side joined. The new Society's propaganda intensified, bills for regulation appeared in the state legislature, and the doctors closed ranks. Soon "medical opposition became extremely bitter and so effective that it was impossible to secure any restrictive legislation." Initially, like Miss Cobbe, the AAVS pressed only for restriction. Failing to secure that, in 1887 it widened its demands to total abolition.[47]

Antivivisection sentiment spread, though not, as in England, in a thunderclap of public excitement. In Boston *Our Dumb Animals* and the MSPCA, though remaining ostensibly open-minded, leaned more and more heavily toward the antivivisection side. Another valuable ally was the Boston *Transcript,* the favored newspaper of Boston's elite.[48] An even more important convert was the Women's Christian Temperance Union (WCTU), probably the largest women's organization in the country. Its Department of Mercy, organized in 1891, immediately set about distributing thousands of diatribes against experimental physiology. The next year a second antivivisection society was formed, in New York City. It did not survive long, but two weeks after its founding the Illinois Antivivisection Society, destined for a more successful career, was organized at Aurora, near Chicago. In 1895 Boston antivivisectionists founded the New England Antivivisection Society, perhaps the most extreme of the lot. Despite (or because of) its radicalism, it claimed two hundred members within a month.[49]

For arguments against vivisection, even for the specific examples to support these arguments, American antivivisectionists drew almost exclusively on the voluminous literature of the English controversy. Caroline White's speeches offered her hearers a thoroughly English diet, and in 1893 she was still lambasting the antique horrors of Alfort and resurrecting the Florentine misdeeds of Miss Cobbe's old foe, the physiologist Moritz Schiff. As late as 1896 the embarrassed advocates of restriction in the District of Columbia, by that time a major research center, could not evince a single local case of alleged abuse. Their failure reflected not the unimpeachable humaneness of Washington scientists but the penchant of American antivivisectionists for letting the English provide their evidence instead of investigating for themselves.[50] In these circumstances, the movement of organized antivivisection toward the English insistence on no compromise became inevitable. But it was also natural for the Americans to look to England, since antivivisection in both nations sprang from the same sources and matured in much the same cultural environment.

Nevertheless, although one in aims and ideology, British and American antivivisectionists pursued divergent strategies. Until the middle eighties, British abolitionists hoped for imminent parliamentary victory. But by 1884 it had become clear that Parliament would give them no more than the restrictions already won in 1876.[51] Miss Cobbe and her allies did not despair, but they did postpone the millennium. A long-term campaign of public education replaced the annual legislative minuet. When the British electorate finally possessed all the facts, when the distortions of physiologists had withered in the light of truth, the parliamentary *coup de grâce* would follow as a matter of course. Exposing the fallacies of vivisection would simply take much longer than at first thought. After 1884, this attempt to evangelize the British public absorbed the entire vigor of the antivivisection societies, and its tempo hardly abated until the turn of the century. If British antivivisection in the nineties achieved no landmarks, reached no great climax, this resulted from its choice of strategy, not from any lack of vitality.

American antivivisection ran a more dramatic course. During the late eighties and nineties, the expansion of physiological and bacteriological research began to make the United States a world center of scientific medicine. Laboratories multiplied, and experiments on animals proliferated. The lay public began to take some notice of the discoveries coming out of the laboratories of institutions like Harvard, Johns Hopkins, and the U.S. Department of Agriculture; antivivisectionists took alarm at the number of animals going in. Agitation, swelling all through the eighties, reached a peak in the middle nineties.

The antivivisection societies, however, took only a secondary part in the accelerated campaign against experimental medicine. Far more powerful organizations intervened. The Department of Mercy of the WCTU lashed out at scientists. More influential (because by now legislators and bureaucrats looked to them as the established authorities on proper treatment of animals) were the major animal protection societies. First among their spokesmen stood the ASPCA (now shed of Bergh's rabid antivivisectionism), the Massachusetts SPCA, and the national federation of humane societies, the American Humane Association. No one could convict their leaders of irrational hatred of science, yet even these men and women looked upon medical research as a serious and growing menace to animal welfare.

State legislatures could brush aside the intemperate demands of extreme antivivisectionists but could not ignore growing pressure for restriction from the SPCAs. These were sensible and respected groups; a history of moderation lent their requests plausibility, and the support of leading politicians and clergymen lent them weight. In 1894, the Massachusetts SPCA scored the first victory, a minor one, with a law banning vivisection in elementary and secondary schools. This in no way obstructed scientific research, so scientists did not seriously object to it. But its passage was for them a worrisome omen. Two years later the Society justified their fears by asking the legislature to mandate to its officers powers of inspection over all animal experimentation in the Commonwealth. This dreadfully alarmed medical men and evoked dire prophecies of the imminent demise of experimental medicine in Massachusetts at the hands of ignorance and sentimentality.[52]

Nor were Massachusetts scientists the only ones worried. The Washington state legislature, prodded by the WCTU, outlawed vivisection in all of the state's schools and colleges, save only medical and dental schools—not that this made much immediate difference in a state still barren of physiology and bacteriology. Unhappily for the scientists, antivivisectionists were not content to stake their claims in the far West. In 1896, U.S. Sen. James McMillan of Michigan introduced a bill to regulate vivisection in the District of Columbia, a leading center of American experimental medicine. It was endorsed by six sitting justices of the Supreme Court, by the cream of the Washington clergy, by such eminent academics as former president John Bascom of the University of Wisconsin and the Harvard historian Albert Bushnell Hart, and, most convincing to nonscientific eyes, by a long list of practicing physicians.[53]

The support for the McMillan bill suggested the breadth of Victorian hostility to vivisection; the growing extremism of the antivivisection societies indicated its depth. Much of their propaganda was pitched on an offensively low level: vicious anonymous letters to physiologists from hysterical women, lurid posters of bloody experiments flaunted on busy streets, efforts to ostracize medical scientists from respectable society. One Englishwoman even circulated to laboratory assistants her prayers for the death of vivisectors—until a sympathizer reminded her that the occult powers of a vivisector beyond the grave might work more evil than even a live physiologist.[54]

The "violent language" and "reckless statements" of such extremists embarrassed more judicious animal protectors.[55] Yet their very embarrassment suggested an uncomfortably close family relationship. The inflated rhetoric of radical antivivisectionists sketched in caricature the lineaments of a widespread fear and dislike of vivisection. Anxieties trembling beneath the surface of Victorian culture erupted now into the full light of day. Most people, even most animal lovers, felt these pressures less strongly. For one reason or another, countervailing values and beliefs moderated their antagonism. Yet even the mildest antivivisectionism echoed faintly the desperate horror of the extremists. All pain was revolting. But to inflict it coolly, deliberately, scientifically was too appalling, and too ominous, to tolerate.

VI
Science and Sensibility

What extreme antivivisectionists despised, many Victorians distrusted. It was none too easy to understand exactly what this was. Pain, surely, for antivivisection was, above all—in every pamphlet, in every speech, in every poster—the starkest manifestation of the waxing Victorian revulsion from pain. Yet the matter was more complex than that. Millions of animals suffered intensely under much commoner practices. Why, for example, did animal lovers not unleash equal wrath against the thoroughly savage conditions prevailing in slaughterhouses? Somehow vivisection put pain in a context that redoubled its horror, made it uniquely and deeply threatening. Vivisectors loomed as dark angels of the Victorian imagination because in embracing pain they, like Satan, committed spiritual treason.

One perhaps expected to find a "half-brutalized and sottish carter . . . furiously flogging his stubborn horse." But "it is men of science—men belonging to the learned professions—who disembowel living horses and open the brains of dogs." How could an educated person remain coldly insensible to the quivering appeal of an anguished dog? That cultivated people could be so callous not only disgusted antivivisectionists; it threatened them. Many Victorians placed an almost childlike faith in the certainty of progress and, above all, moral progress. (Many also harbored serious reservations about the inevitability of progress, but this was a weaker counterpoint.) The promise of a nobler future eased consciences troubled by the apparent selfishness and materialism of their own graspingly commercial society. Perhaps, too, it partly compensated for the loss of an older way of life that grew more idyllic the further it receded into the past. And possibly the prospect of a better society in this world substituted for the increasingly distant hope of a better life in the next. For whatever reasons, the Victorians clung stubbornly to their faith in moral progress.[1]

Vivisection challenged that faith. In the steady upward course of moral evolution, "we find suddenly a break, a pause, nay, a very decided retrograde movement." Civilization's chief glory and central buttress was compassion. Vivisection—"a remnant of primitive savagery"—"engenders cruelty or indifference to suffering. Therefore it reverses the order of the refining forces of civilization." And "if we destroy pity, which it took thousands of years to develop, we have much to fear from the cruelty of a man who has brain but no heart." The arduous climb up the ladder of moral evolution had consumed millennia, and "it is so easy to fall."[2] Cruelty by the ignorant and half-civilized was bad enough. Cruelty by the educated and cultivated, the highest products of evolution, posed an intolerable danger to the upward progress of the race.

Yet this was not the worst of it. Not only cultivation and learning set vivisectors apart. They also belonged to the healing profession. Few medical scientists in the last third of the century practiced medicine, but they were closely identified with physicians in the public mind by the aims of their work—a connection cemented by the medical societies' unanimous defense of vivisection. Moreover, as scientific methods penetrated medical schools, more and more ordinary doctors came to have personal experience of vivisection, and this tendency only promised to accelerate.

That physicians could dabble in, rely on, or even approve of dissecting living animals appalled antivivisectionists. Traditionally, the doctor was "one who approaches human suffering in tenderness and mercy, being only anxious to alleviate it." Prior to the scientific revolution in medicine of the late nineteenth century, the physician's scanty knowledge and fumbling therapies very possibly slowed healing as often as they speeded it. At best he could ease his patient's pain with laudanum or later morphine. Under these circumstances, the doctor's importance as a psychological and physical comforter far outweighed his ineffectual efforts as a healer. Even after science had dramatically advanced therapeutics, this image of the physician-as-consoler lingered. Indeed, much attenuated, it still persists.[3]

Vivisection comported ill with this time-hallowed picture of the doctor. How could one dedicated to comforting the miserable and alleviating pain deliberately torture a sentient fellow creature? Could such a person be trusted with one's sick and suffering spouse or children? Vivisection "makes brutes of those who should be kind and humane in the practice of the healing art." Instead of compassionating pain, doctors were coming to regard it "with curiosity, inquisitiveness, and absolute indifference except as to the character of its various phenomena.[4] Vivisection blighted the very men called on for comfort in the pains of childbirth or the hour of death. Victorians already uneasy about pain looked upon this new-model physician with resentment and suspicion.

Formerly, the "sentiment of Humanity" was "the very life-principle of the body medical"; now "Science is all in all." Antivivisection offered a way to resist the penetration of science into medicine.[5] Reluctance to accept the new medicine did not derive from blind opposition to change. The image of the scientist—cool, calculating, manipulative—clashed fundamentally with the traditional role of the family doctor. Vivisection became the focus of the struggle to prevent the encroachment of science because in the vivisector's laboratory scientific medicine came most radically into conflict with the older stereotype of the physician. Somehow the two had to be reconciled. The strength of antivivisection measured the difficulty of doing so.

This new laboratory doctor often disturbed other physicians as much as laymen. Occasionally uneasiness burst into open hostility. Most doctors understood clinical investigation and comparative anatomy but, if trained before the 1880s, knew little of the new scientific medicine and its experimental methods. Not surprisingly, they often resented it, not least because of the contemptuously superior bearing that medical scientists too often seemed to adopt toward their less up-to-date colleagues.[6] Old-fashioned doctors carped at what they considered endless multiplication of petty specialities and viewed the new scientific spirit with "grave doubts and keen apprehension."[7] Science threatened their standing with the public and within the profession.

Whatever their intramural grumblings, the vast majority of doctors resolutely defended their scientific brethren from antivivisectionist attacks. Professional solidarity overcame any doubts. But for some irritated and anxious physicians, vivisection became an especially powerful symbol of the science they distrusted. Perhaps it seemed inconsistent with their own image of themselves as enemies of pain. Certainly the practice epitomized the experimental method that medical scientists exalted over the traditional techniques of clinical observation and comparative anatomy.[8] Conservative doctors resented vivisection being pushed into the common curriculum of medical schools, with the implied threat that the next generation of physicians would cast their elders into the outer darkness of scientific ignorance. Not by mere chance was Henry J. Bigelow, who led the opponents of President Eliot's remodeling of Harvard Medical School along scientific lines, also a tart critic of vivisection.

From the point of view of practical medicine, there were good grounds for healthy skepticism about the pretensions of medical science. The record of new therapies in the first half of the century did not inspire confidence. The conventional medical wisdom of those years, "active therapy" (drastic bleeding and massive doses of purgatives), had failed dismally. Even doctors began abandoning it around the middle of the century—reluctantly, because they had no more promising alternative until close to 1900. The senior Oliver Wendell Holmes declared in 1860 that "if the whole materia medica, *as now used,* could be sunk to the bottom of the sea, it would be all the better for mankind—and all the worse for the fishes."[9]

Initially, scientific medicine had scarcely more to offer than active therapy or the methods of "irregular" medical sects. Experimental physiology contributed much new knowledge, but even its most ardent early defenders could evince only a scant handful of rather esoteric minor improvements in practice.[10] Ultimately, the vindication of experimental medicine would come from bacteriology in the 1890s. But even bacteriology at first met distrust, and with some reason. True, Lister's introduction of antisepsis, based on the new germ theory, eventually revolutionized surgery. But his careful and skillful contemporary Lawson Tait, an anti-vivisectionist, rejected both Lister's theory and his methods yet claimed equally impressive results. Furthermore, the burgeoning literature of bac-teriology in the eighties and nineties included "much bad and hasty work" that further discredited the new field. Especially since bacteriology held out no immediate help to therapeutics, skepticism was not wholly out of place. Most doctors greeted it with indifference if not hostility. The laity had no reason to respond more warmly.[11]

For a few extreme antivivisectionists, the failures of experimental medicine demonstrated that medical science had already learned all it could.[12] However, most only rejected the so-called advances of experimental medicine achieved through vivisection. Antivivisectionists scoffed at the germ theory and its practical application in "Listerism." After the develop-ment of diphtheria antitoxin in the nineties, they denounced antitoxins and serums as useless, even poisonous.[13] Their most searing vilification they reserved for Pasteur himself, the chief apostle of the germ theory. His treatment for rabies came under especially heavy fire, perhaps because it scotched the belief, beloved of animal protectors for decades, that hydro-phobia resulted from cruelty to dogs and thus executed upon mankind just punishment for brutality.[14]

Antivivisectionists seldom rested their case against experimental medi-cine on these purely negative grounds. They offered a practical alternative in the flourishing and respected field of public health or sanitary medicine. Cleaning up the slums, improving sewerage, providing pure water supplies, upgrading diet, and reducing intemperance and vice were the real answers to disease: "If our doctors would turn their attention more to sanitation among human beings more cures would be effected, and less disease contracted." This faith in sanitary medicine was far from contemptible in the seventies and eighties. Sanitation had probably done more to improve health in the previous half-century than all of clinical and experimental medicine. The experimentalists, not the sanitarians, needed to prove their case. Unfortunately for antivivisection, they did. By the late nineties, only ignorance or willful blindness could defend sanitation as an adequate substitute for experimental medicine. Even the public health movement capitulated and began to apply bacteriological techniques to its own work of sanitation, water supply, and preventive medicine. Nevertheless, the antivivisectionists continued to damn antitoxin and prescribe cleanliness as the sovereign cure for disease.[15] To believe otherwise would capitulate to vivisection and open the floodgates of pain.

Yet the battle against scientific medicine was not only a war on pain; it was a crusade against science—against the kind of science that could, with a clear conscience, accept, inflict, *use* pain as a pathway to knowledge.

Denigration of "ultra scientists" echoed like a bitter chorus through the tracts and pamphlets of antivivisectionists. Even a fairly neutral observer wondered "how much of the antivivisection-cry is but the concealed expression of Science-hatred?"[16]

This seemed perverse. Science, by demonstrating the kinship of man and beast, had paved the way for kindness to animals. In that sense, it had fathered antivivisection. Antivivisectionists in effect conceded this by, for example, citing Darwin to shore up their claims for equal justice for animals.[17] Animal protection owed its success, as one speaker reminded the American Humane Association, "largely to the advance of science."[18] Yet had not science now betrayed the animals that it purported to defend? Animal lovers and biological scientists, who had for long shared an appreciation of human kinship with animals, now parted company over the nature of the obligations created by that relationship. This crisis of conscience was bound to come; in fact, antivivisection was only part of it. But it left many animal lovers with a distaste for science.

The sense of betrayal by science, however, went much deeper and ramified far beyond the fate of animals. The close identification of science with progress meant that the Victorian faith in progress implied equal confidence in science. Since progress presupposed moral evolution even more than material advancement, science must seek not only knowledge of and control over nature but the "practical elimination of physical suffering through medicine, and even of moral evil through the new science of sociology." Vivisection shattered this hope. It was lamentable enough that science, instead of easing pain, inflicted it, but the implications of this seemed grimmer still. In an age highly wrought up about pain, vivisection's infliction of it became a moral evil of demonic dimensions. The admission of vivisection as a legitimate tool of science would dash faith in science as an instrument of moral progress and thereby undermine confidence in moral evolution itself. Antivivisectionists could not permit this. Not only did they deny the legitimacy of vivisection, but they counterattacked by insisting that moral evolution itself would before long "make animal experimentation unthinkable."[19] At a time when other faiths, including faith in God, were in jeopardy, faith in moral progress was too precious to lose. The morality of science must be safeguarded, even against scientists themselves.

Yet scientists obstinately refused to heed these moral injunctions and persistently strayed into irreverent skepticism. Men of science in earlier generations had devoted themselves to revealing the glory of God's creation. But this new-fangled science produced no Bridgewater Treatises, upheld no moral values, recognized no enduring spiritual truths. Its truths were petty physical facts derived from experiment; even its most far-ranging theories remained mired in materialism. Worst of all, its corrosive skepticism was infecting a whole generation. The "spirit of scientific inquiry" was driving out of the schools "the old and long-established ideals of collegiate training" and destroying the willingness of students "to accept facts upon others' testimony."[20]

Bitterness about the amplified influence of science fed partly upon envy. Literary and clerical intellectuals had long dominated cultural life. Now men of science had begun to steal their celebrity. Naturally this bred resentment. But more than simple jealousy underlay anxiety about science. A "moral disease," represented in its most virulent form by vivisection, had stricken science. This distemper hardened, desiccated, and finally withered "the moral nature" of its victims. Public moral health demanded immediate extirpation of the cancer upon science, for science happened to be "that part of our social body which is just now the seat of the highest vitality."[21]

Antivivisectionists diagnosed this disease specifically as "savage materialism," imported from the "Continental laboratory." True, many German scientists did vaunt their materialism. The fact that many Anglo-American scientists repudiated it as indignantly as any antivivisectionist did not still the anxiety. Behind this smokescreen, other men of science remained ominously silent, while a few openly confessed their "agnosticism"—a word coined, significantly, by vivisection's bulldog as well as Darwin's, Thomas Huxley. Faith in the spiritual element in human nature could not long coexist with the materialistic credo that inspired such practices as vivisection. "They may claim that they are Christians, but it seems to me that, in their inmost hearts, they are materialists," concluded Caroline White.[22]

This materialism threatened not only to topple a faith in God already under siege, but to corrode morality as well. The new science taught its devotees "to regard the world as a scene of universal struggle, wherein the rule must be: 'Every one for himself; and no God for any one.'" Such doctrines, it seemed, could only culminate in an anarchic riot of immorality and crime.[23] This antivivisectionist anxiety found reinforcement in the more general Victorian apprehension that religious doubt, by eroding the sanctions of heaven and hell, would unleash a flood of immorality. These two related fears now merged in antivivisection's hostility to science. The conjunction occurred in part because science itself was a prolific source of doubt but also because scientists, especially biological ones, exuded a particularly strong odor of infidelity. Against this background, opposition to vivisection became a holy war. Antivivisection not only combated the most malignant strain of scientific materialism but also undercut that specific group of men who posed, by their theories and personal example, the severest danger to religious belief. It thereby staved off on two fronts the assault on morality.

Science endangered more than the Decalogue. Its coldly rational materialism threatened also to freeze human emotion and sensibility. Frances Power Cobbe compared "our Intellects and Emotions" to "buckets in a well. When our Intellects are in the ascendant, our Emotions sink out of sight. . . ." This fear of the head subduing the heart did not spring up *de novo* in antivivisection. Animal protectors had voiced it often enough before, and they in turn only articulated an anxiety widespread in Victorian society. But this fear tormented antivivisectionists with special intensity. An extraordinary urgency trembled in their fervent pleas that "Goodness and Love" were immeasurably more precious than knowledge.[24]

Most eminent Victorians would have agreed in 1850. Yet, as the century wore on, the enemies of the "heart" multiplied. The heart took on a new, broader role as the fortress not only of the noncognitive side of human nature, but of traditional spiritual and moral beliefs and values. But the battle often seemed to go against it. Science, pure and applied, came to symbolize the profane intellect, questioning, probing, skeptical, irreverent — and its prestige swelled each year, magnified by the revolutionary applications of new technologies and the astonishing progress in unveiling the secrets of nature. The status of science, moreover, benefited from being hitched to the brightest star in the Victorian sky, faith in progress. As the years passed, the conflict between head and heart grew sharper and more agonizing. The higher criticism, the "testimony of the rocks," the works of Darwin battered and often shattered the old confidence in the literal truth of God's Word—and sometimes all faith in God. The soldiers of Christ girded their loins and took up arms against "the doubting intellect." The troops of science defended their new-won realms with equal stoutness.[25]

Animal lovers preached a special gospel of the "religion of the heart." And, while most of them refused to discard science altogether, they relegated it to decidedly secondary rank. The heart, not the head, ultimately made the world go round:

> Humble love,
> And not proud science, keeps the door of Heaven;
> Love finds admission where proud science fails.

Scientific pursuits were not per se evil. But the "severity of [scientific] rationalism" threatened to dry up ordinary human emotions. The man of science needed some countervailing influence "to soften down the hard lines of science engraved on his heart as well as on his brain, to balance reason with sentiment."[26] The promotion of love for animals, of sympathy with all God's creatures, of compassion for pain wherever found, was calculated to meet this need, not so much for individual scientists as for an age of science.

To defend the heart, to cherish compassion, to attack suffering meant to safeguard faith in God and in the spirit within man. To attack the heart, to cast off compassion, to yield to pain, was to sink in a mire of materialism. If science had declared war on the heart, experimental physiology was its shock brigade. Gabriel von Max's painting, "Der Vivisektor," much treasured by George Angell, depicted an aging physiologist staring gloomily at a pair of heavenly scales, in which *"a glowing human heart"* far outweighed *"a human brain covered with laurels."*[27]

Why was physiology singled out from all the sciences for special blame? For one thing, vivisection simply struck many Victorians as incredibly heartless and unfeeling. But the current ran deeper. For their sympathizers, animals had become emblematic of the heart and kindness to them one of the highest expressions of heartfulness. Physiological "torture" of animals thus doubly assaulted the heart. A Black Mass of rationalism, it exalted coldness over kindness in the operator and blasphemed the heart itself, symbolized in the animal victim. So cynical a mockery of cherished and threatened values invited counterattack.

Antivivisection resisted the onslaught of scientific materialism and defended morality against scientific immorality. In that way it shielded the heart, the human spirit, from degradation at the hands of heartless science. Although not the only way of fighting back, for many uneasy about this new-fangled science this response was crucial. Given the tangled complex of Victorian anxieties revolving around these issues, the massive upwelling of antivivisection sentiment in the last three decades of the century—concentrated in the antivivisection societies but widely diffused outside of them—was not surprising.

Science, religious doubt, and hostility to pain: These three were knit together in an emotional web that undergirded antivivisectionist ideology. By spurning compassion, science confessed the corruption of its soul. By coldly inflicting pain in pursuit of mere phenomenal knowledge, science revealed its abandonment of spiritual values, its unconcern for moral progress, its immersion in materialism, its refusal to admit religious truths into the temple of science. Faith did not register on a galvanometer, and a science that could torture animals apparently recognized no other standard of truth.

Dangerous enough when confined to the laboratory, scientific materialism now threatened to infiltrate every home in the person of the trusted family doctor. The purity of medicine had to be preserved. This need explains the allegiance of antivivisectionists to the preachments of sanitary medicine long after bacteriology had done to death its claims. The sanitary reform movement had always tended to preach physical cleanliness as an adjunct to moral sanitation. Morality and physical health went hand in hand; "the danger to health came as much from the corruption of morals as from the contamination of the environment." To fight against "impurity," "pollution," and "filth" (the standard rhetoric of the movement) did not mean merely to build sewers.[28] It was this side of sanitary medicine that really captured the minds of antivivisectionists. "All this dirty stuff, the 'serums' and 'antitoxins'"—byproducts of disease, discovered through the iniquity of vivisection—were identified with filth, both physical and moral. Through disease, God both punished an individual for bad habits and warned against them. Sanitary medicine thus fitted into the natural, provi-

Canine loyalty
("The Long Sleep," from *Harper's Weekly,* February 6, 1869)

dential order of God's world. Experimental medicine violated it. Vivisection befouled the divine plan.[29]

Antivivisectionist complaints about scientific medicine ultimately came down to a moral objection. Revealed indirectly in a devotion to sanitary medicine, it emerged explicitly in denunciations of the fundamental values of the medical profession: Medicine had grown amoral; it had forgotten that neither "knowledge nor freedom from pain nor length of life is an ultimate goal in itself." The new breed of doctors had elevated "Bodily Health into the *summum bonum"* and had accommodated "the standard of right and wrong to that new aim." Many Victorians concerned by the erosion of religious belief shared the antivivisectionist hostility to this "Doctor's Doctrine." John Henry Newman wrote:

> But, after all, bodily health is not the only end of man, and the medical science is not the highest science of which he is the subject. Man has a moral and a religious nature, as well as a physical. He has a mind and a soul; and the mind and the soul have a legitimate sovereignty over the body, and the sciences relating to them have in consequence the precedence of those sciences which relate to the body.

Nowhere was the exalting of materialistic over spiritual values more blatant than in vivisection. Modern medicine failed to comprehend, as one writer put it, that the "contagion of cruelty communicated by vivisectors to their students" and thence to the larger community was "a deadlier malady than any which affect the bodies of men," for it withered their hearts.[30]

Fig. 13, Dog fixed on vivisecting table.
Reproduced from " *La Physiologie Opératoire*," page 125.

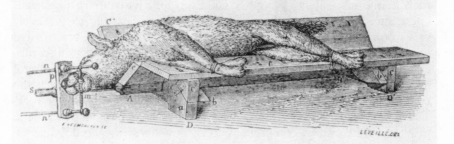

Fig. 22.   Reproduced from "*La Physiologie Opératoire*," page 135.

Scientific treachery
(From Frances Power Cobbe, *Bernard's Martyrs* [London, 1879])

Scientific medicine focused people's minds on the merely physical and averted their thoughts from the spiritual and eternal; it made the senses the "sole criterion of truth and right."[31] Its materialism thus endangered the moral health of the entire society. But medical science did not alone spread this poison. What "criterion of truth and right" did other sciences apply? What ultimate values did Darwinian biology appeal to? Or modern physics? Or chemistry? Men of science no longer labored, in the tradition of their predecessors, to show forth the glory and goodness of God. A sinister materialism had permeated and corrupted all the sciences. And was not science in turn corrupting the very society that had welcomed it and given it high place?

If this was a far-fetched picture of science, that was because antivivisectionists had only the faintest notion of what scientists were actually about. Animal lovers who tried to expose the horrors of vivisection by citing chapter and verse from scientific journals (a favorite ploy) usually only exposed their own incomprehension as they stumbled like babes through the scientific woods. With fresh-faced confidence they invoked medical evidence obsolete for decades: "a ridiculous fagot of antediluvian oracles," as William James put it. They were forever finding themselves the butt of ridicule for their ignorance of the most basic physiological facts, such as the insensibility of the brain. Even antivivisectionist physicians knew amazingly little of the physiological researches that they naively undertook to disparage.[32] Many of the wild charges that scientists attributed to malice and duplicity reflected mere ignorance. Antivivisectionists misunderstood the very method of science. Trapped in the older natural history mentality, like most lay Victorians, they thought of science as the collecting of discrete facts to be slotted into a classificatory framework. They totally failed to realize that scientists now strove, through experiment, to attain a theoretical comprehension of how nature worked.[33] Science simply baffled antivivisectionists.

Bafflement only exacerbated their fears of what science was leading to. Did not vivisectors hide their work in dark corners? "As a general rule the public is carefully excluded from this knowledge. Secrecy is usually enjoined upon the student, and the work is hidden in cellars, in laboratories, and places carefully guarded from the outside spectator." Men of science formed a "new priesthood"—"arrogant, secretive, and merciless." These white-robed monks of science spoke "in a technical dialect more than half of whose words give [the layman] no meaning whatever." More and more people, antivivisectionists feared, had come to believe "that a scientist is no ordinary individual; he is a man set apart, as it were, in a peculiar priesthood, for the discovery and promulgation of scientific truth."[34]

The antivivisectionists, in a perverse way, had uncovered a real truth. As science grew more and more abstruse, it slipped beyond the grasp of the ordinary educated man or woman and fell under the exclusive sway of a small group of experts. "Not so very long ago the whole field of Human Knowledge was . . . conceivably within the grasp of any one first-class human intellect. . . ."[35] Anyone with a modicum of education could read and understand Lyell or Darwin. David Ferrier's researches on cerebral localization, however, were accessible only to specialists. This was particularly galling when it occurred among physicians, where one's own body formed the universe of discourse. Scientists hardly comprised a new priesthood, but most of them now did, willy-nilly, form an exclusive circle whose "secrets" only initiates could fathom. This naturally deepened the suspicions of their befuddled contemporaries.

The accusation of secrecy added the last brush stroke to the image of traitor science evoked by the pains of the vivisector's laboratory. The earliest Victorians had relied on science for the defense of religion; science had wavered and fallen away. Later Victorians still entrusted to science their faith in moral progress; now science seemed to shatter that, too. Yet, when they should have bowed in shame, scientists brazenly strolled into their professional inner sanctum where, shielded from effective reproach by their baffling arcana, they taunted the ignorant *vulgus* outside. Some went so far as to assail religion openly, to deny spiritual truths any standing, and to flaunt their materialism in the face of the most cherished values of an uncertain age. The linkage of pain with this new-fangled science was not coincidental. For Victorians appalled by pain, cruelty was among the worst moral evils. In callously inflicting pain, scientists therefore displayed their amorality, their unconcern for moral progress, and their contempt for the spiritual.

This was a gross caricature, and only the most rabid science haters swallowed it entire. But it captured the flavor of one side of the Victorians' multifarious, ambivalent response to science. Few really believed in this picture, but in irritated or frustrated moments many inclined to it. Antivivisection in this way wedded anxieties about science to the revulsion from pain. Vivisection naturally became one of the tenderest spots in a culture feverish with change, for there the rising vogue of science collided head-on with the new humane sensibility. Or so it seemed to many Victorians.

Scientists did not take the antivivisectionist fury lightly. It threatened the professional lives of some and the dignity and repute of all. Worse, it challenged their very *raison d'être*. Antivivisectionists had no monopoly on compassion. Victorian science, as the age's chief engineer of moral and material progress, was animated by the vision of a better world, purged of suffering and vice. A sense of mission imbued scientists, and high among their ultimate ends stood the diminution of pain. In its own way, science embodied the new sensibility as much as the SPCA did. Scientists and antivivisectionists did not let fly at each other across a vast gulf but struggled hand-to-hand for possession of the same moral terrain. No wonder the opposition's insults raised scientific hackles.

For British physiologists, the limit of toleration was breached in 1881 when the Victoria Street Society prosecuted David Ferrier for alleged violation of the Vivisection Act in his and Gerald Yeo's research on cerebral localization. The prosecution failed, but for future defense the physiologists and their sympathizers organized in 1882 the Association for the Advancement of Medicine by Research (AAMR). Already for a year or two previously scientists had begun to speak out more vigorously, and now the new association launched a full-fledged publicity campaign. But it also attacked practical obstacles to working physiologists at the bureaucratic source. Within months the AAMR had negotiated a comfortable *modus vivendi* with the Home Secretary. The AAMR Council became the vetting agency for all license applications; its support meant virtually automatic approval. The physiologists could hardly have asked for more. Their propaganda suddenly ceased as the AAMR retired into discreet silence.[36] For the next quarter of the century, the British foes of vivisection hurled their wrath at a blank wall.

In America during the seventies and eighties, medical scientists scarcely needed to organize to protect vivisection. The rare and feeble efforts to induce state legislatures to restrict experiments on animals were easily thwarted by *ad hoc* measures. Only in New York, where Bergh's obsession with vivisection manifested itself almost annually in the state legislature, did repeated dangers call for an entrenched defense. To counter "such selfrighteous busy bodies as Bergh and his imitators," the state medical society created in 1880 a standing Committee on Experimental Medicine. Even where the menace seemed remote, American physiologists and their allies assailed antivivisection in books, pamphlets, the reviews, weeklies, popular scientific journals. This barrage partly stemmed from the sensitivity of American scientists to British experience. They read with alarm the warnings of British physiologists, widely reprinted in America, and the personal laments of colleagues across the Atlantic reinforced their trepidations.[37]

When the expansion of American medical research provoked a spate of restrictive bills in the early nineties, the danger suddenly became more urgent. The medical militia mobilized. A loose coalition of physicians and scientists coalesced around the eminent surgeon William Williams Keen in Philadelphia; this later became the Pennsylvania Society for the Protection of Scientific Research. Another *ad hoc* group, eventually organized as the Committee on Experimental Biology, formed in the Boston area under the leadership of Harold Ernst of Harvard Medical School. In Washington Surgeon-General George M. Sternberg acted as local liaison for the scientists.[38]

In 1906 a second Royal Commission, inquiring into the administration of the Vivisection Act, upset the cozy relationship of British physiologists with the Home Office. Forced to carry their case to the public once more, they organized in 1908 the Research Defence Society (RDS), under the guiding hand of Stephen Paget, for twelve years Secretary of the AAMR.[39] In that same year, perhaps inspired by the RDS, the American medical lobby finally created a national propaganda organization, the American Medical Association's Committee for the Protection of Medical Research. Its chairman, the physiologist Walter Cannon, made the most of his contacts in journalism and launched a devastating campaign against the antivivisectionists.[40]

The defenders of vivisection were in an awkward situation. Proving its usefulness as an experimental technique was the least of their difficulties. They also had to acquit themselves of the charge of heartless disregard of pain, while simultaneously clearing science of materialism and immorality. All this they had somehow to demonstrate to people uncertain even of what modern science was all about.

This was a tall order, complicated by the fact that doubts and confusion about scientific medicine were not confined to the laity. Science, in something like its modern sense, had only begun to emerge from the womb of natural philosophy in the early nineteenth century, and the life sciences came last. The older generation of biological scientists, whose early training owed more to the traditional observational style of natural history than to the newer experimental method, squirmed slightly while lending support to the vivisectors. Huxley and Owen, for example, staunchly defended vivisection but still felt personally uncomfortable with it.[41] Within the medical sciences themselves, animal experimentation retained, until near the end of the century, something of the character of a brash newcomer, whose intrusion made the older hands nervous. Vivisection had always been the touchiest point in the program of experimental medicine, and, although few physicians broke the united front against antivivisection, many harbored serious reservations. On vivisection was focused the anxiety that the scientific revolution in medicine created in many physicians of the older type. The confusion and uneasiness about vivisection—and the new science it represented—even among some of its nominal defenders aggravated the lay public's misunderstanding and mistrust.

Dispelling this miasma was essential. Vivisection could not be defended if its role was not understood. The advocates of scientific medicine therefore attempted first to remove some of the mystery from experimental science, by trying to elucidate its method and explain its practical importance. The new science, they pointed out, could no longer rely solely on observation of nature to obtain data. Experiment had become its essential tool. And the experimental method did not mean the verification of isolated facts by isolated scientists in isolated laboratories. Fitted together in "a fine mosaic," the results of many researchers produced a "long chain óf progressive knowledge." Eventually this led to a theoretical understanding of some natural function. Only then did practical breakthroughs result. A fact "laboriously . . . established with no other thought than the noble one of advancing knowledge" could, by extending the boundaries of science, play its small but essential part in the conquest of disease. Even failures helped, by directing researchers away from sterile paths. So ask not for practical results, for *"what is impractical medicine?"*[42] Vivisection was useful to science, and science to humanity. There was no mystery about that.

Yet to judge vivisection by its utility was to undervalue it. Physiologists accepted the pain of vivisection as the unhappy cost, not only of prolonging human life, but of a still higher goal. Animal experimentation was another small step forward in the eternal quest to understand the world. Who could question the nobility of that endeavor? More to the point, who could accuse of materialism and amorality those engaged in that endeavor? The selfless search for knowledge had a salutary effect on the human mind in no other wise attainable. "Of a truth," murmured one self-consciously pious scientist, "the universe is God's, and none can touch his robe in faith without virtue going out from it." Virtue flowed wholesale. "So long as the moral and spiritual development of mankind remains the supreme purpose of creation, medical science can claim equal honors with the science of God."[43]

Scientists could hardly deny that technical complexity had removed their work from the intellectual public domain and that they themselves now constituted an isolated elite. But they could remove the onus of this by linking it to these spiritual aspirations, by outfitting themselves as the vestal virgins of the new age, guarding the temple of science. Science indeed, at least in the hymns of its acolytes, had acquired the attributes of divinity. Omnipotent, ineluctable—"You may retard, but you cannot arrest, the progress of science"—its eternal light o'erwhelmed mere mortals:

> To the science of Nature, indeed, is allotted that one incomparable human day which knows no sunset. In the pure light of its ever-present daybreak, individual workers will pass away, generations will change, but the studies of Nature . . . will surely grow from age to age, and, as on Proserpina's sacred tree, one golden fruit will follow another. . . .

The intellectual and moral advancement of the race depended on constant devotion to research. It insulted scientists to charge them with materialism. In their selfless dedication to the service of science and the elevation of mankind, they willingly sacrificed their own lives on the altar of science.[44] Perhaps the antivivisectionists had not wholly missed the mark when they derided scientists as a "new priesthood." What emerged here, in the scientists' own words, was a remarkable new vision of the scientist as hero, almost saint. This probably persuaded more physiologists than antivivisectionists, but it was impressive nonetheless. And it served its purpose. Accusing a saint of godless materialism inevitably fell flat.

Yet there was still the problem of pain. It was hard to believe in the sanctity of a heartless torturer. Conversely, if physiologists could dissociate themselves from suffering, they would quash the most damning evidence stirring public suspicion of the immorality of their science. The medical scientists rose to the challenge. Deriding the antique medical evidence of antivivisectionists, scientists insisted that anesthetics had made the pain of vivisection largely a thing of the past. Anesthetics may have been employed more freely in their propaganda than in their laboratories, but the point was fundamentally valid. In 1882 Gerald Yeo analyzed data collected under the Vivisection Act of 1876 and concluded, stretching the truth only slightly, that barely one experiment in a hundred caused as much pain as surgery. By 1910 James Warbasse had driven that figure down to the point of absurdity: Only one in a hundred thousand caused any pain at all. Besides, an unreflecting animal did not feel pain as intensely as people.[45]

Those whimpering dogs surely felt something, however. Physiologists could not plausibly claim that they never inflicted pain, and neutral observers were likely to take with a grain of salt their protestations that they seldom did. Medical scientists therefore tried to bolster their image by stressing their professional kinship with ordinary physicians. However unsavory the reputation of physiologists, the public looked upon family doctors as warriors against pain, comforters of the afflicted. Scientists cultivated this connection by directing much of their propaganda through medical societies and general practitioners and by glossing over the gap separating the laboratory from the doctor's office:

> From the ignorant we expect to receive only censure, but from those who "in the valley of the shadow of death" have learned to know what manner of men we are, I have faith to believe the reply will come: We have trusted you with the lives of our loved ones; we intrust to you God's dumb creation.

Antivivisectionists tried to overcome this. They warned against swallowing the family doctor's claims about vivisection, pointing out that the average physician was largely ignorant of laboratory science. On that score they were right, but they might as well have cautioned people against trusting the clergy. The nearly unanimous support of ordinary physicians—whatever their private doubts about scientific medicine—may well have saved experimental physiology when its back was against the wall.[46]

Ultimately, however, the real answer to the argument from pain lay in neither denying nor evading but reversing it. Confronted with the choice, few people would flinch at sacrificing hundreds of animals to save a human life. Perhaps this was merely self-interest. But, even as a matter of principle, which was the greater cruelty: to outlaw vivisection to protect some thousands of animals, or to sacrifice them to prevent the "mental and moral anguish" as well as physical pain "wrought through disease in millions of men and women"?[47]

Antivivisectionists had an answer of sorts. Deliberate infliction of pain corrupted man's spirit, transformed him, like Dr. Jekyll, into a heartless brute. This evil far outweighed any bodily anguish that vivisection might help to ease. This was a confused and perhaps contradictory argument, since it turned upon inflating physical pain into spiritual evil, but its clarity did not finally matter. Although many Victorians—driven by their era's revulsion from pain—worried abstractly about the moral consequences of vivisection, only its most rabid foes convinced themselves that those scientists who, in their striving to conquer disease, had to inflict pain actually turned themselves into moral degenerates. Surgeons and even the family doctor did the same thing.

None of this prevented antivivisectionists from raging against the cruelty and brutality of physiologists. But their targets could at least retort that medical men were "the most humane class of the community." Vivisectors had proved themselves "more sensitive to the sufferings of other people and other animals" than the antivivisectionists, who could not see beyond the pain of a few dogs and rabbits to "the sufferings of thousands upon thousands of human beings of the present and future generations."[48] The logic of this was hard to refute. Moreover, whispered a small voice at the back of the mind, one's own life might be at stake. The medical profession got the benefit of any doubt.

The only weakness in this argument was that it had to be proved. If vivisection was to be justified by its alleviation of suffering, then vivisectionists had to demonstrate significant contributions to medical practice. Scientists had to provide evidence conclusive to nonscientists that the benefits of vivisection outweighed the sufferings of vivisected animals. This was not easy to produce. Defenders of vivisection could demonstrate convincingly to unbiased minds, when available, that experimenting on animals increased physiological knowledge. But their listeners were likely to reply, in effect: What then? Later generations raised on miracle drugs may automatically assume a connection between abstract knowledge and medical progress, but Victorians did not. Given the bizarre and occasionally disastrous succession of medical therapies since 1800, they had a right to a certain skepticism. Besides, how could a physiologist know that he was on the right track if his theories about the human organism did not issue in improved treatment of it?

The scientists met this argument squarely. Throughout the controversy, they confidently asserted that advances in physiology inevitably meant improvements in medical practice. Unfortunately, at first they had little to offer except confident assertions. At the height of the vivisection debate in England, William James frankly admitted that "the therapeutic benefits we have gained by it are as yet minute." Even Lister's new surgery could at first demonstrate no clear advantage over "careful, capable surgeons not using antiseptic techniques."[49]

The first important breakthrough came in the middle eighties with the advent of brain surgery. Previously, doctors had considered abscesses and tumors of the brain invariably fatal. Following upon the path-breaking operation of Hughes Bennett and Rickman Godlee in London in 1884, surgeons rescued a growing number of patients from certain death. Their success created a minor sensation, and, as medical men hastened to emphasize, only vivisection—specifically the work of the much maligned David Ferrier and others on cerebral localization in animals—made it possible.[50] But operations on the brain remained rare and risky. They hardly seemed sufficient justification for rampant, unrestricted vivisection.

Within a few years of Bennett and Godlee's historic operation, physiologists could claim direct authorship of another breakthrough in practical medicine. Myxedema, a cretinous condition occurring most frequently in middle-aged women, had long puzzled physicians. In the late eighties, it was discovered that removal of the thyroid gland in monkeys produced this baffling syndrome. Two years later, inspired in part by the experiments of Miss Cobbe's old *bête noire* Moritz Schiff, Victor Horsley suggested treating myxedema with thyroid tissue from animals. George R. Murray immediately applied the idea, with spectacular results. Animal experimentation, its publicists exulted, had brought "men and women back from myxoedema to what they were before they became thick-witted, slow, changed almost past recognition, drifting toward idiocy." This treatment was a piece of the rawest empiricism, neither Horsley nor Murray having the remotest idea what role the thyroid played. But it worked.[51] However, it was less satisfactory as an argument for vivisection. Myxedema was rare; few people outside the medical profession had even heard of it. The success of thyroid therapy, despite sensational demonstration in dramatic photographs, could not work a radical change in public opinion.

These piecemeal advances did chip away at antivivisectionist support. Moreover, as antiseptic surgery refined its techniques, often through animal experimentation, its superiority over traditional surgery grew increasingly evident. Lister's operating room techniques spread through the profession, and they inevitably carried in their wake the germ theory of disease. This was more a matter of validation-by-association than of logical demonstration; nevertheless, in practice acceptance of the one generally meant acceptance of the other. The germ theory was notoriously the child of animal experimentation. Though bacteriology had as yet failed to contribute significantly to practical medicine, it was becoming difficult to separate experimental medicine from the everyday language and practice of the healing art. But advances in treatment came slowly and in small doses, and their *necessary* connection with vivisection was not always clear, even to many physicians. A wary public still awaited the dramatic therapeutic victory that would clinch the case for experimental medicine.

In this uncertain atmosphere, the vivisection controversy came to a head in the United States in the nineties. State and local antivivisection crusades worried scientists, but not half as much as the drive for federal legislation. The McMillan bill was more than one senator's whim. Behind it lay a campaign carefully orchestrated by the Washington Humane Society since 1894 and promoted by antivivisectionists throughout the country. With its wide support among the capital's elite, however, the bill could not be dismissed as the misguided zealotry of a handful of overwrought pet lovers. The antivivisectionists' trump card was Sen. Jacob H. Gallinger. A homeopathic physician from New Hampshire, Gallinger adopted the bill as a personal crusade. Scientists could hardly take seriously his antediluvian medical pretensions; they could hardly fail to take seriously his chairmanship of the crucial District of Columbia Committee.[52]

The bill itself, a more restrictive version of the British Act of 1876, applied only to the District; vivisection elsewhere fell under state jurisdiction. But, like the abolitionists half a century earlier, antivivisectionists sought to have Congress declare the nation's principles by stamping out vivisection where constitutionally permissible. Moreover, Washington was "perhaps the center of animal experimentation in this country at the present moment." If Congress passed regulatory legislation for the District, antivivisectionists throughout America would take it as an inspiration and a model, and so might state legislatures. The physiologists and their allies could afford to take no chances. William H. Welch of Johns Hopkins and Henry P. Bowditch of Harvard fathered in 1895 a joint committee on vivisection of the American Physiological Society, the American Society of Morphologists, the American Anatomical Society, the American Society of Naturalists, the American Society of Physicians, and the American Society of Surgeons. In February 1896 this committee released a "Statement in Behalf of Science," introduced by the presidents of Harvard, the Massachusetts Institute of Technology, and the Massachusetts Medical Society, and signed by virtually every significant medical scientist in the country.[53]

Then, as the April hearings before Gallinger's committee drew near, resolutions denouncing the McMillan bill descended upon the Senate from the National Academy of Sciences, the American Medical Association, the Joint Commission of the Scientific Societies of Washington, and a phalanx of other medical and scientific bodies. To match this, the antivivisectionists could submit in evidence nothing more impressive than the expostulations of a Dr. Albert Leffingwell. They were beaten down with impressive thoroughness, utterly crushed beneath a landslide of scientific authority.

The sturdy Gallinger, undismayed, reported the bill favorably from his committee on a flood of unrestrained antivivisectionist rhetoric. But the remotest chance of passage had evaporated.[54]

Hearings on the Massachusetts regulatory bill opened in Boston in the same month. Harold Ernst duplicated there, on a smaller scale, Welch's massacre of the antivivisectionists. Not even these routs sufficed. In 1897 Gallinger diligently superintended another regulatory bill on its way to inevitable defeat. With the blood of the 1896 slaughter fresh in congressional nostrils, Welch could have squelched this threat with little fanfare, but he preferred to parade his troops in force again to "strengthen the impression we have made so that no similar bill will be brought up again.[55]

Armageddon was over, and it had turned out to be disappointingly anticlimactic. What had happened was simple. Early in 1894, Emile Roux and A.L.F. Martin announced the development of diphtheria antitoxin, the culmination of ten years of laboratory work following upon the investigations of Friedrich Loeffler and Edwin Klebs. Mortality from diphtheria, the dread scourge of infancy, had hovered for years around forty percent. The use of antitoxin immediately slashed it to ten percent. Dr. J. J. Kinyoun of the U.S. Marine-Hospital Service told Gallinger's committee in 1896 that, had antitoxin been available during the five preceding years, it would have saved "at the lowest estimate 150,000 lives." The world owed this life-giving discovery directly and irrefutably to experiments on living animals. Not only did animal experimentation play a crucial role in the development of antitoxin itself; the theoretical framework that made it possible to conceive of such a thing—and promised more discoveries like it—had been forged in "the torture chambers of science."[56]

The public impact was profound. Before antitoxin, when an infant lay stricken with diphtheria, the family doctor could only throw up his hands, while in four cases out of ten the despairing parents watched their child painfully suffocate to death. Now science had nearly banished that awful scene; a single injection usually restored a healthy child to grateful parents. And only vivisection had made it possible. How could antivivisectionists fight that? They tried to deny flatly the efficacy of antitoxin; they called it a filthy, dangerous poison, but they could not erase the statistics. In 1894 McMillan's bill might have stood a chance; by 1896 it was doomed. By 1898 McMillan himself had deserted.[57]

Medical science continued to add to antivivisection's woes. The early experimenters on the role of the thyroid had, without quite realizing it, begun to stumble toward an understanding of the endocrine system. In 1889 the flamboyant Franco-American physiologist Charles Edward Brown-Séquard enunciated "the modern concept of internal secretions." His attempt to rejuvenate his own seventy-two-year-old body with an extract of sex glands did not pan out (except for the antivivisectionists, who had a field day with the "Brown-Séquard elixir of life"), but at least the crucial concept was now understood. In 1894 a pressor substance was extracted from the adrenal glands; in 1899 its active principle was isolated and two years later was available in pure crystalline form: the drug adrenalin. Real comprehension of adrenalin's role in the body awaited the work of Walter Cannon and his associates at Harvard. In fact, not even the general principles of endocrine function were clearly understood until the 1902 experiments of E. H. Starling and W. M. Bayliss, the pair who coined the word "hormone." Nevertheless, adrenalin was quickly pressed into thera-peutic use.[58] Of its many applications, the most impressive was the dramatic rescue of apparently doomed victims of heart failure. It was hard to argue convincingly against a drug that seemed to bring back the dead, and few antivivisectionists tried.

Endocrinological research dealt another blow to antivivisection in 1922, when, after many years of frustration, the work of Frederick Banting and his associates led to the isolation of insulin and the successful treatment of diabetes. But by that time, animal experimentation had demonstrated its medical importance in so many ways that no fair-minded person could doubt its effectiveness in saving lives and easing pain. The control of tuberculosis, the virtual eradication of yellow fever in the southern United States and of Malta fever in the British armed forces, serum treatment for "spotted fever" (epidemic cerebro-spinal meningitis), public health measures to eliminate typhoid and cholera: All owed much to experiments on animals. Vivisection was no longer a suspect and esoteric laboratory practice of doubtful utility but, as its defenders relentlessly repeated, a scientific tool of immense benefit to the everyday lives of ordinary people. It became harder and harder for those who denigrated it to find sympa-thizers.[59]

Medical advances did not eradicate antivivisection. The irrepressible Gallinger was back with another bill in 1900. And, beginning then, a loose coalition of Massachusetts antivivisectionists brought up almost annually some new measure to limit experiments on animals. This campaign petered out after a decade or so. But, as late as 1919, Senator Henry Meyers of Montana tried to persuade Congress to exempt dogs from vivisection, though evidently no one took him very seriously. In England, too, antivivi-section soldiered on. In the early years of the new century, the National Antivivisection Society (Victoria Street rechristened) still commanded an annual income on the order of £7,000. The flood of pamphlets and posters showed no sign of drying up.[60]

Not only extremists still had qualms about vivisection. Regulatory proposals continued to attract a cautious modicum of impeccably moderate support, though less with each passing year. In 1900 the American Humane Association still had nineteen antivivisection pamphlets in print. Complaints about the administration of the Vivisection Act in England carried sufficient weight to require a second Royal Commission in 1906, and up to about 1910 Massachusetts legislators took restrictive bills seriously—that is, prior to the medical testimony, which invariably induced immediate rejection. Occasionally a major newspaper called for restriction, though never with enough enthusiasm to generate more than an ephemeral editorial. As late as 1919, an assistant secretary of the Navy named Franklin D. Roosevelt delivered a speech urging legal controls over vivisection.[61]

Yet these were reflex twitchings of a mortally enfeebled impulse. Even the leaders of antivivisection sensed this and tried desperately to hang on to the fraying remnants of public sympathy. In 1898 the National Antivivisection Society, headed now by Stephen Coleridge, abandoned its insistence on immediate and total abolition—for twenty years the bedrock of its policy—and declared for the halfway house of restriction. Coleridge's pious assurances that the Society hoped thereby ultimately to end all vivisection failed to placate the ancestral spirits. The aged but still acerbic Miss Cobbe stormed out of her retirement in the mountains of Wales to curse the weak-kneed and form her own British Union for the Abolition of Vivisection. But only about five percent of the National Society's members followed her.[62]

The American Anti-Vivisection Society, still firmly under the guiding hand of Mrs. White, remained untainted by compromise. But its membership apparently trickled away, and its influence among other animal protectors, already considerably reduced, virtually evaporated. Other American antivivisectionists, not committed to total abolition at the cost of extinction, tried to save the cause by breaking their ties with the purists, publicly confessing the usefulness of vivisection and asking only for curbs on its "excesses." These half-hearted antivivisectionists organized several societies for the "humane regulation" of animal experimentation, but by 1907 only three survived, and none ever attracted a substantial membership. Moderation drew scarcely more support than extremism fifteen years earlier.[63]

Antivivisectionists seldom found a friendly hearing now even within the animal protection movement. As early as 1875, the *Animal World* had cautioned against the abusive tone and "unauthenticated charges" endemic among the total abolitionists. "People here go mad," a flustered John Colam wrote Angell. After Henry Bergh's death in 1888, only Mrs. White and Baroness Burdett Coutts, of the major SPCA leaders, refused to compromise with vivisection. Simmering hard feelings exploded openly in the early nineties, with American antivivisectionists and SPCA leaders publicly hurling abuse at one another. After a bitter floor fight at the American Humane Association convention in 1892, moderates voted down an AAVS-sponsored blanket condemnation of vivisection and substituted a call for restriction. After the antitoxin revolution of the middle nineties,

SPCA leaders drove their black sheep out of the fold altogether. In 1900 the International Congress of animal protection societies officially expelled the antivivisection organizations.[64]

As experimental medicine solidified its claim to practical value, not only did opposition dissipate within SPCA ranks, but active supporters appeared in larger and larger numbers. By the early twentieth century, the president of the Research Defence Society (RDS) served also as RSPCA vice-president, while a vice-president of the RDS sat on the RSPCA Committee. Delegates to the 1914 American Humane Association convention in Atlantic City hastened to reassure an observer from the Pennsylvania Society for the Protection of Scientific Research that they wished to "leave vivisection alone."[65]

The attitude of animal lovers toward vivisection came more and more to resemble that of the medical community. By 1912 the president of the Boston Animal Rescue League was commiserating with the foremost American experimental physiologist. "Of course you will understand," Anna Smith wrote to Walter Cannon, "that I am associated with people who are morbid on this subject and who bring accusations that they do not seem to even try to substantiate." Cannon understood. By the First World War, only a handful of animal lovers remained "really rabid"; most had even quietly shelved their schemes for regulation. Along with the rest of the educated public, most animal lovers had come to agree with Harold Ernst of Harvard Medical School:

> It seems to me impossible that anyone who has lived, as it is our privilege to live, in a generation that has seen the labors of a Pasteur, of a Koch, or of a Reed . . . can honestly oppose the continuation of the practice of animal experimentation in the freest possible way.[66]

The weight of medical progress had crushed antivivisection. Here and there the spark continued to flicker into flame. Total abolitionists of Mrs. White's stripe—or even of Stephen Coleridge's—had invested too much of themselves in antivivisection to abandon it now. But they were alone, deserted by other animal lovers and devoid of public sympathy. They continued to peck away at their old foes, but the heart, if not the shrillness, had gone out of it. Unrelenting harassment of researchers could not disguise the fact that the movement had shriveled into a tiny caricature of its former self and had slid decisively into the shadows inhabited by quackery and battiness.

The shock of defeat seemed to loosen the antivivisectionist's grip on reality. The bizarre Bostonian Philip Peabody insisted that the "opponents of vivisection include many of the best known and ablest logicians, doctors and physiologists (including vivisectors themselves) known to fame." An anonymous Chicago "M.D." persuaded himself that diphtheria antitoxin was only a "fad," which "will go as bleeding went, as soon as the truth is known concerning it." Caroline White came to believe that "the enforcing of cleanliness and breathing of pure air" would end all disease. The 1913 international convention in Washington heard Prof. Augustin Levanzin lecture on "The Medicine of the Future: Dietotherapy." Fasting, the professor assured his hearers, was the wave of the future. Except in rare cases, it cured appendicitis without surgery. It also alleviated insanity. Eccentricity did not bother antivivisectionists; at times they seemed to revel in it. Spiritualism and Theosophy became almost as common as vegetarianism. Walter Hadwen, Miss Cobbe's hand-picked successor, exhibited the general drift of antivivisection after 1900 in his own convictions. These ranged from the respectably unusual—a teetotaller, a nonsmoker, a lay preacher for the Plymouth Brethren—to the baldly peculiar: "a furious opponent of all vaccination, a vegetarian, and a believer in the danger of premature burial."[67]

Inevitably, those who brooked no compromise with science grew more estranged from their culture as science more thoroughly permeated it. Much the same process transformed the medical profession. Diphtheria antitoxin and the succeeding triumphs of vivisection discredited the lingering opposition to experimental medicine among doctors. No physician could reject such potent therapeutic tools and retain his patients' confidence or his peers' respect. Physicians had either to submit to science or to retreat into now discredited sects. The handful of antivivisectionist doctors came from these discarded relics of a bygone era. It seemed fitting for Hiram Corson, the oldest practicing physician in the United States, to serve as vice-president of the American Antivivisection Society. Even a less physically decrepit English specimen, Edward Berdoe, lived mentally in the first half of the century: In 1893 he urged his colleagues to take Gall and Spurzheim's phrenology as their textbook on the brain! By around 1900, the scientists had completed the rout of their opponents and unified the profession under their banners. Their few remaining foes had to accept exile into various forms of fringe medicine. Henceforth all physicians had to pledge allegiance to science or be drummed out of the corps.[68]

The victory of science was more than the triumph of a technical method. It heralded a wholly new image of medicine: "experimental, active, manipulating its data by main force, given to speak not of concomitants and symptoms but causes of disease." This picture came to dominate the profession's concept of itself and, partly via the vivisection controversy, was transmitted to the public at large. But the justification of scientific medicine was inextricably intertwined with—in fact was one cause of—the new image of science and the scientist emerging at the same time. No longer passive observers and interpreters of God's design to a public fully competent to understand and share their work, scientists had passed into a new incarnation. They had grown gigantic, the masters of nature, "wresting" her "secrets" from her, "conquering" disease, of both body and soul. The laity, barred from sharing this esoteric knowledge, could only stand back and admire from afar.[69]

The battle over vivisection was perhaps the last major controversy in which lay people pretended to the competence to argue with scientists on their own grounds. From now on, in the few instances in which the purity of their motives or the nobility of their efforts was questioned, scientists could be called to account only through the mediation of other scientists. After Hiroshima, it was atomic scientists who denounced the atomic bomb. Even in the 1960s and 1970s, when a more general disenchantment with science set in, nonscientists looked primarily to "renegade" experts for leadership in the struggles over ecology and genetic research.

In the lay mind, science had grown both above and beyond the everyday world. The scientific response to antivivisection did not create this astonishing new image of the scientist. The changes in science itself and in its relationship to the larger public did that. But the vivisection controversy did offer one of the earliest and most prolific occasions to broadcast it. It would not be far from the mark to say that out of the crucible of antivivisection first emerged the scientist-hero of the twentieth century.

The apotheosis of science culminated a long-term trend in Victorian culture. Two mutually reinforcing tendencies—increasing admiration for the accomplishments of science, coupled with its growing influence as a model for intellectual endeavor of all sorts—had marked Anglo-American thought for decades. The creation of "social sciences" testified to the strength of science's hold on the Victorian mind. This is not to deny that science's path to intellectual preeminence was strewn with obstacles. Ambiguities and reservations usually qualified and sometimes extinguished the admiration of literary intellectuals for their scientific brethren. Especially when the onward march of science threatened to trample religious belief and the values of the "heart," it provoked bitter hostility: Witness the broad sympathy for antivivisection. But, while many Victorians at times suspected science, few rejected it outright, and year by year its vogue expanded. Antivivisection proved to be one of the last convulsive shudders in the arduous effort of digesting science into a culture previously dominated by literary and religious modes of thought. Once that convulsion had exhausted itself, the dominion of science was secure.

Most animal lovers acquiesced in the triumph of science, usually even joining in adulation. This did not mean that they had abandoned the values with which they had invested animals, values that science had once seemed to threaten. Rather, they had reconciled these old attitudes and beliefs with the primacy of science. By working through the disturbing implications of a radically transforming tendency in Victorian culture, they had learned to live with what initially seemed unacceptable and finally made their uneasy peace with it.

This was made simpler because science had won, not by assailing the new humane sensibility, but by appropriating it. In the growing revulsion from suffering, suffering was usually envisioned specifically as physical pain. Perhaps the embodiment of the aversion from pain in compassion for animals encouraged this; after all, we recognize physical pain in animals more readily than mental anguish. In any case, pain commonly meant bodily pain, and this was precisely what scientific medicine alleviated. Scientists thereby turned the tables on antivivisectionists. They made themselves appear comforters of the suffering and their opponents abettors of pain. By doing so, they vindicated the moral status of science and solidified its place in the modern pantheon.

To be fair, this move was more than tactical. Victorian scientists were Victorians, and they felt the revulsion from pain as keenly as anyone else. The purposes of science came to be conceived as including the diminution of suffering, and the prestige of science was thus attached to compassion. Scientists only insisted—and even animal lovers agreed, once the conflict clarified—that people had primacy over animals. Science, in crushing antivivisection, had not defeated the new sensibility but reinforced it, though emphasizing that it had to broaden beyond animals.

VII
Entangled in the Web of Life

During the last two decades of the century, organized animal protection grew noticeably tamer. Always cautious, the major SPCAs eschewed controversy more assiduously than ever. But behind this genteel facade transpired a fundamental shift in the intellectual and moral basis of concern for animals. The sense of kinship with animals, the revulsion from pain, and the newly vindicated respect for science came together to brew a radical redefinition of man's place in nature. All of this drifted rather foggily through the minds of most animal lovers, and only a handful of radicals fully explored the implications. But the Victorian version of compassion for animals was unmistakably fading, and the future was in the air.

After the 1870s, the scope of SPCA work slowly constricted. Contentious issues like field sports and factory farming were avoided in favor of teaching children to be kind to pets and birds and caring for stray dogs and cats. The first animal shelter had opened in London only as recently as 1860. In 1871 this "Dogs' Home" moved to impressive new quarters in Battersea, and the idea soon caught on elsewhere. Liverpool established a "Home for Dogs" in 1883 and Leeds in 1886. Before this, Philadelphia and Boston already had homes for strays, and by the 1920s some thirty-six shelters cared for America's failed pets.[1]

The character of the movement had changed. Work continued for horses and cattle and even expanded to include protection of wild birds and mammals. But by the end of the century most animal lovers had given their hearts to pets. "The protection afforded the smaller animals has been greatly expanded," reported the ASPCA in 1909; other societies responded in the same way. The dog and cat had ousted their larger brethren at the emotional and operational center of the animal protection movement. Some societies began to enroll pets as official members (their dues presumably paid by their owners). By the time of the First World War, most

122

SPCAs had become little more than clubs of cat lovers and dog fanciers. Not until after 1945 would the primacy of pets be challenged.[2]

The failure of antivivisection had something to do with this retreat from broader concerns. The crushing defeat of antivivisection vindicated the wisdom of not straying onto disputed territory. The vivisection controversy also purged SPCA's of their more radical members, many of whom bolted in disgust to the thoroughgoing antivivisection societies, leaving the SPCAs more conservative than ever. But the change cannot be entirely laid at the door of antivivisectionism, if only because the transformation was well under way before the vivisection controversy passed its peak.

In larger part, the fire had gone out of animal protection because the fuel that fed it had dwindled. By the first years of the twentieth century, the anxieties that had spawned kindness to animals had been, if not resolved, tamed. Decades of familiarity with the kinship of human being and beast had drained that uncomfortable idea of some of its terrors. The shock of industrialization and urbanization had faded into daily routine. Science had infiltrated the thinking even of literary intellectuals and clergymen. The tensions induced by changes so fundamental had by no means evaporated—they are still with us—but most educated Victorians had learned to live with them. Indeed, by 1900 most had grown to maturity in their shadow.

Yet a still more basic cause made the winding down of SPCA work, and the compassion for animals that nourished it, almost inevitable. Through much of the century there had been few socially legitimate outlets for humanitarian impulses. Self-interest, custom, and laissez-faire ideologies conspired to discourage, at least among the conventionally minded middle classes, concerted action to ease human suffering. Slum dwellers, the unemployed, factory children, and most other victims of social distress were off-limits to bourgeois benevolence. In consequence, the rising humane sensibility, blocked elsewhere, flowed disproportionately toward animals.

By century's end this had changed. Legislation protecting women and children was on the books; the settlement house had come into its own; social service was emerging as a profession. One no longer needed to pour pity on animals for want of acceptable human objects of compassion. Sympathy for animals did not wane, but it understandably became less central. From the 1880s even members of animal protection societies expanded their work beyond animals; SPCAs metamorphosed into humane societies with broader interests, or societies for the prevention of cruelty to children hived off from them.[3] Since animals no longer provided a major (perhaps the main) outlet for middle-class humanitarianism, concern for them naturally grew more cautious and more restricted.[4] Once the surrogate for a broad spectrum of diverse impulses, kindness to animals had been legitimated as a value in its own right. But in the process it had lost its wider relevance and urgency. For most people, it lapsed from crusade to convention.

Yet, in this atmosphere of ideological retreat, a quiet revolution was occurring. The triumph of the pet did not mean that animal lovers had wholly abandoned efforts to puzzle out the moral standing of man and beast in nature. On the contrary, in the last decades of the century, they began the complex task of delineating a new theory of partnership between human beings and nature, a closer working relationship better fitted to the post-Darwinian world. Only a handful of unusually thoughtful people elaborated these novel ideas and deeply felt their influence. But the new approach won general if superficial assent, and it touched and subtly shaped the attitudes of virtually all animal lovers.

The change began, not with four-legged creatures, but with birds. Tormented titmice and bereaved mother robins had figured, along with furry victims of heartless youth, in admonitory children's books since the late eighteenth century. But cruelty to birds never really concerned early animal protectors, aside from cock fighting and, very rarely, an abused chicken or two. Around the middle of the century, wild birds began to draw more attention. Several American states enacted laws protecting the insectivorous birds useful to agriculture. Across the ocean, a flurry of correspondence provoked a *Times* leader in October 1865 bemoaning the folly of slaughtering small birds. In 1867 the Rev. Francis Orpen Morris, vicar of a rural Yorkshire parish, petitioned Parliament for protection of wild birds. He failed, but the next year his friend, the Rev. H. F. Barnes, organized the first British bird protection society at Bridlington, on the Yorkshire coast. Pressure upon the local M.P. led in 1869 to legal protection of seabirds. This was also the year that the *Animal World* began publishing, and it covered the bird question exhaustively. By May 1870 Morris had organized an Association for the Protection of British Birds. Working with it, the RSPCA secured parliamentary enactment in 1872 of a bill protecting wild birds during the breeding season. A second Wild Birds' Protection Act followed in 1876. "Our native British birds are now more or less sufficiently protected," concluded a satisfied Morris.[5]

America lagged a decade or more behind England. In early 1883 George Angell asked the Massachusetts legislature to require public schools to teach children not to molest birds. In 1884 a wave of newspaper articles manifested wider American interest; soon the WSPCA became heavily involved, and other societies quickly followed. Yet the lead came not from the SPCAs, but from the recently founded American Ornithologists' Union (AOU). Within a few months New Jersey enacted a comprehensive bird law; the next year New York passed the Union's own model statute; and by 1910 all but ten states and territories had adopted the AOU law. In 1886 the ornithologists and their allies at *Field and Stream* magazine organized a national bird protection society named after the pioneer American naturalist

John James Audubon. In little more than a year the Audubon Society burgeoned to more than 38,000 members. A rapid decline after 1888 was checked by the reorganization and reinvigoration of the group in 1896 on its present basis as a federation of state Audubon societies.[6]

By the nineties only pets aroused more intense interest than wild birds among animal lovers. The demands of fashion largely accounted for the wholesale slaughter of birds, a particularly sensitive point for the female majority in the SPCA movement; so animal protection societies labored mightily to discourage the wearing of feathered hats. Women organized groups like the Plumage League, and thousands took the pledge. Margaret Mead recalled that her mother, on principle, never wore any feathers but ostrich plumes, which are plucked almost painlessly from the live bird. Bird protection had evoked so much fervor by 1894 that it dominated the international animal protection congress at Geneva that year to the virtual exclusion of everything else except vivisection.[7]

The whole phenomenon was puzzling. Why should animal lovers have suddenly plunged into a crusade for birds? Occasionally traditional refrains echoed among their arguments: The birds' lovely melodies enriched our lives; they were admirable models of industry and perseverance. But most of the propaganda struck a new note, a strange one for animal lovers. Birds voraciously devoured insects. Decimate the feathered population, warned SPCA magazines, and a plague of grubs and weevils will consume our sustenance. Only the ravenous appetite of millions of small birds maintained the balance of nature and kept starvation from the door. The *Animal World* blamed the *phylloxera* then ravaging French vineyards on the thoughtless destruction of small birds. This was indeed a new line. For the first time animal lovers assailed not cruelty to other creatures but simply the snuffing out of their lives.[8]

An extraordinary thing was happening: the formulation, in primitive, tentative form, of a wholly new ethic for human treatment of other forms of life. It had little immediate impact, except on a handful of radical thinkers. It quietly coexisted alongside older, partially contradictory attitudes. But it lightly touched the thoughts of almost all animal lovers—which meant most educated Englishmen and Americans—and gradually, subtly remolded their beliefs. Ultimately it revolutionized their whole conception of nature and the human role in it. Its progenitors gave no special name to this new outlook, but a later generation would call it "ecological."

Certain elements that eventually merged into this new way of thinking had been commonplace for a long time. The traditional belief in a great chain of being, which lingered on its deathbed through much of the century, had implanted the idea that all of nature, including humanity, was linked together. The assumption of a strict hierarchical ordering disappeared, but the idea of linkage survived.[9] More immediately, the theological argument from design, widely influential in the eighteenth and early nineteenth

An unlikely origin of ecological awareness
("The Utility of Birds," from *The Animal World,* June 1, 1889)

centuries, stressed the intricate ways in which each creature aided others to live: "All [are] created for all, in one comprehensive system of mutual support." Animal lovers used this to encourage kindness to animals: Beasts aid people, so people should aid them.[10]

This suggested a corollary that even the earliest animal lovers accepted. The Divine Planner had not created animals solely for human beings. As trustees of creation, people did have a perfect right to put animals to reasonable use, but beasts also had their own lives to lead, their own happiness to enjoy. Only human needs, not caprice or cruelty, could legitimately interfere with a brute's existence, for "a magpie has as good a right to live as her ruthless destroyer."[11] This put human dependence on animals for food and labor in a rather different light. If, even under stress of necessity, people took from animals their independence, their happiness, and their lives, then people owed them a huge debt of gratitude. Early animal lovers hinted at this; as the century wore on and man's semi-divine uniqueness faded, the hints swelled into resounding proclamations. Since "the human race is under vast obligations to the lower races," the failure to return thanks and reciprocal aid was the blackest ingratitude.[12] Perhaps this belief nourished the sense of moral outrage that later pervaded the end-of-the-century ecological ethic: the feeling that, when human beings abused nature, they not merely damaged their own long-term interests but perpetrated a morally vicious act.

Yet all of these ideas—the linkage of nature, the interdependence of life, humanity's reciprocal obligations to animals and its ingratitude toward them—never quite cohered in the first two-thirds of the century. Writers in behalf of animals played upon each of these beliefs—some of them wearyingly—in constructing their arguments for kindness but always used each separately. Only in the agitation over bird protection did these individual ideas gradually coalesce into a coherent and novel understanding of the human relationship to the structure of the natural order. But why then? There were two catalysts, both generated by the great intellectual revolution conventionally linked, as a kind of shorthand, with Darwin's name. Under the influence of these catalysts (the origins of which are discussed in detail in Chapter IV), the new conception of man's role in nature precipitated out of the older mix of potentially related but independent beliefs. One was the removal of the human being from primacy *over* nature to a humbler place as *part* of nature. Once the uniqueness of people and the subordination of animals to them had been swept away, nature could easily be seen as a seamless web, each tiny segment dependent on every other.

The other catalyst, brewed in a complex reaction to the horrors of this savage nature that human beings had been plunged into, was the belief in the autonomy of animals and of all nature, the "sacredness of life for itself." Since the elaborate, interdependent structure of nature no longer existed solely for human benefit, one could no longer assume that people could with impunity treat it as they willed.

Some animal protectors never really understood this. When a cor-respondent suggested in the *Animal World* in 1875 that India's tiger popula-tion be controlled rather than extirpated, John Colam was puzzled. He could not comprehend "why the noxious, ferocious and deadly enemies of mankind should not be destroyed." The writer replied that tigers kept down other destructive beasts, like the wild pig. But Colam kept insisting that "civilization" demanded "the extermination of noxious animals." Any connection between his task of protecting individual animals and the larger work of protecting the natural order simply escaped him. Even in its obituary of the pioneering conservationist Frank Buckland, the *Animal World* professed that "the good things done by the deceased in furtherance of animal propagation and preservation" were of no concern to the SPCA movement.[13]

However, this older, narrower approach was fast becoming a relic of the dead past. From the first, the bird protection agitation had stressed the birds' role in preserving the balance of nature.[14] By the late 1860s, some animal lovers had generalized this belief:

> Every animal has its duty to perform in preserving the great balance of nature, which is kept *in equilibrio* by the preying of one animal upon another, and if this balance is disturbed we are sure to feel the result.[15]

Through the rest of the century SPCA magazines consciously or uncon-sciously reinforced this belief by printing hundreds of stories warning of the dire consequences of killing insectivorous birds and thus breaking "an important link in the chain of nature." But the lesson applied to more than birds, since "man does not live to himself alone, but exercises a vast and important influence upon both animate and inanimate nature." This pre-sented no problem so long as people behaved like the rest of their animal kin, for "all animals exert a great influence upon each other. The car-nivorous feed upon the herbivorous, and generally in a primitive state all these agencies balance each other pretty fairly." The trouble was that human beings no longer lived in a primitive state. Their ability to destroy now far exceeded that of even their most ferocious animal cousins. The slaughter of small birds provided but one example. Man had exterminated whole species—the moa, the bustard, the wheatears—and now his reck-lessness endangered others: moose, buffalo, seal, walrus, giraffe, zebra; the list grew longer each year. Possibly more frightening, "the thoughtlessness, brutality, and avarice of destructive man" now "imminently threatened" the "delicate balance between animal and vegetable life." "Future scientists will look back at us of today aghast at our blindness and heedlessness."[16]

In this rhetoric, animal lovers struck some of the same notes as the con-servationists who flourished, especially in America, around the turn of the century.[17] Indeed animal protectors and conservationists formed a united front on certain issues; witness the SPCA-Audubon Society alliance. But their common interests disguised fundamentally different ideologies, and identifying those differences is crucial to understanding the emerging ecological ethic. Some conservationists found, in individual confrontation with the wilderness, rich emotional and aesthetic—almost religious—satisfactions dried up by the arid tameness of civilization. They felt, with Thoreau, that "in Wildness is the preservation of the World." Animals and birds usually ranked below mountains and forests, but they too, as wilderness creatures, benefited from the desire to preserve unspoiled nature. These conservationists, led by John Muir of the Sierra Club, tended to gravitate to that minority wing of the movement more accurately called preservationist.[18]

The majority of conservationists worried about the depletion of nature's material rather than spiritual bounties. Saving timber or water for future generations demanded wise management of natural resources. Wildlife, too, comprised a natural resource: the raw material of hunting. Hunters therefore took the lead in protecting it, most notably the Boone and Crockett Club, an exclusive elite of big game hunters led by Theodore Roosevelt. But husbanding game, unlike conserving forests, was hard to justify on economic grounds. Instead, these rifle-toting conservationists invested hunting with urgent moral purpose. The fading of the wide-open West and the growth of commerce and industry threatened to sap Americans of their frontier-bred toughness, self-reliance, alertness, and manliness—an ominous danger to a generation weaned on "the survival of the fittest." But one could still glimpse hope through the sights of a .30-.30. The old American virtues could be honed to their frontier keenness in the pitting of human mind and muscle against the sharp survival instincts of elk or bear. Conservation of wildlife, by preserving hunting for Americans yet unborn, offered an antidote to an overdose of civilization: the moral equivalent of the wild West. Moreover, wildlife conservation itself taught the sportsman a valuable lesson in self-control and self-sacrifice.[19]

This horrified many animal lovers and disturbed almost all. The typical SPCA member admitted, more or less grudgingly, the legitimacy of hunting. But breeding elk or bison simply so that people could shoot them went too far. Significantly, when conservationists spoke of "butchering" wildlife, they meant "hogging game."[20] For animal lovers, on the other hand, the word conjured up grisly images of blood and pain. But revulsion from the suffering inflicted by hunters was only the most obvious manifestation of the fundamental cleavage between animal lovers and conservationists, a gap that separated the former even from less blood-stained preservationists like Muir. Conservationists tried to safeguard endangered species; animal advocates wanted to protect individual animals. It mattered little to most SPCA members whether callously massacred seabirds were the last of their kind or a score out of millions. The point was that each bird had a right to life that, while not absolute, absolutely demanded respect.

Behind this conflict lay a deeper question that troubled many Victorians. What was the value of life, the purpose of life, in the scheme of nature? At times nature seemed "careful of the type" yet "so careless of the single life." At other times, as the fossil record now implied, nature appeared to blast both individual and species with indiscriminate unconcern.[21] Was life then pointless? Darwin posed the issue in its most naked, most frightening form with his vision of a blind, uncaring nature, mindlessly murderous. Yet he also seemed to offer an answer of sorts; at least many readers mined one out of his writings. Nature, however void of deliberate purpose, managed slowly, wastefully, but steadily to stumble upwards. Eons of carnage were not pointless, unredeemed. The sacrifice of billions of lives and perhaps millions of species contributed to the progress of evolution, the gradual perfecting of life, and ultimately the emergence of the human race.

How did man's ruthless killing of other animals fit into this moral framework? Darwinism itself offered no sure guidance. From one point of view, the slaughter of seabirds appeared merely another bloody episode in the painful upward writhing of evolution, no more blameworthy than any other side effect of natural selection. But the matter was more complex. If the population of any species or the number of different species fell below the maximum level that could be supported by a given environment, two results ensued. First, the pool of potential variations, the raw material of natural selection—what nature, so to speak, could choose from—shrank. The chance of an "improved" animal emerging therefore decreased. Second, the competition for survival eased. In this slacker atmosphere, weaker, less "fit" organisms, normally doomed by natural selection, lived and reproduced. Thus, it might be argued, heedless massacres of animal and bird life interfered with the mechanisms of natural selection and retarded the upward struggle of evolution.

On the other hand, was not man, as the highest product of natural selection, not fulfilling evolution by eliminating animals less fit to survive? Perhaps, but did not man's technologically augmented ability to kill not make him different, remove him from the workings of natural selection, and impose on him the need to conserve life, lest he destroy the delicate mechanism of evolution? The questions could continue indefinitely, with the final answer receding forever down an endless hall of mirrors.

However, few Victorians—and no animal lovers—needed to analyze the mechanisms of natural selection to convince themselves that life was sacred. Yet, when they spoke of the sacredness of life, the phrase concealed a crucial ambiguity. Did they mean life or lives? Both conservationists and animal lovers agreed that all life in nature deserved respect. But conservationists took this to mean the preservation of types of life in all its infinite variety. Animal protectors understood it as the sacredness of each life. Conservationists thus adopted a stance closer to the apparent ethics of evolution and subordinated the individual to the species. Yet even they recoiled from the full horror of natural selection, and the slaughter of whole species appalled them. Moreover, for those conservationists spiritually descended from the Transcendentalists (like Muir, who revered with mystic awe a vision of nature rioting in multitudinous life), extirpation of entire species bordered on blasphemy. Conservationist programs of wildlife management aimed to prevent animal species from falling victim to superior human competition, regardless of natural selection. Conservation of species became an end in itself, as a partial refutation of the more ruthless side of Darwinism and as an affirmation of the value and glory of life.[22]

For animal lovers this did not suffice. They insisted on a more thorough exoneration of nature from Darwin's slanders. Perhaps the downgrading of individual existence raised implications for one's own life too frightening to tolerate. To restore faith in the moral purpose of nature was essential. Surely human beings, now part of nature, ought not to contribute to the debacle by abandoning their moral obligations to fellow creatures. By proving themselves "careful of the single life," they could help to refute the libels on nature's morality. However closely animal protectors cooperated with conservationists in practical work, they could never compromise on principle. Respect for each individual life, as an equal partner in the ecology of the planet, had become a way of combating the horrid alternative of a world in which life meant nothing.

The new ecological consciousness hardly saturated the minds of ordinary animal lovers. But they could hardly have avoided it, and it obviously affected them; otherwise the enthusiasm for the ecological aspects of the "bird question" is inexplicable. Nor was this surprising. For decades animal lovers had buttressed their arguments with each of the component beliefs that eventually melded to constitute the new outlook. It was a short step to linking them together. Admittedly, these crudely formulated notions of ecology were never dominant. But they were widely heard.

The ecological approach subordinated both human being and beast to the overarching structure of the natural world, the whole web of life. By doing so, it gave animals a place in nature that, viewed from this angle at least, equaled man's in importance. This new ethic thus demanded the same respect for all life, human or animal. It did not condemn people for killing animals for food or clothing, any more than it blamed cats for preying on mice. But it did ask equal reverence for the existence of all living creatures. How to express this remained, perhaps inevitably, rather vague. But the very existence of such a belief required a thorough reappraisal of one of the earliest fundamentals of the animal lovers' creed: the rights of animals.

The original version of animals' rights was sired by utilitarianism and nurtured by the French Revolution. As their pedigree suggests, these rights derived from the animal's capacity to feel pain. Their substance consisted (according to John Lawrence, one of the sturdiest early advocates of the doctrine) mainly in the right to receive decent food and shelter and to have "no wanton outrage [committed] upon their feelings." Animals' rights, in short, included only the enjoyment of possible pleasure and freedom from unnecessary pain. Moreover, they always remained subject to the superior rights of people. Lord Erskine summed up this older notion of animals' rights in the House of Lords in 1809:

> Their freedom and enjoyments, when they cease to be consistent with our just dominion and enjoyments, can be no part of their natures; but whilst they are consistent, I say their rights, subservient as they are, ought to be as sacred as our own.

This theory by no means disappeared in the latter half of the century. In 1879 Edward B. Nicholson premised his argument for animals' rights on the proposition that "feeling (by which I mean the power of feeling pleasure and pain) gives rights." He claimed both Bentham and John Lawrence as his intellectual forebears. A number of other contemporary animal lovers shared his adherence to the tradition of Bentham and Lawrence.[23]

Yet after the middle of the century this older theory grew increasingly unsatisfactory. The intellectual earthquake that tumbled people down among the animals and raised brutes to new heights also crumbled the traditional foundations of animals' rights. If beasts not only felt like people but thought like them, lived like them, and perhaps even shared human aesthetic and religious sentiments, then were their rights not correspondingly wide? Said one advocate: "Admitting that the so-called lower animals are part of ourselves, in being of one scheme and differing from us only in degree, no matter how they be considered, is to admit that they have equal rights."[24]

That coin had another side. If human beings differed from animals only in degree, then how did one defend equal rights for all persons without also including at least the higher mammals? People also differed in degree from one another; if one could deny rights to a dog or an ape, one could also deny them to a child or an idiot. The Rev. W. C. Gannett glimpsed this when he associated the growing recognition of animals' rights with the new rights acquired by "women, children, the poorer classes, slaves and criminals." Black people, yellow people, Eastern Europeans, women, children, and other groups were all widely regarded as intellectually, and often morally, inferior to full-grown Anglo-Saxon males. If inferiority deprived animals of rights, could the same not be said about the "lower orders" of human beings? Defending animal rights meant standing up for human rights, for "when the rights of dumb animals shall be protected, the rights of human beings will be safe."[25] Clearly the old, restricted utilitarian basis for animals' rights no longer sufficed. But what was to replace it?

Here the new ecological mentality fitted in. Since all creatures formed one seamless, mutually interdependent web of life, the existence of each deserved respect. Man could rightfully use other forms of life when needed to sustain his own proper mode of existence. But he must treat them with care, even reverence. The wholesale slaughter of birds was stupid, but more than stupid. It was wrong—not wrong because the birds suffered (animal lovers, curiously, almost never claimed that), but because man had no right to take life for which he had no need. Such abuse of one's co-partners in nature constituted a grave moral lapse, a failure to respect the holiness of life.

Intimations of this new outlook appeared as early as the late 1840s:

> There is a growing feeling of reverence for the lower creation. . . . we regard them as sharers in one quality, and that the most tangible portion of our inheritance—they share in life, they are living creatures. They are in [this] one particular our brethren.[26]

By the late sixties, the belief that life itself carried rights had grown common enough to figure in this SPCA propaganda aimed at children: "Even if we had no hearts to feel for acts of cruelty, we have no right to destroy any living creature, for everything has an equal right to live." In this case it was only an insect, so it came as no surprise that wild animals, too, were brought within the charmed circle—whatever John Colam might say about tigers:

> One may say, generally, that so long as they do not endanger human life, nor imperil man's means of subsistence, wild animals have the same right to life and liberty which man himself enjoys. Nor should they be treated in any way which would be termed cruel if applied to mankind.

Few animal lovers thought very deeply about all this. Perhaps only a few consciously switched their allegiance from the older theory of animal rights to these new ideas. But ecological rights had become part of their intellectual baggage. All living creatures now held rights that merited respect simply because all dwelt together in the great, mutually supporting house of nature: the "sacredness of life for itself."[27]

How animal lovers got from "the web of life" to the "sacredness of life" remained puzzling. An understanding of ecology seemed to argue for more prudence or intelligence in the treatment of nature, rather than more reverence. Perhaps the "sacredness" of animal life derived in part from a simple transference of a deeply felt, almost religious commitment to animal protection to the more broadly conceived ecological understanding of animals and people. The unease induced by industrialization and urbanization—the fear of alienation from and the consequent desire for reunion with nature—may have lent this commitment its emotional force, otherwise not readily explicable. Possibly modernization reinforced the moral indignation of animal lovers in another way as well. When they talked about wholesale slaughtering of birds, they often referred to it as a shameful waste of life. The needless sacrifice of even the lowest life disturbed them. This note of frugality perhaps echoed the lessons of efficiency taught by modernization and carried over to ecology.[28]

Whatever the truth of these speculations, however, the moralism of animal protectors certainly had roots older than the Industrial Revolution. Advocates of kindness to animals had always warned that cruelty "in every form is the associate of vice"—nay, more, "the parent of murder":

> The Italian peasant who showers blows upon his prostrate horse has a knife for any one who ventures to remonstrate with him. In England the passage from cruelty to assassination is not quite so short, but the records of the police courts show that even here there is too much similarity between the treatment of animals and the treatment of women and children.

Nor was this merely the likeness of two different fruits of the same tree. A direct causal link led from cruelty to animals to bloody crime; "cruelty to animals predisposes us to acts of cruelty towards our own species."[29] This almost obsessive fear of spreading cruelty was not fastidiousness. It grew from the very real and visible brutality of Victorian cities, a deadly and all-too-plausibly contagious disease. For this reason, SPCAs always worked hard to suppress public cruelties, "the sights of which tend to brutalise a thickly crowded population and to debase the children." The RSPCA wanted to move all slaughterhouses to the thinly inhabited outskirts of cities. Henry Bergh tried to persuade the New York authorities to suppress the "Chamber of Horrors" at the Eden Musee, a sort of New World Madame Tussaud's. During the panic created by the grisly work of Jack the Ripper, a London minister proposed, as part of a crime prevention program for Whitechapel (the Ripper's *locus operandi*), the closing of all slaughterhouses in the area.[30]

The observation of cruelty, terrible though its potential effects, dwindled to insignificance beside the act of cruelty. Indulgence in cruelty not only spawned crime; it scarred the perpetrator as horribly as the victim, for "by giving way to such passion, you injure your own character as much, nay more, than you injure your horse. . . ." This remained true regardless of whether the virus of cruelty thus implanted actually broke out in overt crime. "Humane feelings" toward animals "form a natural tie which cannot be rudely broken without doing violence to many of the finer attributes of our nature."[31]

Cruelty also redounded on its agents in less personal disasters. Rabies, a disease much dreaded in nineteenth-century cities, was supposed to prove this. As early as 1828 William Youatt, Honorary Veterinary Surgeon to the RSPCA and an authority attested by Darwin, explained the etiology of the disease definitively: "Caused by Inoculation alone—the Virus must be received on some abraded, or wounded, or mucous surface—the Virus resides in the Saliva alone." If any veterinarian had the credentials to make his writ run in the realm of animal protection, it was Youatt. But most animal protectors refused to believe him, because they wanted to believe something else. Hydrophobia had nothing to do with saliva; it had to do with cruelty. Its "obvious causes," according to Frances Maria Thompson, were "the cruel treatment of dogs, and leaving them to starve about the streets." Another animal lover concluded that "the hard working of [cart] dogs led to hydrophobia." Samuel Wilberforce, Bishop of Oxford, also invoked the tortures of dog carts. A writer in the *Pall Mall Gazette* attributed the disease to chaining up dogs in the hot sun ("A little hydrophobia is not only excusable but perfectly natural . . .").[32]

The same argument did service in explaining another worrisome problem of the age, spoiled and diseased meat. As early as the 1830s, animal protectors claimed that meat from maltreated animals "is extremely unwholesome, and unfit for human consumption." A later writer insisted that Texas fever, a cattle disease, resulted from "the outrageous abuse of the poor animals" during shipment to market. Animal lovers throughout the last two-thirds of the century held as an article of faith the belief that cruelty spoiled meat. As late as 1910, a Mrs. Ivimey suggested to the RSPCA that eating the flesh of ill-treated cattle caused cancer. George Angell considered it a "law that cruelty to the animal injures the meat"; cruelty "avenges itself upon the consumer."[33]

It was not fortuitous that vengeance slipped into Angell's warning. The animating impulse behind all of this speculation about diseased meat, hydrophobia, and the reflex effect of cruelty in general was the conviction that abuse of animals was followed by retribution. Cruelty to animals invariably brought with it "the unfailing Nemesis of human misconduct."[34] For most animal lovers the authorship of this nemesis was not to be found in the purely mechanical working of some blind law of nature but in the purposive hand of providence. Christians had always believed that the wicked will suffer for their misdeeds; often that punishment came in this life as well as the next. Animal lovers believed this, too. Cruelty to animals cried to heaven for retribution, and God rained it down in the form of disease, man's inhumanity to man, and the subtler agonies of a hardened, warped, and blighted character. Taking the life of an "innocent, unoffending animal, solely because we have the wish or power to do so, is an act of wanton wickedness, which, sooner or later, will bring upon us the punishment that inevitably awaits on sin."[35]

This proffered a powerful argument against cruelty. But it also unintentionally laid bare the roots of the intense moralism with which animal lovers invested the ecological mentality. To the new, scientifically based understanding of nature as an intricate web of life, animal lovers brought an older, essentially Christian and nonscientific morality. By grafting these ethical values onto a more or less value-free, purely explanatory conception of nature, they had created an entirely new approach to the natural world and the human role in it. The perilous human stake in maintaining the balance of nature became a sacred trust, and the practical need to treat other species with care became an ethical duty to respect all forms of life.

Guilt about human transgressions against nature may well have reinforced this moralism—again, perhaps, the scars of industrialization. From a scientific point of view, the wholesale slaughter of, for example, small birds was stupid and dangerous. But animal protectors saw it as wrong and sinful, an immoral aggression against life forms to which people owed reverence. This slaughter profaned the temple of life. At a time when the higher nature of human beings had been called into question by scientific insistence on their animality, disrespect for the spiritual values inherent in the animal world could not be taken lightly. The ecological understanding of nature, which seemed to plant people more firmly than ever among the beasts, had paradoxically become a way of reinforcing human spirituality. Clothed in the garb of compassion and armed with the scales of justice, ecology stood now as a new morality.[36]

An occasional radical thinker carried this to unpalatably logical extremes. Henry Salt, a former Eton master who had thrown over his adolescent charges for a Thoreauvian life in the wilds of Surrey, demanded that animal lovers surrender their pets. "There is no more miserable being than a lap-dog, and the lap-dog is the sign and symbol of that spurious humanity which is the final outcome of 'petting.'" Salt insisted that "petting" and patronizing animals prevented recognition of their independent moral status. Animal lovers must shake off the habit and "make animals our friends not our pets." However, as Salt's own case showed, this did not preclude inviting these friends to live in one's home in a suspiciously pet-like capacity. But whatever Salt's practice, he preached that the proper attitude toward all animals was neither petting nor persecution, but benevolent neutrality. Let animals lead their own, natural lives rather than act out human wishes. Even the "artificial thralldom" of domestication, while possibly justifiable under some circumstances, Salt viewed with suspicion. Actually eating animals passed all bounds of tolerance.[37]

Salt's American friend J. Howard Moore shared his passion for vegetables as well as his insistence on the moral equality of animals and man. But he seemed to delight more in denouncing people than in defending animals. Human beings were assuredly not half-divine, as they had for so long ludicrously assumed. Moore had no illusions about this "talkative and religious ape" who was "not a fallen god, but a promoted reptile." In some respects, man represented the nadir of the animal kingdom: "the most unchaste, the most drunken, the most selfish and conceited, the most miserly, the most hypocritical, and the most bloodthirsty of terrestrial creatures." For better or worse, "man is an animal in the most literal and materialistic meaning of the word." Moore managed to find this chill vision bracing. If people looked these stark truths full in the face, they would have to cast aside their ragged illusions of uniqueness, admit that they were in the same boat with their animal cousins, and reorganize their relations with other animals on a basis of reciprocity, mutual help, and fraternity.[38]

Most people, perhaps understandably, looked askance at such notions. Few were ready to give up roast beef, much less to "go the whole orang," as Charles Lyell put it, and admit themselves to be nothing more than beasts. Still, somewhere between the proto-ecological gropings of bird protectors and the uncompromising naturalism of Moore and Salt, one catches a glimpse of a new cast of mind—a new understanding of the workings of nature and our place in them—emerging from the unlikely womb of Victorian love for animals.

Epilogue

One of the commonest yet deepest tragedies of human life in a period of rapid change is the mutual incomprehension of parents and children. No matter how informed and sympathetic, one generation cannot reproduce the flavor and feel and impact of the experiences of another. Fathers and mothers, sons and daughters only fumble toward a grasp of one anothers' lives. The effort is always vain, yet never completely. Out of the struggle comes a partial, uncertain, even speculative knowledge, from which grows the clumsy understanding that we build our lives on.

The historian's work is like this, though without the poignancy of personal loss. But the raw material is even more intractable, for our great-great-grandparents' lives (not to mention Hildebrand's or Xenophon's) are far more opaque than our parents' or children's. Yet the way in which their values and beliefs affected their lives has also shaped ours, and we cannot —and should not—cease speculating as to how. Kindness to animals long ago receded to the status of a conventional reflex, which we now accept unthinkingly. Victorians were very conscious of it; it was then a cause that rallied the rich, famous, and powerful, and legions who were none of these. At least in small ways, it must have influenced their world view. Exactly how love for animals helped to reorient their thinking, and thus ours, we can never know with certainty. But we can conjecture.

In the twilight of their era, our Victorian ancestors had begun to drift uncertainly toward a new comprehension of their relationship to the rest of nature, a surprising foreshadowing of the ecological concerns of our own time. They lacked the scientific paraphernalia of food chains and eco-systems. But they had dead aim on the morality of living with one's environment. If people transgressed against nature, if they insisted on mastery over their environment, they would end by lording it over a dead world—until they, too, died for their sins. In cooperation with nature lay salvation.

The unexpected modernity of this ecological ethic is heard elsewhere in the legacy of Victorian love for animals. We live with the unspoken assumption that we are one with other animals. Whatever their religious or

138

metaphysical convictions, few of our contemporaries question that our minds as well as bodies are more complex and sophisticated versions of the "minds" and bodies of other animals. If anything, the tendency today is to play down the gap that does exist: Witness the enthusiasm for talking chimpanzees. Our thoughts, our feelings, our impulses, even our values and mores, we try to understand against the background of our animality. But we did not invent this view of human nature. The Victorians did. And learning kindness to animals was part of the process of learning to live with their own animality. Partly they redefined the animal, but they also redefined themselves.

And by nurturing compassion for animals, they had nourished as well a broader humane impulse, a hostility to pain and suffering in human being and animal alike. In 1800 sympathy was a tenuous, fitful, and often superficial response to the distress of others. By 1900 compassion for suffering was second nature. It is hard to overestimate the importance of that revolution in feeling. On it depends much of our literature, a great deal of our religion, and not a little of our politics. The revulsion from pain energizes the welfare state at home and relief programs abroad. To attribute all of this to Victorian concern for animals would be ludicrous. But to ignore the critical role of love for animals in shaping and disseminating this modern sensibility would be blind.

After all, SPCA leaders were the first to organize societies to prevent child abuse—to breach, in the name of compassion, the sacred sanctuary of the home. More generally, the animal protection movement first mobilized the humane sensibilities of those among the English and American middle classes too timid to venture into more controversial efforts to relieve suffering. Eventually, when that reticence diminished, the compassion once lavished mainly on animals helped to found settlement houses, to abolish child labor, to enact old-age insurance, to endow medical research.

To comprehend the nature and limits of our sympathies today, we need to understand their origins. For example, physical suffering seems to us—as opposed to Hindus or, for that matter, to Samuel Johnson—more urgent than spiritual distress. We have worried (though perhaps not excessively) about feeding and clothing the poor for decades; only recently have we thought much about educating them. Likewise, mental illness has long been the underfed orphan among serious diseases vying for government research monies. This is only natural. The needs of the body are more basic than the needs of the soul. But why do we think so? The reasons are complex. Perhaps one of them is that our ancestors learned compassion by practicing it on animals, whose spiritual anguish, if any, is obscure to us. Perhaps, too, in coming to think of ourselves as animals, we have unconsciously tended to stress our "higher" capacities less.

Consider another example. Our compassion today often flourishes as a rather abstract sentimentality—at times cant is not too strong a word. Our hearts bleed for people whom we have never seen; indeed, they usually bleed more freely for the plight of the elderly in a column of newsprint than for the crotchety old woman across the street. Television tugs at our sympathies nightly with its symbolic sufferers. The fashions change: now perhaps teenaged runaways; next season possibly the victims of chattel slavery or of Hitler. Our sympathy for suffering also reaches out to real people, but why does it frequently take the form of this curiously detached and insubstantial sentimentalism? It may only be human nature, but it may also reflect the nurturing of our pity in Victorian love for animals. Establishing a real and solid bond of sympathy with a mute beast was difficult, if not impossible, whatever the professions of Victorian animal lovers. The somewhat awkward and artifical compassion developed could easily have drifted into a disembodied sentimentalism, especially in an age that did not shrink from sentiment. If love for animals appeared to many as the purest type of compassion (as it did), it may have helped to embed in Anglo-American culture this detached and impersonal sympathy for suffering. When contemporary indignation about suffering occasionally seems more ritual than real, one might reflect on its ancestry.

These speculations prove nothing—except that we have thought too little about the shape and sources of our most basic attitudes. We tend now, with good reason, to smile at the sentimentality and anthropomorphism of Victorian animal lovers. But we cannot afford to let our amusement turn to condescension. We are their children.

Notes

Abbreviations in Notes

SPCA = Society for the Prevention of Cruelty to Animals
ASPCA = American SPCA. New York, N.Y.
MSPCA = Massachusetts SPCA. Boston, Mass.
PSPCA = Pennsylvania SPCA. Philadelphia, Pa.
RSPCA = Royal SPCA. Horsham, Sussex (until 1973, London)
WSPCA = Women's Branch of the PSPCA. Philadelphia, Pa. (now Women's SPCA of Pennsylvania)
Buffet = Edward P. Buffet, "Bergh's War on Vested Cruelty," 8 vols., typescript, in ASPCA archives. (Since this work is not paginated, citations give only volume and chapter title.)
RSPCA Records = "Records of Proceedings in Parliament, Letters and Articles in the 'Times' and other Publications, and of the general Progress of Public Opinion, with reference to the Prevention of Cruelty to Animals . . . , 1800-1895," 17 vols., typescript, in RSPCA archives

The printed annual reports of the societies listed above are cited in the following form: ASPCA, *1885 Annual Report,* p. 47. Minute Books are cited by volume number and either page or date, depending on the arrangement of the particular minutes. In the case of the RSPCA minutes, the first, unnumbered volume is cited as [First] Minute Book and the succeeding volumes by the number on the spine of the book; thus, Minute Book No. 1 is actually the second volume in chronological order, and so forth. Full references are in the bibliographic note.

Chapter I

1. For a discussion of the significance of these paintings, see Joseph Campbell, *Primitive Mythology,* vol. 1 of *The Masks of God* (New York, 1959), pp. 299-312.

2. F. E. Zeuner, "The Origins and Stages of Animal Domestication," in *Animals and Man in Historical Perspective,* ed. Joseph and Barrie Klaits (New York, 1974), pp. 121, 138-39.

3. The role of animals in premodern thought, especially in the visual arts, is treated at length in Francis Klingender, *Animals in Art and Thought to the End of the Middle Ages* (London, 1971) and Karl Sälzle, *Tier und Mensch, Gottheit und Dämon: Das Tier in der Geistesgeschichte der Menschheit* (Munich, 1965). Klingender concentrates on Western

Europe; Sälze deals with both western and nonwestern cultures. For a different perspective on medieval and early modern attitudes toward animals, see Lynn White, Jr., "The Historical Roots of Our Ecologic Crisis," *Science* 155 (1967): 1203-7. Kenneth Clark's recent *Animals and Men* (New York, 1977) is an attractive picture book with a brief and superficial text.

4. Keith Thomas, *Religion and the Decline of Magic* (New York, 1971), chap. 2, mentions several such magico-religious rituals common in late medieval England. The other side of this coin was the ritual punishment of animals for various crimes, most commonly witchcraft and sodomy. Such criminal prosecutions, in proper judicial form, were not unusual in premodern Europe. They rested on a variety of religious and quasi-religious beliefs rather than on any notion that animals were capable of personal moral responsibility. See E. P. Evans, *The Criminal Prosecution and Capital Punishment of Animals* (New York, 1906). Certain animals, cats most notoriously, are traditionally the familiars of witches.

5. Bronislaw Malinowski made this suggestion in *Magic, Science and Religion* (Boston, 1948), pp. 27, 29. Cf. the old Russian prayer quoted in Karl A. Menniger, "Totemic Aspects of Contemporary Attitudes toward Animals," in *Psychoanalysis and Culture,* ed. George B. Wilbur and Warner Muensterberger (New York, 1951), p. 49.

6. A typical statement of the orthodox, indeed virtually unchallenged, interpretation of this passage is in St. Augustine, *The City of God against the Pagans,* vol. 6, trans. William Chase Greene (Cambridge, Mass., 1969), p. 187 (lib. xix, cap. xv). Augustine's general position on human obligations to animals was that they did not exist. "Since beasts lack reason . . . we need not concern ourselves with their sufferings." He apparently derived this from the Stoics, who consistently taught that no moral or legal bonds of any sort exist between men and animals. See John Passmore, "The Treatment of Animals," *Journal of the History of Ideas* 36 (1975): 196-98. (Passmore's article is the best single source for the ideas of first-rank thinkers on the question of human obligations to animals. Unfortunately, his coverage is sketchy at best—inevitable in so short an essay—and becomes positively haphazard by the time he reaches the eighteenth century.) The medieval Christian interpretation of Genesis 1:26-28 ignored other obvious ways of construing the text more favorable to animals. See John Passmore, *Man's Responsibility for Nature: Ecological Problems and Western Traditions* (London, 1974), pp. 5-12, and Clarence J. Glacken, *Traces on the Rhodian Shore: Nature and Culture in Western Thought from Ancient Times to the End of the Eighteenth Century* (Berkeley, 1967), pp. 166-68.

7. Cited in John Lawrence, *A Philosophical and Practical Treatise on Horses, and on the Moral Duties of Man towards the Brute Creation* (London, 1796), vol. 1, pp. 8-9.

8. Dix Harwood, *Love for Animals and How It Developed in Great Britain* (New York, 1928), p. 60; Steen Eiler Rasmussen, *London, the Unique City* (New York, 1937), p. 77; D. W. Robertson, Jr., *Chaucer's London* (New York, 1968), p. 117; Robert W. Malcolmson, *Popular Recreations in English Society, 1700-1850* (Cambridge, Eng., 1973), pp. 56-71. Malcolmson describes a number of these sports on pp. 45-51.

9. On this obscure but important subject, see Robertson, *Chaucer's London,* pp. 9, 106, 122. Note also the comment by Kenneth Clark in his television lectures *Civilisation* (London, 1969), and cf. Hannah Arendt's discussion of the opposition between classical and modern views of compassion in *Men in Dark Times* (New York, 1968), p. 15. The Italian Renaissance's version of Stoicism, at least as filtered through Neoplatonism, may have constituted a limited and late exception to my generalization. See Paul Oskar Kristeller, *Renaissance Thought: The Classic, Scholastic, and Humanist Strains* (New York, 1961), pp. 132-33. In any case, animals were by definition excluded from *humanitas.*

10. Sir Thomas Browne, *Religio Medici* (1642), in *Works,* ed. Geoffrey Keynes, 2d ed. (London, 1964), vol. 1, p. 72. Cf. the related comment in Robertson, *Chaucer's London,* p. 191.

11. St. Francis of Assisi may seem an obvious exception, but his almost pantheistic vision of nature lumped animals together with Brother Sun and Sister Moon. Seeing God in everything is not the same as sympathizing with the actual sufferings of actual animals.

12. Harwood, *Love for Animals,* pp. 13, 40. Cf. the longer discussion of Thomas Aquinas in Passmore, "Treatment of Animals," pp. 198-201. However, Steven Ozment quotes a late-fifteenth-century manual for guiding the confessions of children that apparently construes the stoning of chickens and ducks as a sin against the Fifth Commandment: See *The Reformation in the Cities: The Appeal of Protestantism to Sixteenth-Century Germany and Switzerland* (New Haven, Conn., 1975), p. 23. Was the clerical author concerned with protecting the animals or with molding the character of the children?

13. See *De Anima,* trans. J. A. Smith (Oxford, 1931), especially book 2, pp. 414a-415a; *De Motu Animalium,* trans. A.S.L. Farquharson (Oxford, 1912). Cf. *Historia Animalium,* trans. D'Arcy Wentworth Thompson (Oxford, 1910), book 8, pp. 588a-588b.

14. Arthur O. Lovejoy, *The Great Chain of Being* (Cambridge, Mass., 1936), pp. 186-87 (note especially the quotations from the *Book of Sentences* and Bacon); A. C. Crombie, *Medieval and Early Modern Science* (Cambridge, Mass., 1961), vol. 1, pp. 139-40, 172-73.

15. H. W. Janson discusses exhaustively such symbolic use of one animal in *Apes and Ape Lore in the Middle Ages and the Renaissance* (London, 1952). Beryl Rowland, *Animals with Human Faces* (Knoxville, Tenn., 1973) is a veritable encyclopedia of animal symbolism, principally in the literature and art of the Middle Ages. Cf. Glacken, *Traces on the Rhodian Shore,* pp. 309-11.

16. James Fisher, *Zoos of the World* (London, 1966), chaps. 1-2; Harwood, *Love for Animals,* pp. 15-23. The standard history of the zoo is still Gustave Loisel, *Histoire des ménageries de l'antiquité à nos jours* (Paris, 1912).

17. Robertson, *Chaucer's London,* p. 33 n; Harwood, *Love for Animals,* pp. 23-26, 28, 37; Brian Vesey-Fitzgerald, *The Domestic Dog: An Introduction to Its History* (London, 1957), pp. 92-93. The quotations are from the Tudor writer William Harrison, in Harwood, p. 26.

18. Klingender, *Animals in Art and Thought,* passim but especially pp. 490-91; Fisher, *Zoos,* pp. 44-48. Clarence Glacken points out instances of direct and careful observation of nature by the Emperor Frederick II and Albertus Magnus (*Traces on the Rhodian Shore,* pp. 224-29), but the extraordinary work of these two unusual men only emphasizes its rarity.

19. Michel Eyquem de Montaigne, "Apology for Raimond Sebond," in *The Essays of Montaigne,* trans. George B. Ives (Cambridge, Mass., 1925), vol. 2, pp. 201-44. George Boas discusses Montaigne's "theriophilism" and its subsequent fortunes in *The Happy Beast in French Thought of the Eighteenth Century* (Baltimore, 1933). See also Boas's article "Theriophily," in the *Dictionary of the History of Ideas* (New York, 1973), vol. 4, pp. 384-89. As he notes there (p. 388), such notions prior to the eighteenth century usually represented "an appraisal of human life" rather than "a feeling for the sufferings of animals." Cf. Francis Bacon, "De Dignitate et Augmentis Scientiarum," lib. viii, cap. ii, in *Works,* ed. James Spedding et al. (Boston, n.d. [1860-65]), vol. 3, pp. 70-71 (translation in ibid., vol. 9, pp. 249-50).

20. Basil Taylor cites these developments in explaining the origins of the English school of animal painting. See *Animal Painting in England, from Barlow to Landseer* (Harmondsworth, Middlesex, 1955), p. 12.

21. Quoted in Gertrude Himmelfarb, *Darwin and the Darwinian Revolution* (New York, 1959), p. 263.

22. Wallace Shugg, "Humanitarian Attitudes in the Early Animal Experiments of the Royal Society," *Annals of Science* 24 (1968): 228. I know of no full discussion of these developments, but see Emile Guyénot, *Les sciences de la vie aux XVIIe et XVIIIe siècles*

(Paris, 1957), chap. 2, and chap. 4, sec. vi; and M. F. Ashley Montague, *Edward Tyson, M.D., F.R.S., 1650-1708* (Philadelphia, 1943), esp. chaps. 4-6 and 8.

23. Harwood, *Love for Animals,* p. 78; Ernest Lee Tuveson, *Millennium and Utopia: A Study in the Background of the Idea of Progress,* rev. ed. (New York, 1964), pp. 104-5.

24. For an example of the diffusion of this knowledge and its impact, see [Bernard Mandeville], *The Fable of the Bees; or, Private Vices Publick Benefits* (London, 1714), p. 147. Sir Michael Foster discussed seventeenth-century physiological theories of the nervous system in his *Lectures on the History of Physiology during the Sixteenth, Seventeenth, and Eighteenth Centuries* (Cambridge, Eng., 1901), chap. 10. This work, however, is dated and must be used with caution. See especially, as a corrective to Foster's jaundiced view of Thomas Willis, Sir Charles Symond's biographical sketch in *The Royal Society: Its Origins and Founders,* ed. Harold Hartley (London, 1960), pp. 91-97.

25. *The British Apollo, or Curious Amusements for the Ingenious* 1 (1708), supernumerary paper for April, quoted in Wallace Shugg, "The Cartesian Beast-Machine in English Literature (1663-1750)," *Journal of the History of Ideas* 29 (1968): 284. Cf. David Hume, *Enquiries concerning the Human Understanding and concerning the Principles of Morals,* ed. L. A. Selby-Bigge, 2d ed. (Oxford, 1902), pp. 104-8.

26. Shugg, "Beast-Machine," p. 292. Locke's authority reinforced this idea, and the growing appeal of the concept of the Great Chain of Being may have made the notion more plausible. See Lovejoy, *Chain of Being,* chap. 6 (esp. pp. 184 and 195-98) and pp. 228-29. Descartes had tried to rescue human uniqueness by arguing that beasts were only machines that appeared to feel but were actually as incapable of pain as a steam pump. His ingenious hypothesis, however, was not seriously entertained in England, though whether this was a triumph of common sense or of British chauvinism, I cannot say. Cf. Shugg, "Beast-Machine," 279-92; also idem, "Humanitarian Attitudes," p. 237. The fullest discussion of this Cartesian theory and reactions to it is in Leonora C. Rosenfield, *From Beast-Machine to Man-Machine,* 2d ed. (New York, 1968). Rosenfield believes the theory to have been "vigorous" in England (p. 65), but my own research supports Shugg.

27. I refer here to the human type of soul: immortal, fully rational, and made in the divine image. Animals were still widely believed to possess a lower sort of soul (like the Aristotelian "sensitive" soul); how else account for their voluntary motion? Indeed, the attempt to locate the seat of this soul was an academic industry for two millennia. See Roger K. French, *Robert Whytt, the Soul, and Medicine* (London, 1969), esp. chaps. 8-12.

28. W. Lee Ustick, "Changing Ideals of Aristocratic Character and Conduct in Seventeenth-Century England," *Modern Philology* 30 (1932-33): 161-66.

29. R. S. Crane, "Suggestions Toward a Genealogy of the 'Man of Feeling,'" *ELH: A Journal of English Literary History* 1 (1934): 208-9. For more on the Latitudinarians and their forebears, the Cambridge Platonists, see G. R. Cragg, *From Puritanism to the Age of Reason* (Cambridge, Eng., 1950), chaps. 3-4.

30. R. S. Crane and M. E. Prior, "English Literature, 1660-1800," *Philological Quarterly* 11 (1932): 204.

31. Crane, "Man of Feeling," pp. 208-29.

32. Isaac Barrow, "Sermon XXX," in *Theological Works* (Oxford, 1830), vol. 2, pp. 140-42 (preached sometime before 1677), quoted in Crane and Prior, "English Literature," p. 205.

33. Cf. Cotton Mather, *Bonifacius: An Essay Upon the Good,* ed. David Levin (1710; Cambridge, Mass., 1966). Mather's book actually represented a later development in the progress of benevolence: the practical but—in the eyes of many contemporaries—perversely uncharitable implementation of the doctrine in societies for the reformation of manners, which flourished in the sober reigns of the last two Stuarts. For this story, see Dudley W. R. Bahlman, *The Moral Revolution of 1688* (New Haven, Conn., 1957).

34. C. A. Moore, "Shaftesbury and the Ethical Poets in England, 1700-1760," *PMLA* 31 (1916): 264-325.

35. Edward C. Mack, *Public Schools and British Opinion, 1780-1860* (New York, 1939), pp. 60-63; M. G. Jones, *The Charity School Movement: A Study of Eighteenth Century Puritanism in Action* (Cambridge, Eng., 1938).

36. James Baldwin Brown, *Memoirs of the Public and Private Life of John Howard, the Philanthropist* (London, 1818), esp. pp. 123 ff.; John Aikin, *A View of the Character and Public Services of the late John Howard, Esq., LL.D., F.R.S.* (London, 1792); Samuel L. Knapp, *The Life of Thomas Eddy* (London, 1836); David Owen, *English Philanthropy, 1600-1660* (Cambridge, Mass., 1964), pp. 61-65.

37. Betty Fladeland, *Men and Brothers: Anglo-American Antislavery Cooperation* (Urbana, Ill., 1972), p. 5; Frank J. Klingberg, *The Anti-Slavery Movement in England: A Study in English Humanitarianism* (New Haven, 1926), pp. 32-33, 39.

38. Robin Furneaux, *William Wilberforce* (London, 1974), p. 87; Klingberg, *Anti-Slavery Movement,* p. 73.

39. Owen, *Philanthropy,* pp. 67-68.

40. Cragg, *Puritanism to the Age of Reason,* pp. 53, 72-73.

41. Harwood, *Love for Animals,* p. 72. The baiting sports were occasionally denounced by Puritans from the early seventeenth century — and were even half-heartedly suppressed during the Commonwealth — but because they occasioned drunkenness and other vices rather than because they abused animals. Similarly, Samuel Pepys found bull baiting distasteful because of its coarse, ungentlemanly character and the rowdiness it provoked. See J. Leslie Hotson, "Bear Gardens and Bear Baiting during the Commonwealth," *PMLA* 40 (1925): 276-88; Edward G. Fairholme and Wellesley Pain, *A Century of Work for Animals: The History of the RSPCA, 1824-1924,* 1st ed. (London and New York, 1924), pp. 3-4; Harwood, *Love for Animals,* pp. 71-72. Keith Thomas has suggested that Puritan opposition to "ritual sports bordering on animal sacrifice (such as bear-baiting and bull-baiting)" may reflect a more general hostility to primitive social patterns. See "History and Anthropology," *Past and Present,* no. 24 (1963), p. 8. This may be true but is hardly necessary to explain the relevant data.

42. Howard H. Brinton, *Quaker Journals: Varieties of Religious Experience Among Friends* (Wallingford, Pa., 1972), chap. 11. I owe this reference to Mr. George Smith.

43. Fairholme and Pain, *Century of Work for Animals,* pp. 3-4; Harwood, *Love for Animals,* p. 72. Cf. Shugg, "Humanitarian Attitudes."

44. Cf. Harwood, *Love for Animals,* pp. 180-83, 275-78.

45. George Williams, "On Sentimentality," *Rice University Studies* 51 (1965): 136; Crane, "Man of Feeling," p. 206; Crane Brinton, "Humanitarianism," in *Encyclopedia of the Social Sciences,* vol. 7 (New York, 1932), p. 547. For a typical example of the cult of benevolence in its fully developed form, see William L. Brown, *An Essay on Sensibility: A Poem in Six Parts,* 2d ed. (London, 1791).

46. Moore, "Shaftesbury," pp. 281, 319; Harwood, *Love for Animals,* pp. 180-90.

47. See, e.g., *Gentleman's Magazine* 5 (1735): 124, and 6 (1735): 10. Cf. Harwood, *Love for Animals,* pp. 194-200.

48. Winthrop D. Jordan discusses Linnaeus's influence in this respect in *White Over Black: American Attitudes toward the Negro, 1550-1812* (Chapel Hill, N.C., 1968), pp. 218-19. For Linnaeus's own concept of species, see William T. Stearn's Introduction to the Ray Society facsimile edition of Linnaeus, *Species Plantarum* (1753; London, 1957), pp. 156-61.

49. Lovejoy, *Chain of Being,* pp. 228-31; Paul L. Farber, "Buffon and the Concept of Species," *Journal of the History of Biology* 5 (1972): 259-84. Toward the end of his career, Linnaeus also wavered on the fixity of species, but his public (and influential) position remained his earlier one.

50. Soame Jenyns, *Disquisitions on Several Subjects* (Dublin, 1782), pp. 8-9.

51. The idea of the Great Chain of Being, and especially the principle of continuity, was central to this belief. See Lovejoy, *Chain of Being,* pp. 233-36.

52. E. L. Cloyd, *James Burnett, Lord Monboddo* (Oxford, 1972), pp. 44-47, 126-27, 161-68. But Monboddo's concept of species was more inclusive than the accepted Linnaean version. By the way, the orang-outang, in particular, seems to have been classified often as a member of the human family.

53. Lovejoy, *Chain of Being,* pp. 233-36; Jordan, *White Over Black,* pp. 228-39; Harwood, *Love for Animals,* pp. 224-25. For French views on the relation of ape to man, see Hester Hastings, *Man and Beast in French Thought of the Eighteenth Century* (Baltimore, 1936), part 2, chap. 3.

54. For the diffusion of these biological theories, see Lovejoy, *Chain of Being,* chap. 6. For an example of a direct link between belief in the chain of being and concern about cruelty to animals, see Jenyns, *Disquisitions,* Disquisitions 1 and 2; cf. Harwood, *Love for Animals,* p. 144. It is perhaps more than coincidence that the veterinary practitioner (as a medical man rather than a farrier handy with herbs) first appeared in England in the eighteenth century. See Lawrence, *Horses,* pp. 25-35.

55. Isaac Hawkins Browne, *De Animi Immortalite* (1754), quoted in Moore, "Shaftesbury," p. 315. Cf. Adam Smith, *Theory of Moral Sentiments* (1759), part 2, sec. 3, chap. 1, and David Hartley, *Observations on Man* (London, 1749), vol. 2, pp. 222-23, both cited in Harwood, *Love for Animals,* pp. 134, 144.

56. James McLachlan, *"The Choice of Hercules:* American Student Societies in the Early 19th Century," in *The University in Society,* ed. Lawrence Stone (Princeton, 1974), vol. 2, p. 484; Joseph Butler, *The Analogy of Religion, Natural and Revealed, to the Constitution and Course of Nature* (1736), chap. 1, cited in Coleman Parsons, "The Progenitors of *Black Beauty* in Humanitarian Literature," *Notes and Queries* 192 (1947): 191; Soame Jenyns, *Free Inquiry into the Nature and Origin of Evil* (1757), letter 3, cited in Harwood, *Love for Animals,* pp. 152-53; Toplady cited in *Animal World* 15 (1884): 162.

57. John Wesley, "The General Deliverance" (1788), in *Works* (London, 1872), vol. 6, pp. 241-52; John Hildrop, *Free Thoughts upon the Brute Creation,* 2 vols. (London, 1742-43); Richard Dean, *An Essay on the Future Life of Brutes,* 2 vols. (Manchester, 1767). For a specific refutation of these views, see James Rothwell, *A Letter to the Rev. Mr. Dean, of Middleton* (n.p. [London], 1769). Eighteenth-century French opinions on the subject are discussed in Hastings, *Man and Beast,* part 1.

58. See, e.g., *London Magazine* 22 (1753): 279-80, and 31 (1762): 94-95; John Hawkesworth's essay in *The Adventurer* (1753), cited in Parsons, "Progenitors," p. 192; and the *Pennsylvania Magazine* 1 (1775): 231-32 (a poem attributed to Thomas Paine).

59. M. Dorothy George, *London Life in the XVIIIth Century* (London, 1925), p. 17; Parsons, "Progenitors," p. 192; Harwood, *Love for Animals,* pp. 243-44. Hogarth averred that, if the engravings were effective, he was "more proud of having been the author than I should be of having painted Raffaele's cartoons." See George, *London Life,* p. 17. Hogarth, by the way, painted a self-portrait with his dog Trump. See Vesey-Fitzgerald, *Domestic Dog,* p. 70.

60. *Annual Register* 4 (1761): 196-98; Abraham Smith, *A Scriptural and Moral Catechism,* 2d ed. (Birmingham, n.d. [1833?]), p. xxii (mentions annual sermons by Rev. Richard Amner about the 1780s). The first published sermon on the subject seems to have been James Granger's *An Apology for the Brute Creation* (London, 1772). See Parsons, "Progenitors," p. 193, for the musical piece.

61. The same thing was happening in France, though to a lesser degree. See Hastings, *Man and Beast,* part 3.

62. John Woolman, *Journal and Essays,* ed. Amelia Mott Gummere (Philadelphia, 1922), p. 306, and Joshua Evans, *Journal of the Life, Travels, Religious Exercises, and*

Labours in the Work of the Ministry (Byberry, Pa., 1837), pp. 27-38, both cited in Brinton, *Quaker Journals*, pp. 89-91.

63. Adams to James Warren, October 13, 1775, in Massachusetts Historical Society, *Warren-Adams Letters, Being Chiefly a Correspondence among John Adams, Samuel Adams, and James Warren . . . 1743-1814* (Boston, 1917-1925), vol. 1, p. 137; John Adams, *Diary and Autobiography,* ed. Lyman H. Butterfield (Cambridge, Mass., 1961), vol. 3, pp. 320-21. I owe these references to Prof. Jack Rakove.

64. Journal of Samuel Dexter, October 11, 1779, quoted in *Our Dumb Animals,* 13 (1880-81): 27. The horse's pension plan was adequately funded and protected by a written contract.

65. Humphrey Primatt, *A Dissertation on the Duty of Mercy and Sin of Cruelty to Brute Animals* (London, 1776). Note that the term "Anglo-American" is ambiguous, especially in an eighteenth-century context. It will be used throughout this book to signify the inhabitants, taken together, of England, its American colonies from Maine to Georgia, and later the United States.

66. Primatt, *Dissertation,* pp. ii-iv, 1-14.

67. Ibid., pp. 7-8.

68. Ibid., pp. 321-22.

69. Ibid., pp. 4, 47-48, 103-4.

70. For a twelfth-century example, see Rasmussen, *London,* p. 77.

71. The Evangelicals will make a more extended appearance in the next chapter; for a brief assessment of their influence, see Standish Meacham, "The Evangelical Inheritance," *Journal of British Studies* 3, no. 1 (1963): 88-104. On the subject of child-rearing practices, as complex as it is opaque, see especially Philippe Ariès, *Centuries of Childhood,* trans. Robert Baldick (New York, 1962) and David Hunt's answer to Ariès, *Parents and Children in History: The Psychology of Family Life in Early Modern France* (New York, 1970), as well as the recent collection of essays edited by Lloyd deMause, *The History of Childhood* (New York, 1974), particularly the contributions of Joseph Illick and John Walzer.

72. *London Magazine* 16 (1747): 605-6, and Granger, *Apology,* pp. 17-18, illustrate the diffusion of these concerns. For the role of animals in eighteenth-century children's literature, see Florence V. Barry, *A Century of Children's Books* (London, 1922), pp. 135-44, and Frederick Darton, *Children's Books in England: Five Centuries of Social Life,* 2d ed. (Cambridge, Eng., 1958), pp. 130-34, 158-62.

73. Darton, *Children's Books,* pp. 130-134, 158, 161. For the longevity of *Fabulous Histories,* see *Animal World* 11 (1880): 173, or the British Museum catalogue. Interestingly, Mrs. Trimmer and her cohorts were, like Primatt, "acutely conscious of the superiority of man to the brute creation" (Darton, *Children's Books,* pp. 159, 161). Other readily available examples of these books are Thomas Day, *The History of Sandford and Merton* (1783-89), Mary Wollstonecraft, *Original Stories from Real Life* (1791), and Edward Augustus Kendall, *Keeper's Travels in Search of His Master* (1798).

74. Jenyns, *Disquisitions,* pp. 18-19; "Young Philemon accused by his Sister of Cruelty," in *Poems on Various Subjects for the Amusement of Youth* (1789), quoted in Harwood, *Love for Animals,* p. 256.

75. Elie Halévy, *The Growth of Philosophic Radicalism,* trans. Mary Morris (London, 1928), chap. 1. The doctrine of benevolence, to cite one example, certainly had these overtones.

76. Jeremy Bentham, *An Introduction to the Principles of Morals and Legislation,* ed. J. H. Burns and H.L.A. Hart (1780; London, 1970), pp. 282-83 n. Bentham drew an analogy to human slavery. Later, if Dumont's notoriously inaccurate edition of the *Traités de législation civile et pénale* (1802) can be trusted, Bentham retreated somewhat from this extreme position. In the *Traités* he argued against cruelty to animals on the ground, shared with Kant, that it led to cruelty to people. In the *Constitutional Code* he relied instead on

the assertion that "mature quadrupeds are more moral and more intelligent than young bipeds." At no point, however, did he actually repudiate his earlier argument in the *Introduction.* See David Baumgardt, *Bentham and the Ethics of Today* (Princeton, 1952), pp. 338-39, 362-63, and Passmore, "Treatment of Animals," p. 211. Incidentally, Mill, despite his criticisms of Bentham, was fully as anxious as his intellectual godfather to defend animals from cruelty. See the *Principles of Political Economy* (Boston, 1848), vol. 2, pp. 534-35 (book 5, chap. 11, sec. 9).

77. He was also fond of cats and "became once very intimate with a colony of mice"; he said it was hard "to reconcile the two affections." See Harwood, *Love for Animals,* p. 168.

78. Bentham, *Introduction,* p. 283 n.

79. Herman Daggett, *The Rights of Animals: An Oration Delivered at the Commencement of Providence-College, September 7, 1791* (1792; New York, 1926); here one suspects the influence of the American Revolution as well. Lawrence, *Horses,* vol. 1, chap. 3; for the French Revolution's impact on Lawrence, see ibid., vol. 2, p. 33.

80. John Oswald, *The Cry of Nature; or, An Appeal to Mercy and to Justice, on Behalf of the Persecuted Animals* (London, 1791); *Dictionary of National Biography,* s.v. "John Oswald"; Thomas Paine, *The Age of Reason* (1794), in *Complete Writings of Thomas Paine,* ed. Philip S. Foner (New York, 1945), vol. 1, p. 512.

Chapter II

1. Wilberforce to Hannah More, April 25, 1800, quoted in Robert I. and Samuel Wilberforce, *The Life of William Wilberforce* (London, 1838), vol. 2, p. 366; Hansard, *Parliamentary History,* vol. 35, p. 202. Pulteney, a rich Scot, sat in Parliament from 1768 until his death in 1805. His "independence, and his competence as a speaker, gave him considerable standing in the House": Sir Lewis Namier and John Brooke, *The House of Commons 1754-1790* (London, 1964), vol. 3, pp. 341-43.

2. The debate is in Hansard, *Parliamentary History,* vol. 35, pp. 202-13.

3. Wilberforce to More, in the Wilberforces, *Life,* vol. 2, p. 366; Hansard, *Parliamentary History,* vol. 36, pp. 829-54.

4. Edward Barry, *Bull Baiting! A Sermon . . . Inscribed to John Dent, Esq., M.P.* (Reading, n.d. [1802]); Percival Stockdale, *A Remonstrance Against Inhumanity to Animals* (Alnwick, 1802).

5. *The Times* [London], May 9, 1802, quoted in RSPCA Records, vol. 1, pp. 16-17; *Hansard,* July 11, 1805, cited in ibid., vol. 1, p. 37.

6. Hansard, *Parliamentary History,* vol. 36, p. 833; *Hansard,* vol. 14, pp. 553, 557, 806, 807, 852-53.

7. *Dictionary of National Biography,* s.v. "Thomas Erskine."

8. *The Times* [London], May 30, 1809, quoted in RSPCA Records, vol. 1, pp. 103-4; cf. *Gentleman's Magazine,* quoted in RSPCA Records, p. 106; *Hansard,* vol. 14, pp. 806-8, 989, 1031*-*32, 1071, and vol. 16, p. 883 (asterisks *sic;* they distinguish duplicate page numbers resulting from printer's error).

9. *Cruelty to Animals. The Speech of Lord Erskine . . .* (London, 1809); *Hansard,* vol. 14, pp. 806, 853; vol. 16, pp. 726, 880-84, 1017; vol. 17, pp. 304-5; vol. 29, p. 338; and vol. 34, p. 1265.

10. Dudley W. R. Bahlman, *The Moral Revolution of 1688* (New Haven, Conn.: 1957); Ford K. Brown, *Fathers of the Victorians: The Age of Wilberforce* (Cambridge, Eng., 1961). Similar American organizations are discussed in M. J. Heale, "Humanitarianism in the Early Republic: The Moral Reformers of New York, 1776-1825," *Journal of American Studies* 2 (1968): 161-75.

11. For an attack on such spying, see *Edinburgh Review* 13 (1809): 333-34, 339-41.

12. Arthur W. Moss, *Valiant Crusade: The History of the R.S.P.C.A.* (London, 1961), pp. 20-21; Liverpool *Mercury,* April 28, 1825, quoted in Buffet, vol. 1, "Contents of an Old Scrapbook."

13. See, for example, the review of John Styles, *Sermons on Various Subjects,* in *Eclectic Review* 10 (1813): 635-45. The reviewer treats Styles's attack on cruelty as in no way unusual. Cf. Lord Erskine's comment in *Hansard,* vol. 14, p. 556.

14. Diary of John Evelyn, cited in Howard Williams, *The Ethics of Diet* (London, 1883), p. 107. The excellent biography, *John Ray* (Cambridge, Eng., 1942), by the eminent Anglican naturalist-theologian Charles Raven, does not mention this belief. Cf. Hester Hastings, *Man and Beast in French Thought of the Eighteenth Century* (Baltimore, 1936), pp. 254-65, for eighteenth-century French vegetarians, though most of these appear to have been vegetarians only "in principle." There were also celebrated classical and oriental precedents for vegetarianism.

15. *Dictionary of National Biography,* s.v. "George Cheyne" and "William Lambe"; Williams, *Ethics,* pp. 120-28, 198-206. Cheyne's ideas are discussed more generally in Lester S. King, "George Cheyne, Mirror of Eighteenth Century Medicine," *Bulletin of the History of Medicine* 48 (1974): 517-39. For the classic statement of the theories of this school of vegetarians, see John Frank Newton, *The Return to Nature; or, a Defence of the Vegetable Regimen* (London, 1811).

16. Joshua Evans is mentioned in the previous chapter. The seventeenth-century Anabaptist Thomas Tryon, whose *The Way to Health* (London, 1683) influenced young Benjamin Franklin, was an isolated earlier example: Williams, *Ethics,* 309-14; *The Autobiography of Benjamin Franklin,* ed. Leonard W. Labaree et al. (New Haven, 1964), pp. 63, 87. On the Dorrilites, see Alice Felt Tyler, *Freedom's Ferment* (Minneapolis, 1944), p. 68.

17. *Dictionary of National Biography,* s.v. "William Cowherd"; Williams, *Ethics,* pp. 258-64; Gerald Carson, *Cornflake Crusade* (New York, 1957), pp. 15-17.

18. John Oswald, *The Cry of Nature; or, An Appeal to Mercy and to Justice, on Behalf of the Persecuted Animals* (London, 1791). Several earlier writers had discussed the question, but Oswald was, to my knowledge, the first to come down squarely and definitively against killing animals for food. See also *Dictionary of National Biography,* s.v. "John Oswald"; Williams, *Ethics,* pp. 179-80.

19. [Bernard Mandeville], *The Fable of the Bees: or, Private Vices Publick Benefits* (London, 1714), pp. 146-50.

20. *Dictionary of National Biography,* s.v. "Joseph Ritson"; Joseph Ritson, *An Essay on Abstinence from Animal Food, as a Moral Duty* (London, 1802); the quotation is from p. 159.

21. *Dictionary of National Biography,* s.v., "Richard Phillips" and "George Nicholson." Phillips's dates were 1767-1840, Nicholson's 1760-1825.

22. The frequent conjunction of radical political beliefs with eccentric ideas about other matters in the early 1800s is not often dwelt on by historians (perhaps because they wish to preserve a respectable ancestry for the later Left), but it is a striking fact nonetheless. Nor is it really surprising. Political, religious, and scientific orthodoxies were then much more intertwined than is now the case, and these radicals were, after all, drastically alienated from the accepted verities of their society.

23. Brian Vesey-Fitzgerald, *The Domestic Dog: An Introduction to Its History* (London, 1957), pp. 95-97; Joseph Taylor, *The General Character of the Dog* (London, 1804), pp. iii-iv.

24. James Fisher, *Zoos of the World* (London, 1966), pp. 55-56.

25. See, for example, Anonymous, *The Hare; or, Hunting Incompatible with Humanity* (Philadelphia, 1802); [Samuel Jackson Pratt], *Pity's Gift: A Collection of Interesting Tales, to Excite the Compassion of Youth for the Animal Creation* (Philadelphia, 1808). Herman

Daggett's *The American Reader* (Sag-Harbor, N.Y., 1806) was the work of a native son. On the House of Bishops denunciation, see *Our Dumb Animals* 7 (1874-75): 51.

26. Thomas C. Amory, *Life of James Sullivan* (Boston, 1859), vol. 1, pp. 294-95; [Baltimore] *Federal Republican,* December 30, 1816, quoted in William J. Shultz, *The Humane Movement in the United States* (New York, 1924), p. 12; *Digest of New York Statutes and Reports . . . to the year 1860,* vol. 1, p. 124, quoted in Emily S. Leavitt et al., *Animals and Their Legal Rights,* 2d ed. (New York, 1970), p. 15; Francis H. Rowley, *The Humane Idea* (Boston, 1912), pp. 40-41; Case of Isaac Ross, 3 *New York City Hall Recorder* 191, quoted in Buffet, vol. 1, "Humane Conditions"; Dr. Chalmers, "Cruelty to Animals," [American] *Methodist Magazine* 9 (1826): 259-66; Jennie Holliman, *American Sports, 1785-1835* (Durham, N.C., 1931), pp. 129-30, 134; Bruce Laurie, "'Nothing on Impulse': Life Styles of Philadelphia Artisans, 1820-1850," *Labor History* 15 (1974): 346; John C. Miller, *The Federalist Era, 1789-1801* (New York, 1960), p. 265.

27. See, for example, Richard Steele's attack at the beginning of the eighteenth century on the evils of cock fighting, cited in Dix Harwood, *Love for Animals and How It Developed in Great Britain* (New York, 1928), p. 275. At the century's end, see Thomas Young's onslaught against all the baiting sports (*An Essay on Humanity to Animals* [London, 1798], pp. 61-72), as well as virtually every anticruelty tract published between these two works.

28. Although practiced in America, the sport never took hold there as strongly as in England: Holliman, *Sports,* p. 131. I suspect two reasons for this: (1) America never developed a traditional style of village life comparable to England's, and (2) by the time America was reasonably well-populated, the sport was already coming into disrepute.

29. Cf. Keith Thomas, *Religion and the Decline of Magic* (New York, 1971), p. 65.

30. Young, *Essay,* pp. 70-71; Robert W. Malcolmson, *Popular Recreations in English Society, 1700-1850* (Cambridge, Eng., 1973), p. 123; M. Dorothy George, *London Life in the XVIIIth Century* (London, 1925), pp. 97, 351. Throwing at cocks, a traditional village sport associated with Shrove Tuesday celebrations, was also attacked in the eighteenth century as cruel to animals but suffered a much earlier demise than bull baiting. Malcolmson explains its rapid disappearance in *Popular Recreations,* pp. 119-22.

31. Malcolmson, *Popular Recreations,* pp. 100-7; Wilberforce to Hannah More, April 25, 1800, quoted in the Wilberforces, *Life,* vol. 2, p. 366; Hansard, *Parliamentary History,* vol. 35, pp. 203-4, and vol. 36, pp. 831, 844-46.

32. Hansard, *Parliamentary History,* vol. 35, pp. 202-3, and vol. 36, pp. 833, 852-53; George, *London Life,* p. 97.

33. Holliman, *Sports,* pp. 129-30; Stockdale, *Remonstrance,* p. 12; *Hansard,* vol. 14, pp. 553-54.

34. Hansard, *Parliamentary History,* vol. 36, pp. 836, 848-49; *Hansard,* vol. 14, pp. *1026-27*, 1030-36, and vol. 16, p. 884 (asterisks *sic;* see note 8 above).

35. Hansard, *Parliamentary History,* vol. 36, p. 853. Cf. also vol. 35, p. 209, and vol. 36, pp. 847-48.

36. *Hansard,* vol. 14, pp. 571, 1031*; Ritson, *Essay,* p. 124.

37. Darwin's *Botanic Garden* appeared in 1791, his *Zoonomia* (2 vols.) in 1794-96, and his *Temple of Nature* in 1803. Lamarck's *Philosophie zoologique* was published in 1809. For the popularity of Darwin's books, see Gertrude Himmelfarb, *Darwin and the Darwinian Revolution* (New York, 1959), pp. 16-17.

38. Erskine, *Cruelty,* p. 3; *Hansard,* vol. 14, p. 555. Erskine thought that the recognition of this principle of respect for the animal's feelings "deserved to be considered as an aera in legislation." See *Hansard,* vol. 16, p. 881.

39. See, for example, Hansard, *Parliamentary History,* vol. 36, pp. 845, 847, 848; *An Address to the Public from the Society for the Suppression of Vice* (London, 1804), pp. 71-72, quoted in *Edinburgh Review* 13 (1809): 340 n. Cf. the description of a bull bait in the New York *Spectator,* July 8, 1801, quoted in Holliman, *Sports,* p. 135. For Jenyns, see Chapter I.

40. *Address to the Public,* pp. 71-72, as cited in note 39 above; Hansard, *Parliamentary History,* vol. 36, pp. 845, 848, 851.

41. See Chapter I and Hastings, *Man and Beast* (although Hastings herself does not draw this comparison).

42. Malcolmson, *Popular Recreations,* pp. 107-17; in addition to these vaguer influences, he refers specifically to Evangelicalism and the emphasis on work discipline.

43. See the petitions against the sport in *Commons Journals,* April 13, 14, 15, 23, 26, 28, and May 7 and 24, 1802. Bull baiting seems to have been more commonly practiced in the Black Country than elsewhere, but it was by no means limited to industrial areas. Even its apparently greater prevalence there may in part simply reflect the fact that stronger opposition brought more instances to light. For the geographic distribution of the sport, see Malcolmson, *Popular Recreations,* p. 123. Significantly, the last bull baits to be suppressed in England were in nonindustrial areas. RSPCA Minute Book no. 2, pp. 179-80, 195-202, 220-21; no. 3, pp. 33-41, 189-91, 223-36; no. 4, pp. 44, 51-56, 212, 326; no. 5, pp. 22-24, 166-67.

44. *Commons Journals,* May-June 1821, May 1822, February-April and June 1824, March and May-June 1825, passim; *Lords Journals,* July 1821, May-July 1822, March-April and June 1824, March and May 1825, passim.

45. Cf. the interesting comments of "Raynor Creighton" in Ronald Blythe, *Akenfield* (London, 1969), p. 170. All through the century animal protection societies were overwhelmingly urban organizations. Brian Harrison goes so far as to suggest that much RSPCA activity of the nineteenth century constituted, in effect if not intent, "urban attacks on rural culture." See "Animals and the State in nineteenth-century England," *English Historical Review* 88 (1973): 790. I am *not* claiming that city dwellers in fact treat animals better than rural people.

46. It is no coincidence that bull baits were typically held in November or December, a slack period following the intense labor of the harvest. Cf. Keith Thomas, "Work and Leisure in Pre-Industrial Society," *Past and Present,* no. 29 (1964): 54. On the development of time discipline during the Industrial Revolution, see E. P. Thompson, "Time, Work-Discipline, and Industrial Capitalism," *Past and Present,* no. 38 (1967): 56-97. For a fuller and more broadly conceived discussion of the fitting of men to machines, see Sidney Pollard, *The Genesis of Modern Management* (Cambridge, Mass., 1965). Evangelical objections to bull baiting must be seen in this context.

47. *Commons Journals,* April 23 and 28, 1802 (petitions from the Shropshire towns of Wellington and Wenlock and the Staffordshire towns of Tipton and Sedgeley).

48. The close similarity in wording of many of these petitions indicates concerted action. See especially the petitions from Walsall, Wolverhampton, Wednesbury, and Darlaston in *Commons Journals,* April 13-15 and April 26, 1802.

49. *Hansard,* vol. 14, pp. 559-60.

50. Hansard, *Parliamentary History,* vol. 35, pp. 202, 207-9, vol. 36, pp. 836, 838-39.

51. See the comments of Brian Harrison in the symposium "Work and Leisure in Industrial Society," *Past and Present,* no. 30 (1965): 101. I am indebted to him for some of what follows, but more to various comments of Oscar Handlin over the past several years. See specifically Handlin, "The Modern City as a Field of Historical Study," in *The Historian and the City,* ed. Oscar Handlin and John Burchard (Cambridge, Mass., 1963), pp. 13-14.

52. Brian Harrison, "Work and Leisure," p. 101.

53. Hansard, *Parliamentary History,* vol. 35, p. 204, vol. 36, pp. 837-38, 840-41, 844. Cf. Windham's almost identical arguments against Erskine's Cruelty to Animals Bill: *Hansard,* vol. 14, pp. 1038-40.

54. These paragraphs draw on all the bull-baiting debates, and only wide reading in them can re-create the full picture behind the fragmentary comments of Windham and his allies. However, for representative passages see Hansard, *Parliamentary History,* vol. 35, pp. 203, 205-6, vol. 36, pp. 833-34, 846, 849, 851.

55. Ibid., vol. 36, pp. 833-35.

56. The issues of industrial morality and discipline have only in the last few years attracted as much attention from American as from English historians. The best study in the antebellum period is Paul Faler, "Cultural Aspects of the Industrial Revolution: Lynn, Massachusetts, Shoemakers and Industrial Morality, 1826-1860," *Labor History* 15 (1974): 367-94. Faler does not touch on animal sports, but he deals with the same general issues central to my argument. See also Herbert Gutman, "Work, Culture, and Society in Industrializing America, 1815-1919," *American Historical Review* 78 (1973): 531-88, especially 544-46 (reprinted in Gutman's book of the same title [New York, 1976]).

57. *Our Dumb Animals* 7 (1874-75): 51; Boston *Daily Evening Transcript,* April 16 and May 4, 1846 (I owe this reference to Prof. Henry Binford); Holliman, *Sports,* pp. 129-130, 134-36.

58. This conclusion depends in part on who is counted as a manufacturing worker. See George Rogers Taylor, *The Transportation Revolution, 1815-1860* (New York, 1951), p. 267.

59. Modernization is, of necessity, a term rather loosely used. I mean to include within it three distinguishable though related developments: (1) industrialization, (2) large-scale urbanization, and (3) the accompanying rationalization of economic and social structure and habits, meaning chiefly the *tendency* to organize human activities not along customary lines but in ways thought out to achieve particular ends.

60. Raymond Williams points out that the "unnaturalness" of industrialism was "the keystone of a continuing criticism of the new industrial civilization": *Culture and Society, 1780-1950* (New York, 1958), p. 15.

61. Caroline Tisdall, "Natural Philosophy," *Manchester Guardian Weekly* 109, no. 22 (December 22, 1973): 23; Louis Legrand Noble, *The Life and Works of Thomas Cole,* ed. Elliot S. Vesell (1853; Cambridge, Mass., 1964), pp. 145-46. On the revolution in animal painting, see Basil Taylor, *Animal Painting in England, from Barlow to Landseer* (Harmondsworth, Middlesex, 1955).

62. Tisdall, "Natural Philosophy," p. 23; Sydney George Fisher, Farm Journal, May 24, 1846, in box B-32 of the Sydney George Fisher Papers (Historical Society of Pennsylvania).

63. Basil Willey, *The Eighteenth Century Background: Studies on the Idea of Nature in the Thought of the Period* (London, 1940), pp. 207-8.

64. Oswald, *Cry of Nature,* pp. 57-58. Bentham is the most celebrated example of this view (see Chapter I), but see also John Lawrence, *A Philosophical and Practical Treatise on Horses, and on the Moral Duties of Man towards the Brute Creation* (London, 1796), vol. 1, p. 119.

65. Speech of Dr. George Loring to MSPCA Annual Meeting, March 29, 1870, printed in *Our Dumb Animals* 3 (1870-71): 1. Was it not contradictory to attack rural sports like bull baiting while clinging to the old agrarian world? Of course, at least to some extent. But people are not always consistent, and the situation itself had no wholly consistent solution.

66. B. L. Hutchins and A. Harrison, *A History of Factory Legislation,* 3d ed. (London, 1926), chaps. 1-5; Carroll Davidson Wright, "Labour Legislation: United States," *Encyclopedia Brittannica,* 11th ed. (Cambridge, Eng., 1911).

67. The Ragged School movement is dealt with in the standard works on British education in the period, but the most interesting approach is Jo Manton, *Mary Carpenter and the Children of the Streets* (London, 1976). The American campaign for public education is adequately summarized in R. Freeman Butts and Lawrence A. Cremin, *A History of Education in American Culture* (New York, 1962).

68. Brian Harrison, *Drink and the Victorians: The Temperance Question in England, 1815-1872* (Pittsburgh, 1971); Norman H. Clark, *Deliver Us from Evil: An Interpretation of American Prohibition* (New York, 1976), chaps. 1-4.

69. Edward C. Mack, *Public Schools and British Opinion, 1780-1860* (New York, 1939), pp. 165-66, 214-15, 226, 257-58.

70. Derek Beales, *From Castlereagh to Gladstone, 1815-1885* (London, 1969), pp. 132-33; Tyler, *Freedom's Ferment,* pp. 265-68; David Rothman, *The Discovery of the Asylum* (New York, 1971), chaps. 3-4. Rothman pursues his thesis so single-mindedly that he slights the complexity of the motives of prison reformers; their humanitarian side is brought out more—perhaps too—emphatically in Tyler's brief account.

71. The standard work on British antislavery is still Frank J. Klingberg, *The Anti-Slavery Movement in England: A Study in English Humanitarianism* (New Haven, 1926). There is no truly equivalent work for America, but a good synthesis of the literature on abolitionism is James Brewer Stewart, *Holy Warriors: The Abolitionists and American Slavery* (New York, 1976). David Brion Davis's magisterial volumes thus far extend only to 1823.

72. See, for example, Eric Foner, *Free Soil, Free Labor, Free Men: The Ideology of the Republican Party before the Civil War* (New York, 1970); Rothman, *Discovery of the Asylum,* chaps. 3-4; Joseph Adshead, *Prisons and Prisoners* (London, 1845), esp. pp. vi-xi; Edwin Hodder, *The Life and Work of the Seventh Earl of Shaftesbury, K.G.* (London, 1886), vol. 1, chaps. 3, 5, 8-11, and vol. 2, chap. 12-15, passim.

73. Hodder, *Shaftesbury,* vol. 1, pp. 95-99, and chaps. 3, 5, 8-11; Manton, *Carpenter,* passim; Gilbert Hobbs Barnes, *The Antislavery Impulse, 1830-1844* (1933; Gloucester, Mass., 1957), pp. 66-67.

74. Manton, *Carpenter,* p. 249.

Chapter III

1. For details of attempts to start animal protection societies, see James Crewdson Turner, "Kindness to Animals: The Animal-Protection Movement in England and America during the Nineteenth Century" (unpub. diss., Harvard University, 1975), pp. 39, 77-78.

2. *Commons Journals,* May 17, 19, June 13-29, 1821; *Lords Journals,* July 2-11, 1821. Little information about Martin survives, but from it Shevawn Lynam has pieced together an engaging, if partisan, biography: *Humanity Dick: A Biography of Richard Martin, M.P., 1754-1834* (London, 1975); see also *Dictionary of National Biography,* s.v. "Richard Martin."

3. *Commons Journals,* May 7-June 5, 1822; *Hansard,* 2d ser., vol. 7, pp. 758-59, 874; *Lords Journals,* June 10-July 22, 1822. The Act can be found in the *Statutes at Large* at 3 Geo. 4, c. 71. When the bill reached Lords, the venerable Lord Erskine was there to express his satisfaction and to present petitions in support of it: *The Times* [London], June 11, 1822.

4. *Hansard,* 2d ser., vol. 10, p. 133, vol. 12, p. 660, and vol. 14, p. 650; RSPCA, *1837 Annual Report;* Wellesley Pain, *Richard Martin* (London, 1925), pp. 77-97. The best brief survey of English animal protection legislation up to 1900 is J.E.G. de Montmorency, "State Protection of Animals at Home and Abroad," *Law Quarterly Review* 18 (1902): 31-48.

5. *John Bull* [London], November 3, 1822; *The Times* [London], June 17, 1824.

6. Accounts of this meeting can be found in *The Times* [London], June 17, 1824, and in RSPCA [First] Minute Book, pp. 1-3. The lives of all of the men mentioned are chronicled in the *Dictionary of National Biography,* except for Broome, about whom virtually nothing is known, and C. Carus Wilson, a brief account of whom can be found in Frederic Boase, *Modern English Biography* (London, 1892-1921), vol. 3, pp. 1404-5.

7. RSPCA [First] Minute Book, pp. 1-2. For a fuller account, see Turner, "Kindness to Animals," pp. 84-85.

8. RSPCA [First] Minute Book, pp. 7, 12, 17, 19, 22, 27, 34-61; Edward G. Fairholme and Wellesley Pain, *A Century of Work for Animals: The History of the R.S.P.C.A., 1824-1934,* 2d ed. (London, 1934), p. 54; RSPCA, *1866 Annual Report,* pp. 33-34; [Lewis

Gompertz], *Objects and Address of the Society for the Prevention of Cruelty to Animals* (London, 1829), pp. 5-6; [idem], *Report of an Extra Meeting of the Society for the Prevention of Cruelty to Animals. January 13th, 1832* (London, n.d. [1832]), p. 8.

9. Mackinnon, born in 1784, took an M.A. at Cambridge (St. John's) in 1807. A Fellow of the Royal Society, of the Society of Antiquaries, and of the Geological Society, he served in Commons ("a hard-working and useful member") for more than thirty years, as a Tory until 1852 and a Liberal thereafter. His 1828 treatise was rewritten in 1846 as a two-volume *History of Civilisation,* "a work of merit." See *Dictionary of National Biography,* s.v. "William A. Mackinnon." Mackinnon was a member of the SPCA from 1828 to 1833 and a vice-president thereafter until his death in 1870. He may have been involved with the SPCA prior to 1828, although I cannot verify that claim in Fairholme and Pain, *Century of Work for Animals,* 1st ed. (London and New York, 1924), p. 291.

10. RSPCA [First] Minute Book, pp. 68-70. Gloucester lent his name to many moral-reform societies of an Evangelical stripe. Ford K. Brown, *Fathers of the Victorians: The Age of Wilberforce* (Cambridge, Eng., 1961), p. 343.

11. RSPCA [First] Minute Book, passim. The City office is mentioned on the title page of [Gompertz], *Report of an Extra Meeting.* One witness (whose memory, however, was dimmed by half a century) claimed that Gompertz had been the foremost SPCA leader from the outset: S. C. Hall, *Retrospect of a Long Life: From 1815 to 1883* (London, 1883), vol. 1, pp. 228-29.

12. *Dictionary of National Biography,* s.v. "Lewis Gompertz" and "Benjamin Gompertz." For Gompertz's inventions, see his *Index to 38 Inventions of Lewis Gompertz, Esq.* (London, n.d. [1837]), a four-page promotional leaflet. His ideas about animals were set forth, sometimes a bit obscurely, in *Moral Inquiries on the Situation of Man and of Brutes* (London, 1824) and *Fragments in Defence of Animals* (London, 1852), a collection of his pieces from *The Animal's Friend.*

13. [Lewis Gompertz], *Remarks on the Proceedings of the Voice of Humanity and the Association for Promoting Rational Humanity to the Animal Creation* (London, n.d. [1831]), passim; RSPCA [First] Minute Book, pp. 85, 100, 113-14; [Gompertz], *Objects,* pp. [4] and 11; *The Voice of Humanity* 1 (1830): 168.

14. "Prospectus," p. 1, in *A Report of the Proceedings at the Annual Meeting of the Association for Promoting Rational Humanity towards the Animal Creation, Held at Exeter Hall, May 23, 1832* (London, 1832).

15. "Report of Annual Meeting," p. 13, in ibid.; [Gompertz], *Report of an Extra Meeting,* pp. 4, 14; *The Standard* [London], January 12, 1832, quoted in RSPCA Records, vol. 5, pp. 15-17; undated newspaper clipping (March 1829), pasted in front of RSPCA [First] Minute Book.

16. "Report of Annual Meeting," p. 13, in *Report . . . of the Association for Promoting Rational Humanity; The Animal's Friend* 1 (1833): 21; [Gompertz], *Report of an Extra Meeting,* p. 16.

17. RSPCA [First] Minute Book, pp. 139-41, 144-46; [Gompertz], *Report of an Extra Meeting,* pp. 9-11.

18. RSPCA Minute Book No. 1, pp. 25, 27, 30-37, 38, 47; "Report of Annual Meeting," pp. 14, 17, 21, in *Report . . . of the Association for Promoting Rational Humanity;* RSPCA [First] Minute Book, pp. 151-54, 158-59; [Gompertz], *Fragments,* p. 176.

19. RSPCA Minute Book No. 1, pp. 38, 40-41. This declaration was explicitly adopted only to lay to rest the charge of "Pythagorean doctrines" (ibid., p. 53), but there is little doubt that its unspoken target was Gompertz's Jewishness. Otherwise, why assert Christian principles generally, rather than simply repudiate vegetarianism? Gompertz later repeatedly insisted that the declaration was designed to ease non-Christians out of the SPCA.

20. RSPCA Minute Book No. 1, pp. 53-54; cf. *The Animals' Friend* 1 (1833): 8. Gompertz finally resigned from the SPCA Committee in June 1833: RSPCA Minute Book No. 1,

p. 90. By the late 1830s, the SPCA had again begun to employ inspectors (RSPCA Minute Book No. 2, p. 263), but they were never again as central to the Society's operations.

21. *The Animals' Friend* 1 (1833): 5, 10; 2 (1834): 5-7; 3 (1835): 3-4; 5 (1837): 1. For the takeover of the SPCA offices by the AFS, compare the title page of ibid., 1 (1833), with RSPCA Minute Book No. 1, p. 4; [Gompertz], *Fragments,* pp. 177-79; RSPCA, *1862 Annual Report,* p. 163. For a year or two around 1833, there were actually four competing animal protection societies: (1) the SPCA; (2) the AFS; (3) the Rational Humanity group; and (4) a rather dubious outfit—probably a confidence racket—founded by a former SPCA inspector of evident energy, if questionable character, named Charles Wheeler. Wheeler pops up in RSPCA Minute Book No. 1, p. 29, and *The Animals' Friend* 1 (1833): 9, and 3 (1835): 8-9, 19. The 1864 merger is recorded in RSPCA Minute Book No. 9, pp. 217-18, 221.

22. RSPCA Minute Book No. 1, pp. 26, 55, 133, 144-45, 240-41; RSPCA, *1832 Annual Report,* pp. 3-4, *1833 Annual Report,* pp. 3-4, and *1834 Annual Report,* pp. 3-4. Note that the philanthropic Gurneys were linked to the Society at several points. Besides Samuel and his son, there was Samuel's brother-in-law T. F. Buxton, already mentioned as a founder of the SPCA. One of Samuel's nieces married Joseph Pease, M.P., who served for years on the (R)SPCA Committee (one of the new faces of 1834). A sister of Samuel married into the Fry family, which produced Samuel Gurney Fry, another Committee member. William Fry, a Quaker SPCA leader, may have become related by this same marriage, although I cannot trace his family connections.

23. RSPCA Minute Book No. 1, pp. 44-45, 56, No. 2, p. 211, and No. 3, pp. 5, 281.

24. RSPCA, *1833 Annual Report,* p. 28, *1838 Annual Report,* pp. 13-14, *1839 Annual Report,* pp. 13-14, *1843 Annual Report,* p. 124, *1844 Annual Report,* p. 20, *1860 Annual Report,* p. 12; RSPCA Minute Book No. 1, p. 5, No. 4, pp. 233-34, No. 7, pp. 356-57, No. 8, pp. 51, 58, 148-49, 210, 311-12, 428. Of course, not every scheme had only the lower orders in view. A hundred-pound prize offered in 1838 for the best essay on cruelty to animals elicited thirty-four fat manuscripts, of which the winner was published as a 350-page book; the judges surely did not delude themselves that it would enjoy a wide circulation among carters and drovers. Likewise, a song based on Landseer's "Old Shepherd's Chief Mourner" was obviously aimed at the artist's middle-class devotees. See RSPCA Minute Book No. 2, pp. 181-83, 289, No. 3, pp. 59, 70-71. The winning essay was John Styles, *The Animal Creation* (London, n.d. [1839]). But these were sidecurrents off the mainstream of the RSPCA program.

25. Francis Wayland, *The Elements of Moral Science,* ed. Joseph L. Blau (1837; Cambridge, Mass., 1963), p. 365 (early date is that of the second and standard edition; the first edition actually appeared in 1835); *New York Revised Statutes 1828,* part IV, chap. 1, title 6, sec. 26; *Massachusetts Revised Statutes 1835,* part 4, title 1, chap. 130, sec. 22; *Report of the Commissioners of the Revision of the Statutes,* Mass. Senate Document no. 7, 1835 (Boston, 1835), p. 3; Emily Leavitt et al., *Animals and Their Legal Rights,* pp. 15-18. New York and Ohio also specifically outlawed animal baiting and fighting, while several cities enacted local anticruelty ordinances: Buffet, vol. 1, "Humane Conditions." The Boston *Daily Evening Transcript,* April 16, 1846, complained about nonenforcement (I owe this reference to Prof. Henry Binford).

26. *The Spirit of Humanity and Essence of Morality* (Albany, N.Y., 1835); a second edition appeared in 1855.

27. MSPCA, *1877 Annual Report,* p. 29; Boston *Daily Evening Transcript,* April 16, 18, 23, 25, and May 4, 1846 (I owe these references, too, to Professor Binford); *Our Dumb Animals* 3 (1870-71): 9, and 5 (1872-73): 209.

28. RSPCA Minute Book No. 9, p. 14; *Our Dumb Animals* 3 (1870-71): 69; M.V.B. Davis, *A Brief History of the Pennsylvania Society for the Prevention of Cruelty to Animals* (Philadelphia, 1902), p. 4; Sydney H. Coleman, *Humane Society Leaders in America*

(Albany, N.Y., 1924), p. 147. There is some evidence of an ephemeral animal protection society in Donega, Pa., sometime before 1865: Buffet, vol. 1, "Humane Conditions."

29. It was typical of Bergh's vanity that in later years he consistently lied about his age, with the result that his birth date is usually given as 1823. There is a full-length "popular" biography by Zulma Steele, *Angel in Top Hat* (New York, 1942), as well as a chapter in Coleman, *Humane Leaders;* a biographical appendix in Roswell C. McCrea, *The Humane Movement: A Descriptive Survey* (New York, 1910); and an article by McCrea in the *Dictionary of American Biography.* But the fullest and most reliable source for Bergh's life, rich in primary materials otherwise lost, is Buffet, especially the first two volumes. However, one must tread with caution; Buffet was under the impression that he had communicated with Bergh's spirit in the hereafter. Fortunately, most of his information can be definitely traced to more mundane sources. See also Turner, "Kindness to Animals," pp. 130-37.

30. *Our Dumb Animals* 20 (1887-88): 126; *New York Press,* March 15, 1888, quoted in Buffet, vol. 2, "Bergh's Funeral"; Clara Morris, "Riddle of the Nineteenth Century: Mr. Henry Bergh," *McClure's Magazine* 18 (1902): 414-22; Bergh to Charles A. Roberts, November 18, 1879, quoted in Buffet, vol. 1, "Beginnings of Henry Bergh."

31. Buffet, vol. 1, "Beginnings of Henry Bergh" and "Life's Summer"; New York *Mirror,* n.d. (1888?), quoted in ibid., vol. 2, "Bergh's Funeral." For Bergh's career in Russia, see ibid., vol. 1, "Life's Summer," and especially the eleventh (and last) volume of Bergh's diaries (ASPCA archives). On his time in London, see Bergh, Diary, vol. 11, November 17, 1864, through June 3, 1865; Bergh to M. Richards Mucklé, May 2, 1866 (PSPCA archives); Bergh to Earl of Harrowby, June 12, 1866, in Letter Book No. 1 (ASPCA archives), pp. 30-31 (hereafter cited as ASPCA Letter Book No. 1, 2, 3, etc.); *Animal World* 3 (1871-72): 129, 209-10.

32. Morris, "Riddle of the Nineteenth Century," 417-18, 422; Buffet, vol. 1, "Beginnings of Henry Bergh."

33. Buffet, vol. 1, "The Work Started." The newspaper articles appeared on September 30, October 28, and December 9, 1865. (They are quoted in ibid.) It is possible that Bergh had already made up his mind by September 1865 and that he induced Frank Leslie (who was by 1866, if not earlier, a friend and co-worker) to run these articles as an opening shot in the campaign for animal protection in New York. The precise dating of Bergh's activities in the latter half of 1865 is impossible to unravel.

34. W.C.H. Waddell to [illegible: W. Beach?], September 17, 1867, in ASPCA Letter Book No. 3, pp. 52-53; Coleman, *Humane Leaders,* pp. 38-40. The question of the authorship of the law is confused but can be sorted out from information in ASPCA Letter Book No. 1, p. 49, and No. 3, p. 305, and in Buffet, vol. 4, "Medical Students" (Tucker letter). On the group's membership policies, see Buffet, vol. 1, "New Laws," and a flyer dated June 14, 1866, inserted in front of ASPCA Letter Book No. 1.

35. On the fashionable aspects of animal protection, see Bergh to M. Richards Mucklé, May 2, 1866 (PSPCA archives). As for press support, the great exception was James Gordon Bennett's New York *Herald,* though even Bennett eventually saw the light: Buffet, vol. 1, passim. Support for the ASPCA outside New York City was not so reliable, and the loyalty of the city press to the Society was dramatically illustrated in 1870 when the papers banded together to oppose a bill to abolish the ASPCA. The bill actually passed the Assembly and failed in the Senate by only two votes. However, John T. Hoffman, an early enthusiast for the ASPCA, was then governor and would probably have vetoed it. Buffet, vol. 1, "Burns Bill."

36. Buffet, vol. 1, "Vivisection Controversy." A $7,500 income compared very favorably with the RSPCA's funding around the same time, especially since the ASPCA was a citywide organization and the RSPCA a national one. For the quotation, see Bergh to George Bancroft, May 21, 1867, in ASPCA Letter Book No. 1, p. 10.

37. Coleman, *Humane Leaders,* pp. 143-46; Davis, *Brief History,* pp. 4-5; W.C.H. Waddell to M. Richards Mucklé, November 21, 1866, in ASPCA Letter Book No. 1, pp. 366-69; Bergh to Mucklé, May 2 and November 21, 1866, and Waddell to Mucklé, January 16, 1867 (all in PSPCA archives). Waln will be remembered as the gentleman who had written to the RSPCA in 1860 to inquire about founding an American society. It is of interest that for some time after the founding of the ASPCA, Bergh suggested to animal protectors in other cities (as he does in the above letters) that their societies be organized as branches of the ASPCA. Perhaps this is nothing more than Bergh's imperial instincts cropping out, but I suspect that it also represents conscious imitation of the RSPCA's organizational structure.

38. There is no direct evidence that White was on her way to Nantucket when she saw Bergh, but this is an almost inescapable conclusion from the pattern of her activities. Her father was no small fish; he wrote Pennsylvania's new constitution and ran for vice-president on the Liberty party ticket in 1840. Her own life can be partially reconstructed from the short account in *Brief History of the Movement for the Protection of Animals in the State of Pennsylvania* (n.p., n.d. [Philadelphia, c. 1905]), pp. 1-3; from her obituaries in the Philadelphia *Inquirer* and the *Record,* September 8, 1916; and from the accounts in Coleman, *Humane Leaders,* pp. 145-46, 178-85, 204-6. Her books included *Love in the Tropics, A Modern Agrippa, Patience Barker, Letters from Spain and Norway, and An Ocean of Mystery.* She achieved her greatest importance in a movement (antivivisection) no longer intellectually respectable, and she herself became increasingly quirky as she grew older. Even so, she was a very influential woman. Her omission from Edward T. James and Janet Wilson James, *Notable American Women,* 3 vols. (Cambridge, Mass, 1971), is more than a little surprising.

39. Davis, *Brief History,* pp. 4-5; *Brief History of the Movement,* pp. 2-5; Coleman, *Humane Leaders,* pp. 144-46.

40. "Report of the President & Secretary . . . September 18, 1867" and "2d Report of the President & Secretary . . . December 30, 1867" (mss. in PSPCA Papers, Historical Society of Pennsylvania); Coleman, *Humane Leaders,* p. 145; *Our Dumb Animals* 1 (1868-69): 76; PSPCA, *1870 Annual Report,* p. 4; Davis, *Brief History,* p. 7.

41. W.C.H. Waddell to Dio Lewis, December 26, 1866, in ASPCA Letter Book No. 1, pp. 461-62. Lewis, a homeopathic physician, was a well-known temperance lecturer, physical culturist, and dress reformer, living at that time in Lexington, outside of Boston. He later was for a brief time president of the Oakland, Calif., SPCA: Mary F. Eastman, *The Biography of Dio Lewis, A.M., M.D.* (New York, 1891), p. 345. Lewis deserves serious biographical attention. His life says a lot about nineteenth-century medicine, among other things.

42. Bergh to Mrs. William Appleton, August 16, October 5 and 29, December 31, 1867, and January 11, 1868, in ASPCA Letter Book No. 3, pp. 10-11, 91-94, 137, 241-42, and 256; Bergh to Wilson Swann, October 29, 1867, in ibid., pp. 140-41; George T. Angell, *Autobiographical Sketches and Personal Recollections* (Boston, n.d. [1908]), pp. 9-10. Angell's book is the most accessible source for the early history of the MSPCA. It went through several printings, and each time new material was tacked on at the end; 1908 is the latest printing that I have been able to locate.

43. Angell, *Autobiographical Sketches,* pp. 7-11; Bergh to Angell, February 26, 1868, and Bergh to Pliny Earle Chase, March 25, 1868, in ASPCA Letter Book No. 3, pp. 318-19, 350. Three years later, after the MSPCA was firmly established, Mrs. Appleton was elected a director.

44. Angell, *Autobiographical Sketches,* pp. 12-13; *Our Dumb Animals* 1 (1868-69): 1, 8; Bergh to S. Morris Waln, April 24, 1868, in ASPCA Letter Book No. 3, p. 399.

45. The earlier attempts were *The Voice of Humanity,* a London quarterly that apparently collapsed in 1833 after three years' publication, and an annual, *The Animals'*

Friend, published by Lewis Gompertz's society from 1833 to 1841. The Paris Société Protectrice des Animaux also seems to have briefly published a *Bulletin mensuel* around the middle of the century.

46. Angell, *Autobiographical Sketches,* pp. 13-14, 39; Bergh to Angell, June 4, 1868, in ASPCA Letter Book No. 3, p. 439; *Our Dumb Animals* 1 (1868-69): 17, 33, and 2 (1869-70): 44, 111. *Our Dumb Animals* is still published by the MSPCA, though its title has been shortened to *Animals.* The early reception and subsequent treatment of the MSPCA in the Boston press can be followed conveniently in the George Angell Scrapbooks (MSPCA archives).

47. Angell, *Autobiographical Sketches,* pp. 1-4. This is virtually the only source for Angell's early life, and all of the information in other accounts seems to be drawn from it. For Angell's career after the founding of the MSPCA, however, readers should consult the article in the *Dictionary of American Biography;* the chapter on Angell in Coleman, *Humane Leaders;* and Guy Richardson, "Apostle of Peace and Justice to Animals—Centenary of George T. Angell," *Zion's Herald* 101 (1923): 731-32. Richardson was secretary (i.e., managing director) of the MSPCA in Angell's last years.

48. *Our Dumb Animals* (which was virtually Angell's personal paper) chronicles the traits described in this paragraph in more than adequate detail. For his unremitting devotion to the gospel of work, see also Angell to a Mr. Sawyer, April 10, 1882, in Angell Scrapbook No. 11.

49. Coleman, *Humane Leaders,* pp. 179-80; *Brief History of the Movement,* p. 6; WSPCA Minute Book No. 1, April 14, 1869.

50. For the sake of consistency, I refer to this organization throughout as the Women's SPCA or WSPCA. Actually, its proper title until 1897 was Women's Branch of the PSPCA (although it was separately incorporated soon after its founding). In 1897 the name was changed to Women's PSPCA; today it is known as the Women's SPCA of Pennsylvania.

51. WSPCA Minute Book No. 1, May 12 and 19, 1869; Mary F. Lovell, *Outline of the History of the Women's Pennsylvania Society for the Prevention of Cruelty to Animals* (Philadelphia, 1908), pp. 4-5; *Our Dumb Animals* 2 (1869-70): 58-59. A "Refuge for lost & homeless dogs" had been a major concern from the outset. In the fall of 1869, the WSPCA sought advice about this from Angell; he encouraged them to establish one as "a model for other cities": WSPCA Minute Book No. 1, June 2 and November 24, 1869.

52. WSPCA Minute Book No. 1, April 28 and June 16, 1869; *Our Dumb Animals* 2 (1869-70): 58-59, 87; Lovell, *History of WSPCA,* pp. 4-5; WSPCA, *1871 Annual Report,* p. 18.

53. The first Canadian SPCA was also organized in 1869, in Montreal. It was quickly followed by Quebec (1870), Ottawa (1871), and Toronto (1873). For Montreal, see Beatrice Johnston, *For Those Who Cannot Speak: A History of the Canadian Society for the Prevention of Cruelty to Animals, 1869-1969* (Laval, Quebec, 1970), pp. 1-2. See the lists of American Societies in *Our Dumb Animals* 3 (1870-71): 90-91, and 6 (1873-74): 102-4. (But the date of founding of the San Francisco Society is given incorrectly, and Brooklyn is altogether omitted.) By 1874, animal protection organizations had been founded in, among other places, the following major cities: Albany, Baltimore, Boston, Buffalo, Chicago, Cincinnati, Cleveland, Columbus (Ohio), Davenport, Denver, Detroit, Hartford, Louisville, New Orleans, New York, Newark, Oakland, Philadelphia, Pittsburgh, Portland (Maine and Oreg.), Portsmouth, Providence, Rochester, St. Louis, St. Paul, San Francisco, Toledo, Washington, and Wilmington (Del.). The founding of several of these can be followed in *Our Dumb Animals,* the ASPCA Letter Books, and Angell's autobiography. It is hard to judge how large these groups usually were, but some were substantial: Davenport had two hundred members (*Our Dumb Animals* 2 [1869-70]: 40).

54. Angell, *Autobiographical Sketches,* pp. 83-85; WSPCA Minute Book No. 1, 1874-75, passim; Lovell, *History of WSPCA,* p. 12; *Our Dumb Animals* 4 (1871-72): 85;

Animal World 12 (1881): 44. The *Animal World*'s observation should be taken with several grains of salt, but it does reflect the spectacular rapidity of the growth of animal protection in the United States.

55. The social status of the SPCA leadership should be obvious from the foregoing pages. Even the sympathetic Roswell McCrea admitted to "an element of truth in the characterization of the annual report of a humane society as 'a few pages of statistics, several half-tone cuts and a copy of the Social Register.'" (*Humane Movement,* p. 25.) The RSPCA, ASPCA, MSPCA, PSPCA, and WSPCA annual reports bear him out. For other societies, see John P. Heap, "History of the Washington Humane Society," *Records of the Columbia Historical Society* 25 (1923): 57-61, and Gerald Carson, "In Chicago: Cruelty and Kindness to Animals," *Chicago History* 3 (1974-75): 156. (I owe this last reference to Prof. Henry Binford.)

The character of the membership is necessarily more difficult to establish with absolute certainty because of the anonymity of most members. However, the SPCA annual reports and minute books and the accounts of SPCA activities in both the SPCA press and other newspapers leave no doubt in my mind that the membership was solidly middle-class. Exactly what this means is not so obvious. As Kitson Clark has said, "the conception [of a Victorian middle class] is too important and significant to be abandoned, and too indefinite and subjective to be used with any comfort." (*The Making of Victorian England* [Cambridge, Mass., 1962], p. 119.) In the Victorian era, "middle-class" was very nearly as much a moral category as a social and economic one, and I believe that contemporaries understood this. It encompassed behavior as well as status, and in fact the one often depended on the other. In socioeconomic terms, I take it to mean, roughly, that a person did not engage in manual labor, usually (though not always, especially in America) had some formal education, and worked in an occupation from which one normally could (not necessarily would) derive sufficient income either (in America) to purchase a home or (in England) to maintain servants at home. I would also restrict the use of the term to town dwellers; the application of the concept in this period to rural society seems to me to make little sense. Morally, middle-class meant, above all, respectability, that great Golden Calf of the Victorians; regular habits of work; sobriety (often abstinence from liquor); faithful attendance at church or chapel; personal and domestic cleanliness; fastidiousness of language, especially with respect to bodily functions; and the centrality of family life. Not a few qualified as middle-class on socioeconomic but not moral grounds; many more qualified morally but not socioeconomically. It was the combination of the two that made one middle-class.

56. There is a very intelligent discussion of the response of intellectuals to some of these anxieties in part I of Raymond Williams, *Culture and Society, 1780-1950* (New York, 1958).

57. Gompertz, *Moral Inquiries,* pp. 35-43. Cf. Walter Houghton's analysis: "A business society dedicated to the political principle of laissez-faire and the economic principle that there must be no interference with the iron laws of supply and demand needed to feel that in spite of appearances its heart was tender." Moreover, "the tears make it *unnecessary* to make any efforts for alleviation": *The Victorian Frame of Mind* (New Haven, 1957), pp. 277-78.

58. RSPCA, *Domestic Animals and Their Treatment* (London, 1857), pp. vii-ix; William H. Drummond, *The Rights of Animals* (London, 1838), pp. 11, 16, 20; RSPCA Minute Book No. 2, p. 29; *Our Dumb Animals* 11 (1878-79): 73; Henry S. Salt, ed., *Cruelties of Civilization: A Program of Humane Reform,* vol. 1 (London, n.d. [1894]), pp. vi-vii.

59. RSPCA, *1833 Annual Report,* p. 29; W[illiam] Youatt, *The Obligation and Extent of Humanity to Brutes* (London, 1839), p. 35; Drummond, *Rights,* pp. 2, 90; T[homas] Forster, *Philozoia* (Brussels, 1839), p. viii; *Our Dumb Animals* 1 (1868-69): 73; B. P. Avery, "Our Speechless Friends," *Overland Monthly* 1 (1868): 240.

60. See the undated newspaper clipping (March 1829) pasted in the front of RSPCA [First] Minute Book. There is a similar hint in James Macauley, *Essay on Cruelty to Animals* (Edinburgh, 1839), pp. 9-10.

61. Again, Williams, *Culture and Society,* part I, is an excellent starting place for understanding these fears. See also Houghton, *Victorian Frame of Mind,* chap. 3, sec. 1. The quoted words are from RSPCA, *1843 Annual Report,* p. 32.

62. *Society for the Prevention . . .* [SPCA prospectus], p. 1; MSPCA, *1877 Annual Report,* p. 17; Ralph Fletcher, *A Few Notes on Cruelty to Animals* (London, 1846), p. 50; *Address of the Committee appointed by the Pennsylvania Society for the Prevention of Cruelty to Animals, held May 6, 1867* (Philadelphia, 1867), p. 4; RSPCA, *1839 Annual Report,* p. 51.

63. *Journal of Zoophily* 1 (1892): 71; Buffet, vol. 2, "Bergh's Anti-Celtic Letters"; George T. Angell, *Bands of Mercy Information* (Boston, 1884), p. 10 (printed as appendix to Angell, *Autobiographical Sketches*); *Hansard,* 2d ser., vol. 12, p. 1013.

64. *Society for the Prevention . . .* [SPCA prospectus], p. 2.

65. Angell, *Autobiographical Sketches,* appendix, p. 5; *The Times* [London], June 17, 1824.

66. RSPCA, *1859 Annual Report,* pp. 18-19; Drummond, *Rights,* p. 187; Angell, *Autobiographical Sketches,* appendix, p. 31; David Mushet, *The Wrongs of the Animal World* (London, 1839), p. 19.

67. George Angell, quoted in McCrea, *Humane Movement,* p. 99. The powerful concern for order in an industrializing society, discussed in the last chapter, is obvious here as well. I suspect, too, that the image of the bestial masses rising in savage revolt owes something to the fear of the animal nature of man, treated also in the preceding chapter. For SPCA efforts in humane education, see Turner, "Kindness to Animals," pp. 166-74.

68. Macauley, *Essay on Cruelty,* p. 41; RSPCA, *1860 Annual Report,* pp. 58-61; *Remarks of Edwin Lee Brown, Esq., of Chicago, President of the American Humane Association . . . upon the subject of the transportation of living animals over our railways* (n.p., n.d. [Chicago, 1880]), p. 5; RSPCA, *1836 Annual Report,* pp. 40-42; *Our Dumb Animals* 11 (1878-79): 65-66; John Styles, *The Animal Creation* (London, n.d. [1839]), pp. 21-22.

69. Mushet, *Wrongs,* p. 79.

70. Gompertz, *Moral Inquiries,* p. 43.

71. The fashionable character of RSPCA annual meetings was already noticeable by the 1830s; by midcentury they positively bristled with titles. Brian Harrison stresses the Society's links with the social elite in "Religion and Recreation in Nineteenth-Century England," *Past and Present,* no. 38 (1967): 108. SPCA meetings in America were fashionable affairs from the beginning: see the accounts in *Our Dumb Animals.*

72. Brian Harrison makes precisely this point in "Animals and the State in nineteenth-century England," *English Historical Review* 88 (1973): 786-820.

73. Turner, "Kindness to Animals," pp. 176-78; RSPCA Minute Book No. 9, p. 187.

74. Turner, "Kindess to Animals," pp. 115-18, 166-74.

Chapter IV

1. Jacob W. Gruber, "Darwinism and Its Critics," *History of Science* 3 (1964): 121; *Animal World* 4 (1873): 47; Kenneth Garlick, "Landseer in the Diploma Galleries," *Burlington Magazine* 103 (1961): 143-44.

2. Gertrude Himmelfarb, *Darwin and the Darwinian Revolution* (New York, 1959), pp. 280, 290-93, 336-42; Alvar Ellegård, *Darwin and the General Reader: The Reception of Darwin's Theory of Evolution in the British Periodical Press, 1859-1872,* Göteborgs Universitets Årsskrift 64, no. 7 (1958): 33. Later in the century skepticism about Darwin's theories grew, especially as a result of Kelvin's calculations of the age of the earth, but my

point here is that educated people were very quickly willing to entertain seriously the ideas of the *Origin.*

3. See M.C.F. Morris, *Francis Orpen Morris, A Memoir* (London, 1897), pp. 213-31, and the following tracts by Francis O. Morris, all published in London: *Difficulties of Darwinism* (1869), *A Double Dilemma in Darwinism* (1870?), *All the Articles of the Darwin Faith* (1877), *A Guard against "The Guardian"* (1877?), *Demands of Darwinism on Credulity* (1890); *Animal World* 1 (1869-70): 123; 4 (1873): 157; and 25 (1894): 83-84.

4. See, for example, B. P. Avery, "Our Speechless Friends," *Overland Monthly* 1 (1868): 236-37; E. P. Evans, "The Nearness of Animals to Man," *Atlantic Monthly* 69 (1892): passim; Henry C. Mercer, "Men of Science and Anti-Vivisection," *Science,* n.s., 9 (1899): 221-24; Lawson Tait, *The Uselessness of Vivisection upon Animals as a Method of Scientific Research* (Birmingham, 1882), p. 123; Edward Maitland, "An Appeal to Hearts and Heads," in *Cruelties of Civilization: A Program of Humane Reform,* ed. Henry S. Salt, vol. 2 (London, n.d. [1896]), p. 26.

5. "Darwinism" and "evolution" signified complex sets of ideas and, in both substance and emotional overtone, meant different things to different people, especially when those people were not scientists. A certain amount of oversimplification is inevitable here. But one can say, with reasonable accuracy, that both terms usually conveyed to animal protectors a conglomerate of ideas with two basic components: (1) Higher animals, including man, had evolved from lower forms as a result of (2) a competitive struggle. The first part typically received more emphasis than the second.

6. *Our Dumb Animals* 11 (1878-79): 9; RSPCA, *1865 Annual Report,* p. 34; *Animal World* 8 (1877): 167. The book mentioned was E. B. Hamley, *Our Poor Relations: A Philozoic Essay* (Boston, 1872). Darwinism was equally susceptible to an opposite interpretation: that nature's law was the exploitation of the weak by the strong. Yet animal lovers generally ignored this, even though on occasion it was pointed out to them. See, e.g., *The Times* [London], January 17, 1896, reproduced in RSPCA Records, vol. 17, pp. 193-94.

7. Frances Power Cobbe, *Life of Frances Power Cobbe by Herself* (London, 1894), vol. 2, pp. 126-27, 176; James Freeman Clarke, "Have Animals Souls?" *Atlantic Monthly* 34 (1874): 421; Frances Power Cobbe, *The Ethics of Zoophily* (London, n.d. [1895]), p. 10.

8. Clarke, "Have Animals Souls?" p. 421; Mattoon M. Curtis, "Sympathy with the Lower Animals," *Bibliotheca Sacra* 54 (1897): 38-49. I owe this reference to Mr. Jon Roberts.

9. This could be taken to absurd lengths. William Hosea Ballou suggested, apparently seriously, in the pages of the *North American Review* (!) that some wealthy philanthropist donate $100,000 as a prize for the first person to open communication with the animal world. The trick was to select the smartest beasts, train them to the limits of their intelligence, then do likewise with their offspring, and so forth. The animals' natural evolution would thus be immensely speeded up. Ballou, "Are the Lower Animals Approaching Man?" *North American Review* 145 (1887): 522-23. Had Darwin lived to read this, he might have regretted all his loose talk about domestic selection in the *Origin.* Frances Power Cobbe, incidentally, thought that such a rapid evolution of animals' mental faculties might occur in heaven: *Ethics of Zoophily,* pp. 6-7.

10. Godfrey Lienhardt, *Social Anthropology,* 2d ed. (London, 1966), chap. 1; J. W. Burrow, *Evolution and Society* (Cambridge, Eng., 1966), pp. 80-81, 115-16, 118-36, 228-59; Fred Eggan, "One Hundred Years of Ethnology and Social Anthropology," in *One Hundred Years of Anthropology,* ed. J. O. Brew (Cambridge, Mass., 1968), pp. 121-27. There is a general survey of developments in anthropology and related disciplines during this period, but without reference to their impact on the larger public, in T. K. Penniman, *A Hundred Years of Anthropology,* rev. ed. (London, 1952), chap. 4.

11. Lienhardt, *Social Anthropology,* p. 3. The same question had been asked much earlier about black Africans (see Chapter I). But it had never had much urgency except in

the United States and had at least temporarily faded there before the animal protection movement got under way. The common humanity of blacks and whites was no longer in serious doubt, though blacks were often depicted as racially inferior or even vicious: William Stanton, *The Leopard's Spots: Scientific Attitudes towards Race in America, 1815-1859* (Chicago, 1960); George M. Fredrickson, *The Black Image in the White Mind: The Debate on Afro-American Character and Destiny, 1817-1914* (New York, 1971), chaps. 3, 8-9.

12. Gavin de Beer, ed., *Darwin's Notebooks on the Transmutation of Species,* part 4 (*Bulletin of the British Museum [Natural History]*, historical series, vol. 2, no. 5) (London, 1960), p. 163.

13. L. Perry Curtis, Jr., *Apes and Angels: The Irishman in Victorian Caricature* (Newton Abbot, Devon, 1971) discusses this cartooning convention. For examples, see p. 24-25, 42, 44, 49 (English artists) and pp. 60, 63-65, 67 (American artists). Note that cartoons of this stamp must be distinguished from the graphic tradition, exemplified by Grandville, in which men were depicted as beasts in order to symbolize certain *human* traits—a sort of visual Aesopian fable. The caricatures of the Irish derived instead from a belief that men actually shared in animal characteristics.

14. Speech by Angell, February 14, 1884, quoted in appendix to American Humane Education Society edition of Anna Sewell, *Black Beauty* (Boston, n.d. [1890]); RSPCA, *1896 Annual Report,* p. 167.

15. Developments in physiology of the nervous system between roughly 1800 and 1850 are outlined in Edwin G. Boring, *A History of Experimental Psychology,* 2d ed. (New York, 1957), chaps. 2, 4-6. For an example of utter confusion as to the meanings of "feeling" and "instinct," see "Have Animals Souls?" *Putnam's Monthly Magazine* 7 (1856): 362-63. "Illustrations of Instinct," *Christian Remembrancer* 14 (1847): 440-41, attacks the "alleged distinction between Reason and Instinct."

16. A typical lesser light was Joseph F. James, "The Reasoning Faculty of Animals," *American Naturalist* 15 (1881): 604-15. For the British Association, see "Animal Intelligence," *Westminster Review* 113 (1880): 454-55. Peirce's views are described in Thomas S. Knight, *Charles Peirce* (New York, 1965), pp. 159-60.

17. A fair sample might include John Burroughs, "Do Animals Think?" *Harper's Monthly Magazine* 110 (1905): 354-58; William J. Long, "The Question of Animal Reason," ibid. 111 (1905): 588-94; and P. Evans, "The Aesthetic Sense and Religious Sentiment in Animals," *Popular Science Monthly* 42 (1893): 472-81.

18. L. S. Hearnshaw, *A Short History of British Psychology* (London, 1964), pp. 96-100; Boring, *History of Experimental Psychology,* pp. 562-63. Cf. Edward L. Thorndike's "Do Animals Reason?" in *Popular Science Monthly* 55 (1899): 480-90, for an attempt to put this over to a wider audience.

19. Henry Jacob Bigelow, "Vivisection," in *Surgical Anaesthesia: Addresses and Other Papers* (Boston, 1900), pp. 374-75.

20. *Animal Heroes* (New York, 1905) is a characteristic work by Seton. Representative books by more scrupulous popularizers are John Burroughs, *Ways of Nature* (Boston, 1905), and J. G. Wood, *Nature's Teachings* (London, 1877). For the "nature-faker" controversy, centered on Seton's methods, see Peter J. Schmitt, *Back to Nature: The Arcadian Myth in Urban America* (New York, 1969), chap. 4.

21. George T. Angell, *Autobiographical Sketches and Personal Recollections* (Boston, n.d. [1908]), p. 28.

22. *Animal World* 4 (1873): 47, and 8 (1877): 167-68. Cf. George L. Cary, "The Mental Faculties of Brutes," *North American Review* 108 (1869): 37.

23. Frances Power Cobbe, "The Consciousness of Dogs," in *False Beasts and True: Essays on Natural (and Unnatural) History* (London, n.d. [1876]), p. 109.

24. Charles Darwin, *On the Origin of Species* (London, 1859), p. 84. I do not mean to suggest, here or elsewhere, that this was the only attitude toward nature held by Victorians.

25. Gavin de Beer indicates Lyell's influence on Darwin in *Charles Darwin* (London, 1963), pp. 10, 159-60; his impact on Tennyson is pointed out in E. B. Mattes, *In Memoriam: The Way of a Soul* (1951), cited in Christopher Ricks, ed., *The Poems of Tennyson* (London, 1969), p. 911 n.

26. Donald Fleming, "Charles Darwin, the Anaesthetic Man," *Victorian Studies* 4 (1961): 219-36; Walter Houghton, *The Victorian Frame of Mind* (New Haven, 1957), chap. 3, sec. 5.

27. Hamley, *Our Poor Relations*, p. 39; J. Howard Moore, *Better-World Philosophy: A Sociological Synthesis* (Chicago, 1906), pp. 124-25.

28. Concern about man's animality was not confined to England and America and sometimes appeared in subtle ways and unexpected places. Karl Marx characterized alienation of workers from their labor thus: "What is animal becomes human and what is human becomes animal." See "Economic and Philosophic Manuscripts of 1844," in *The Marx-Engels Reader*, ed. Robert C. Tucker (New York, 1972), pp. 60-62. Auguste Comte thought that human evolution consisted in "l'ascendant croissant de notre humanité sur notre animalité." *Cours de philosophie positive*, 2d ed. (1864), quoted by George Lichtheim, *Short History of Socialism* (New York, 1970), p. 175.

29. Robert Louis Stevenson, *The Strange Case of Dr. Jekyll and Mr. Hyde* (London, 1886), pp. 24-25, 37, 140; H. G. Wells, *The Island of Dr. Moreau* (London, 1896), especially the last chapter. Certainly Wells and possibly Stevenson were also making hay with the vivisection controversy, more of which is in Chapters V and VI. For the *Times* review, see *The Times* [London], April 8, 1871, quoted in Himmelfarb, *Darwin*, p. 337.

30. C. Bernaldo de Quiros, *Modern Theories of Criminality* (London, 1911), pp. 10-15, 41-42; Gina Lombroso Ferrero, *Criminal Man According to the Classification of Cesare Lombroso* (New York, 1911), pp. 6-8; Courtney Kenny, "The Italian Theory of Crime: Cesare Lombroso," in *The Modern Approach to Criminal Law*, ed. Leon Radzinowicz and J.W.C. Turner (London, 1945), pp. 2-4; Leon Radzinowicz, *Ideology and Crime: A Study of Crime in its Social and Historical Context* (London, 1966), pp. 29-30, 38-39, 46-48.

31. Thomas Hughes, *Tom Brown at Oxford* (1861), quoted in Houghton, *Victorian Frame of Mind*, p. 354, where Houghton also notes the typicality of the metaphor of the beast representing sexual desire. Houghton discusses Victorian attitudes toward sex perceptively and at length in chap. 13, sec. 3.

32. Ronald Pearsall, *The Worm in the Bud: The World of Victorian Sexuality* (London, 1969), pp. xi, 106, 175, 232.

33. U.S. Senate Committee on the District of Columbia, *Report and Hearing on the Bill (S.1552) for the Further Prevention of Cruelty to Animals in the District of Columbia* (Washington, 1896), p. 9. Cf. Ronald Walters, *The Antislavery Appeal: American Abolitionism after 1830* (Baltimore, 1976), pp. 77-78. Richard D. French offers an explicitly Freudian reading of the relationship of English antivivisectionism to sex in *Antivivisection and Medical Science in Victorian Society* (Princeton, 1975), pp. 384-89. A broader Freudian analysis of the role of animals as symbols of man's "lower" nature can be found in Smith Ely Jellife and Louise Brink, "The Role of Animals in the Unconscious, with Some Remarks on Theriomorphic Symbolism as Seen in Ovid," *Psychoanalytic Review* 4 (1917): 253-71, especially pp. 255-56.

34. Letter to Springfield *Republican*, July 23, 1903, quoted in Ralph Barton Perry, *The Thought and Character of William James* (Boston, 1935), vol. 2, p. 317.

35. *Animal World* 5 (1874): 6.

36. Bergh to George Angell, March 1868, in Letter Book No. 3 (ASPCA archives), pp. 334-37.

37. [L. A. Jones?], "The Immortality of the Brute World," *Christian Examiner* 74 (1863): 200; Frances Power Cobbe, "The Rights of Man and the Claims of Brutes," in *Studies New and Old of Ethical and Social Subjects* (London, 1865), p. 254.

38. Contemporaries were not wholly unaware of these fine points of language, and a few recommended dropping terms like "brute." See "Have Animals Souls?" *Putnam's Monthly Magazine* 7 (1856): 361; speech by Phillips Brooks in *Our Dumb Animals* 11 (1878-79): 83; Henry S. Salt, *Animals' Rights Considered in Relation to Social Progress* (London, 1892), pp. 17-19. It is a curious fact that the supposedly inferior dark-skinned races in Africa and Asia generally got stuck with the "beasts."

39. For a good example of this imaginative attempt to humanize animals, see "Our Poor Relations," *Blackwood's Edinburgh Magazine* 107 (1870): 531-53.

40. Basil Taylor, *Animal Painting in England, from Barlow to Landseer* (Harmondsworth, Middlesex, 1955), pp. 49-50; a copy of "The Dairy Farm" owned by the Old Print Shop, Inc., of Boston was exhibited at the DeCordova and Dana Museum, Lincoln, Mass., in May 1972.

41. Francis O. Morris, *Dogs and Their Doings* (London, n.d. [1870]), passim; Animal Rescue League (Boston), *1902 Annual Report,* p. 17.

42. *Animal World* 19 (1888): 35; cf. Caroline Bray, *Little Mop: And Other Stories* (London, 1886), pp. 51-61. This theme was not new. A similar incident on Helvellyn, a peak in the Lakes District, was a favorite subject of earlier Romantic poets. Canine steadfastness was also celebrated in a curious subgenre of melodrama called the dog drama, which flourished on the London stage from about 1803 through the 1850s: Simon Trussler, "A Chronology of Early Melodrama," *Theatre Quarterly* 1, no. 4 (October-December 1971): 19; Michael R. Booth, *English Melodrama* (London, 1965), pp. 86-87. (I owe these references to Mr. Stephen J. C. Shea.) However, the old theme took on new life when animal lovers could view the dogs' behavior as not merely dumb instinctual loyalty but equivalent to human faithfulness, the product of intelligently informed choice.

43. Hamley, *Our Poor Relations,* pp. 5-6; Myron B. Benton, "Shy Friends," *Putnam's Monthly Magazine* 14 (1869): 85-86.

44. Henry Childs Merwin, "Vivisection," *Atlantic Monthly* 89 (1902): 322; *Our Dumb Animals* 9 (1876-77): 33.

45. *Animal World* 14 (1883): 30; *Our Dumb Animals* 3 (1870-71): 17. The consequences of this new reverence for nature will be discussed in the last chapter.

46. "Illustrations of Instinct," *Christian Remembrancer* 14 (1847): 437.

47. Charles and Sarah Tomlinson, *Lessons Derived from the Animal World* (London, n.d. [1862?]), vol. 1, p. [4], and vol. 2, pp. [4], 7; Charles Dickens, *Our Mutual Friend* (London, 1967 [1865]), p. 93.

48. *Our Dumb Animals* 1 (1868-69): 37, and 10 (1877-78): 49; Caroline Bray, *Paul Bradley: A Village Tale, Inculcating Kindness to Animals* (London, 1876), pp. 131-32; *Our Animal Friends* 19 (1892): 158-59; Ralph Waldo Trine, *Every Living Creature, or Heart-Training through the Animal World* (New York, 1899). For some interesting though rather airy speculations about the symbolic role of animals in popular entertainment around this time, see Albert F. McLean, Jr., *American Vaudeville as Ritual* (Lexington, Ky., 1965), pp. 139, 142, 144-45, 151, 164.

49. George M. Fredrickson, *The Black Image,* pp. 111-12; David Brion Davis, "The Movement to Abolish Capital Punishment in America, 1787-1861," *American Historical Review* 63 (1957): 29; *Harvard University Gazette,* September 20, 1974, p. 8; George T. Angell, *Autobiographical Sketches and Personal Recollections* (Boston, n.d. [1908]), p. 29.

50. Trine, *Every Living Creature,* p. 5; Merwin, "Vivisection," 323-24; Frederic Rowland Marvin, *Christ Among the Cattle: A Sermon Preached in the First Congregational Church, Portland, Oregon* (New York, 1899), p. 36; Hamley, *Our Poor Relations,* p. 15; Sewell, *Black Beauty,* p. 62 and appendix, p. iii; Cobbe, *Life,* vol. 2, p. 242. There is a penetrating discussion of the animals in *Hard Times* in F. R. Leavis, *The Great Tradition* (London, 1948), chap. 5.

51. *Our Dumb Animals,* 2 (1869-70): 79, 111; 4 (1871-72): 194; and 13 (1880-81): 55. For a more detailed account of the changing role of pets, especially in the animal protection movement, see James Crewdson Turner, "Kindness to Animals: The Animal-Protection Movement in England and America during the Nineteenth Century" (unpub. diss., Harvard University, 1975), pp. 244-54.

52. Turner, "Kindness to Animals," pp. 112-13, 176-83; J. A. and Olive Banks, *Feminism and Family Planning in Victorian England* (Liverpool, 1964), pp. 59, 61; Cobbe, *Ethics of Zoophily,* pp. 3-4. There is now a large literature on the Victorian ideology of womanhood and the cult of domesticity within it, to which I am referring here. The seminal essay in this area is probably Barbara Welter, "The Cult of True Womanhood, 1820-1860," *American Quarterly* 18 (1966): 151-74. According to George Fredrickson, "romantic racialists" in the nineteenth century claimed a like similarity between the moral and spiritual gifts of women and blacks: *Black Image,* p. 114. Since blacks were sometimes considered in racialist scientific theories as links between human beings and anthropoid apes, it was hardly surprising that they were assimilated to animals morally as well.

53. Frances Power Cobbe, *The Moral Aspects of Vivisection* (London, 1875), p. 4; Trine, *Every Living Creature,* title page.

Chapter V

1. William James, *The Varieties of Religious Experience* (New York, n.d. [1902]), p. 292; Frances Power Cobbe, "The Rights of Man and the Claims of Brutes," in *Studies New and Old of Ethical and Social Subjects* (London, 1865), p. 220; idem, "What is Cruelty?" in *The Modern Rack: Papers on Vivisection* (London, 1889), p. 62; E. B. Hamley, *Our Poor Relations: A Philozoic Essay* (Boston, 1872), p. 30. A number of reasons might justify killing surplus animals, but there is no doubt that the dominant motive of Victorian animal protectors was to spare the animals future pain. For more on the origins of animal shelters, see James Crewdson Turner, "Kindness to Animals: The Animal-Protection Movement in England and America during the Nineteenth Century" (unpub. diss., Harvard University, 1975), pp. 251-54. Cf. the roughly contemporary efforts in the United States to render capital punishment less painful by the introduction of electrocution.

2. Cf. the comments of E. M. Forster in *Goldsworthy Lowes Dickinson* (New York, 1962 [1934]), p. 84. The entire subject of pain, slippery though it is, demands scholarly attention. The only work that I know of focused squarely on the historical dimension of the problem of pain is an article by Daniel de Moulin, "A Historical-Phenomenological Study of Bodily Pain in Western Man," *Bulletin of the History of Medicine* 48 (1974): 540-70, a superficial survey of the tolerance by individuals of their own pain. De Moulin, incidentally, appears to agree with me in dating the revolution in attitudes toward pain from the nineteenth century.

3. Advertisement for Eno's Fruit Salt in *Animal World* 22 (1891): back cover of volume binding.

4. Gertrude Himmelfarb, *Darwin and the Darwinian Revolution* (New York, 1959), p. 35; [William Sturgis Bigelow], *A Memoir of Henry Jacob Bigelow, A.M. LL.D.* (Boston, 1900), p. 79; Henry Jacob Bigelow, "Address at the Dedication of the Ether Monument" (1868), in Bigelow, *Surgical Anaesthesia: Addresses and Other Papers* (Boston, 1900), p. 104.

5. William Lawrence, "Vivisection and a Humane Spirit," *Outlook* 76 (1904): 873. For Bigelow's original report of the first use of ether in surgery, see "Insensibility during Surgical Operations Produced by Inhalation," *Boston Medical and Surgical Journal* 35 (1846): 309-16. The controversies produced by the introduction of anesthetics into medical practice are detailed and analyzed in Martin Pernick, "A Calculus of Suffering: Pain and Professionalism in the Practice of American Medicine and Surgery, 1840-1867" (unpub.

diss., Columbia University, 1978). Pernick points out that most physicians, surgeons, and dentists used anesthesia almost immediately after its discovery, but only on some patients and in some types of operations. There was a difference between "abolitionists" and "restrictionists," between those who wanted to abolish all pain and those who wanted to mitigate the worst pains, and the latter were often the majority. (I am grateful to Professor Pernick for providing a summary of the conclusions of his dissertation, which I have not been able to read as of this writing.) This conflict, I suspect, reflected the new sensibility wrestling with older attitudes toward pain; the eventual victory of the abolitionists represented a further entrenchment of hostility to pain in the Anglo-American mind.

Morphine was isolated by F.W.A. Sertürner, who first described the process in *J. Pharm.* (*Lpz.*) 14 (1806): 47-93. Instrumental in introducing it into general medical use was François Magendie, *Formulaire pour la préparation et l'emploi de plusieurs nouveaux medicamens* (Paris, 1822), which was translated into English in 1824. Aspirin, the most successful of a long succession of antipyritics and analgesics derived from coal tar, was very quickly pressed into service after its introduction in 1899. A general study of the introduction and medical use of painkillers in the last two centuries is very much needed.

Nitrous oxide ("laughing gas") was well known by around 1800 and very commonly used at parties by the friskier sort of medical student as a mild intoxicant. Yet the possibility of applying its anesthetic properties in surgery—explicitly suggested by Humphry Davy—was ignored until the 1840s. It is tempting to speculate (though it is nothing more than speculation) that the growing concern about pain intensified the search for an effective anesthetic and thus brought to attention what had been overlooked before.

6. James Granger, *An Apology for the Brute Creation* (London, 1772), p. 8; RSPCA, *1852 Annual Report,* p. 40; *Our Dumb Animals* 1 (1868-69): p. 6; Cobbe, "Rights of Man," p. 225.

7. RSPCA, *1847 Annual Report,* p. 30, *1852 Annual Report,* p. 30, *1854 Annual Report,* p. 62, *1866 Annual Report,* pp. 44-51; Sir Arthur Salusbury McNalty, *A Biography of Sir Benjamin Ward Richardson* (London, 1950), p. 35; RSPCA Minute Book No. 10, pp. 58-59, 91, 113; *The Times* [London], March 14, 1867, in RSPCA Records, vol. 9, p. 101; *Our Dumb Animals* 2 (1869-70): 89; *Animal World* 3 (1871-72): 55-56, 227-28, and 5 (1874): 30.

8. *Hansard,* 2d ser., vol. 10, pp. 133, 488, and vol. 11, p. 1096; RSPCA, *1843 Annual Report,* pp. 22-23.

9. *Our Dumb Animals* 1 (1868-69): 26, and 2 (1869-70): 57, 61; James Peter Warbasse, *The Conquest of Disease through Animal Experimentation* (New York, 1910), p. 15.

10. Strictly speaking, vivisection means a cutting operation on a living animal. Most early vivisections seem to have been of precisely this character. But as physiology advanced and particularly after the development of bacteriology, cutting operations came to comprise only a small fraction of the total number of experiments on living animals. Nevertheless, the term survived in lay usage as a general expression for experiments on living animals of whatever character. After the middle of the century, scientists began to prefer some such term as "animal experimentation"—partly on grounds of accuracy but more, I suspect, because of the unpleasant associations that "vivisection" had acquired in the public mind. John C. Dalton, *Vivisection: What It Is, and What It Has Accomplished* (New York, 1867), pp. 4-5; Charles Darwin to Professor Holmgren of Uppsala, April 14, 1881, in *The Times* [London], April 18, 1881; Hubert Bretschneider, *Der Streit um die Vivisektion im 19. Jahrhundert* (Stuttgart, 1962), p. 1.

11. *Hansard,* 2d ser., vol. 12, pp. 658-59, 1002, 1004-7, 1011; RSPCA [First] Minute Book, p. 163; Richard D. French, *Antivivisection and Medical Science in Victorian Society* (Princeton, 1975), pp. 18-23. This thorough and intelligent study is the indispensable source for the nineteenth-century English antivivisection movement.

12. Bretschneider, *Streit um die Vivisektion,* p. 3; French, *Antivivisection,* pp. 15-16, 18-19, 21; Richard Owen, *Experimental Physiology: Its Benefits to Mankind* (London,

1882), pp. 10-51; Wallace Shugg, "Humanitarian Attitudes in the Early Animal Experiments of the Royal Society," *Annals of Science* 24 (1968): 227-38.

13. For general eighteenth-century hostility, see French, *Antivivisection*, pp. 16-17, and Dix Harwood, *Love for Animals and How It Developed in Great Britain* (New York, 1928), pp. 297-98. For opposition specifically by early animal protectors, see Thomas Young, *An Essay on Humanity to Animals* (London, 1798), pp. 170-72, and John Lawrence, *A Philosophical and Practical Treatise on Horses, and on the Moral Duties of Man towards the Brute Creation* (London, 1796), vol. 1, pp. 129, 132-33. Young did not oppose all vivisection; Lawrence did.

14. Auguste Comte, *Philosophie première [Cours de philosophie positive, Leçons 1 à 45]*, ed. Michel Serres, François Dagognet, and Allal Sinaceur (1830-42; Paris, 1975), pp. 691-92; Wilhelm Haberling, *Johannes Müller: Das Leben des rheinischen Natursforscher* (Leipzig, 1924), pp. 51, 57, 158-59, 228-29, 231; Gottfried Koller, *Das Leben des Biologen Johannes Müller* (Stuttgart, 1958), pp. 28-29, 39, 47.

15. Anonymous, *The Voice of Humanity* (London, 1827), p. 15; Buffet, vol. 1, scrapbook section at beginning of volume. For Magendie's visit see French, *Antivivisection*, p. 20, and pp. 18-23 for more instances of medical or scientific hostility to vivisection.

16. See, for example, Thomas Forster, *Philozoia* (Brussels, 1839), p. 33; Robert W. Fraser, *Rights of Instinct: A Poem* (London, 1838), pp. 106-9; David Mushet, *The Wrongs of the Animal World* (London, 1839), pp. 189-249; John Styles, *The Animal Creation* (London, n.d. [1839]), p. 89; [Andrew Robert Fausset], *The Faculties of the Lower Animals and Their Claims on Man* (London, 1858), pp. 25-26. I exclude from this generalization works written to protest some specific cruelty, like bull baiting.

17. William H. Drummond, *The Rights of Animals* (London, 1838), pp. 148, 150, 166-67; James Macauley, *Essay on Cruelty to Animals* (Edinburgh, 1839), pp. 68-72; W[illiam] Youatt, *The Obligation and Extent of Humanity to Brutes* (London, 1839), pp. 195-96.

18. *Society for the Prevention of Cruelty to Animals* [prospectus] (London, 1824), p. 2; RSPCA [First] Minute Book, p. 48; *Voice of Humanity*, p. 15; Mushet, *Wrongs*, pp. 209-10; RSPCA Minute Books, No. 1, pp. 45-46, No. 2, p. 108, and No. 5, pp. 128, 143; *Animals' Friend* 7 (1839): 61-64, 69; French, *Antivivisection*, pp. 28-29; RSPCA, *1837 Annual Report*, pp. 20-21, and *1844 Annual Report*, pp. 27-28.

19. Claude Bernard almost alone among the first-rate physiologists of his time avoided mechanistic materialism. On English physiology in this period, see French, *Antivivisection*, pp. 36-39, as well as his article "Some Problems and Sources in the Foundations of Modern Physiology in Great Britain," *History of Science* 10 (1971): 28-55; see also Gerald L. Geison, "Social and Institutional Factors in the Stagnation of English Physiology, 1840-1870," *Bulletin of the History of Medicine* 46 (1972): 30-58. On contemporary Continental physiology, see J.M.D. Olmsted's biographies, *François Magendie* (New York, 1944) and *Claude Bernard* (New York, 1938), and William Coleman, *Biology in the Nineteenth Century: Problems of Form, Function, and Transformation* (New York, 1971), pp. 150-54, as well as the brief summary in Bretschneider, *Streit um die Vivisektion*, pp. 7-9. More generally, on the emergence of physiology as a science in its own right, see Joseph Schiller, "Physiology's Struggle for Independence in the First Half of the Nineteenth Century," *History of Science* 7 (1968): 64-89.

20. French, *Antivivisection*, p. 25; RSPCA Minute Book No. 8, pp. 227, 230-31, 323, 325, 385-86, 389-90, No. 9, pp. 2, 7, 18-21, 26-27, 32-33, 42-44, 52-55, 118-19, 180, and No. 10, pp. 67-68; RSPCA Records, vol. 8, pp. 23, 121-22, 127-33, vol. 9, pp. 114, 118-35; Bretschneider, *Streit um die Vivisektion*, pp. 25-26; RSPCA, *1863 Annual Report*, pp. 127-34; Frances Power Cobbe, *Life of Frances Power Cobbe by Herself* (London, 1894), vol. 2, pp. 246-47. The vivisections practiced at French veterinary schools at this time had nothing to do with physiological research but were designed to improve the manual dexterity of the student surgeons. This was not an uncommon practice in the days before

anesthesia, when speed was at a premium in surgery, animal or human. But this sort of vivisection quickly became obsolete after the discovery of ether anesthesia in 1846. Even in its heyday the practice was widely frowned upon even within the medical profession, at least in the English-speaking world.

21. Cobbe, *Life,* vol. 2, pp. 248-50; RSPCA Minute Book No. 9, pp. 219, 234; Bretschneider, *Streit um die Vivisektion,* pp. 14-16.

22. ASPCA Letter Book No. 1, pp. 153-54, 198-200, 228, 243, 296-315, 330-31, and No. 3, pp. 130, 135; Olmsted, *Bernard,* pp. 48-49; Buffet, vol. 1, "Vivisection," and vol. 4, "Vivisection" and "Legislative Attempt"; John C. Dalton, *Experimentation on Animals as a Means of Knowledge in Physiology, Pathology, and Practical Medicine* (New York, 1875), pp. 50-62; [William James], "Vivisection," *Nation* 20 (1875): 128.

23. *Our Dumb Animals* 1 (1868-69): 50, 58, 66, 90; 2 (1869-70): 110; and 12 (1879-80): 61; WSPCA Minute Book No. 1, November 9 and 11, 1870; Dalton, *Vivisection;* Dalton, *Experimentation,* especially pp. 48-63; J. Dickson Bruns, *Vivisection* (New Orleans, 1867).

24. This is amply documented in the *Report of the Royal Commission on the Practice of Subjecting Live Animals to Experiments for Scientific Purposes; with Minutes of Evidence and Appendix* (London, 1876) (hereafter cited as *Royal Commission 1876*) and U.S. Senate Committee on the District of Columbia, *Report and Hearing on the Bill (S.1552) for the Further Prevention of Cruelty to Animals in the District of Columbia* (Washington, 1896). Cf. Bretschneider, *Streit um die Vivisektion,* p. 117.

25. *Journal of Zoophily* 1 (1892): 28, and 4 (1895): 45; Ouida [Marie Louise de la Ramée], *The New Priesthood* (London, 1882), p. 3; U.S. Senate, *Report and Hearing* (1896), p. v; Arthur de Noé Walker, *The Right Reverend Father in God the Bishop of Peterborough, on Vivisection* (Norwich, 1882), p. 11; Henry Jacob Bigelow, "Medical Education in America," (1871), in *Surgical Anaesthesia,* p. 311.

26. U.S. Senate, *Report and Hearing* (1896), p. xviii; *Royal Commission 1876,* p. 183; Huxley to Charles Darwin, October 30, 1875, in Leonard Huxley, *Life and Letters of Thomas Henry Huxley,* 2d ed. (London, 1903), vol. 2, pp. 171-72; William Smith to Huxley, March 4, 1876, in Thomas Henry Huxley Papers (Imperial College Archives, London), vol. 26, pp. 138-39.

27. Huxley to J.F.D. Donnelly, February 12, 1874, in Huxley Papers, vol. 30, p. 85; Huxley, *Life and Letters,* vol. 2, pp. 159, 163; Lloyd G. Stevenson, "Science Down the Drain: On the Hostility of Certain Sanitarians to Animal Experimentation, Bacteriology, and Immunology," *Bulletin of the History of Medicine* 29 (1955): 3; Darwin to E. Ray Lankester, March 22, 1871, in *Life and Letters of Charles Darwin,* ed. Francis Darwin (London, 1887), vol. 3, p. 200; Nora Barlow, ed., *The Autobiography of Charles Darwin, 1809-1882* (London, 1958), pp. 26-27, 90.

28. Barlow, ed., *Autobiography of Darwin,* p. 90; Donald Fleming, "Charles Darwin, the Anaesthetic Man," *Victorian Studies* 4 (1961): 219-36. John Angus Campbell has challenged Fleming's view of Darwin in "Nature, Religion and Emotional Response: A Reconsideration of Darwin's Affective Decline," *Victorian Studies* 18 (1974): 159-74. Campbell seems to me to have misunderstood Fleming and attacked a straw man, but in any case he does not question that portion of Fleming's argument which bears on my point here.

29. The American botanist Asa Gray, apostle of Darwin to the orthodox, is a good example of the gradual isolation of science from religion in the life of the individual scientist. Indeed, he may have served as the model for Chauncey Wright's theory of "the neutrality of science." See A. Hunter Dupree, *Asa Gray, 1810-1888* (Cambridge, Mass., 1959), especially chaps. 14-15, 18.

30. Frances Power Cobbe, "The Right of Tormenting," in *Modern Rack,* pp. 57-58. Cf. *Our Dumb Animals* 13 (1880-81): 75.

31. For a typical summary, see George Macilwain, *Vivisection, Being Short Comments on Certain Parts of the Evidence Given Before the Royal Commission* (London, 1877), pp. 3-4.

32. Cobbe, *Life,* vol. 2, pp. 290-91; [Sir John Duke Coleridge], *The Lord Chief Justice of England on Vivisection* (London, n.d. [1882?]), pp. 10-11; Henry Jacob Bigelow, "Vivisection," in Bigelow, *Surgical Anaesthesia,* p. 368.

33. U.S. Senate, *Report and Hearing* (1896), p. 8; *Our Dumb Animals* 9 (1876-77): 25, and 13 (1880-81): 75; Hamley, *Poor Relations,* p. 34; Ouida, *New Priesthood,* pp. 13-14.

34. Mark Thornhill, *The Morality of Vivisection* (London, 1885), pp. 11, 18; Henry Childs Merwin, "Vivisection," *Atlantic Monthly* 39 (1902): 323; *Our Dumb Animals* 13 (1880-81): 13.

35. See, for example, *Our Dumb Animals* 13 (1880-81): 75; U.S. Senate, *Report and Hearing* (1896), p. v. As the bulk of animal experimentation shifted from physiology to bacteriology, dogs and cats were replaced by guinea pigs as the typical experimental animals in the popular imagination. One wonders whether this had something to do with the decline of antivivisection toward 1900.

36. French, *Antivivisection,* pp. 41-48; Lady [Ghetal] Burdon Sanderson, *Sir John Burdon Sanderson, A Memoir,* ed. J. S. and E. S. Haldane (Oxford, 1911), pp. 31-35, 91; Mark N. Ozer, "The British Vivisection Controversy," *Bulletin of the History of Medicine* 40 (1966): 162; *Royal Commission 1876,* pp. vii-viii. The best single source for the institutional development of British physiology in this period is French, "Problems and Sources in Physiology." In the early eighties, Foster's praelectorship was elevated into a professorship, while Burdon Sanderson was elected the first Waynflete Professor of Physiology at Oxford.

37. French, *Antivivisection,* pp. 47-51; *Royal Commission 1876,* passim; *The Times* [London], December 24, 29, 31, 1873, and January 6, 1874, in *RSPCA Records,* vol. 13, pp. 137-45, 148-49, and vol. 14, pp. 80-82. For intensified RSPCA concern about vivisection in England at this time, see Minute Book No. 12, passim.

38. French, *Antivivisection,* pp. 55-57, Bretschneider, *Streit um die Vivisektion,* p. 17 n; RSPCA Minute Book No. 13, p. 68; account of trial abridged from *Norfolk Chronicle,* December 12, 1874, in RSPCA Records, vol. 14, pp. 83-89.

39. A. J. Munby, Diary, June 7, 1866, in Derek Hudson, *Munby, Man of Two Worlds: The Life and Diaries of Arthur J. Munby, 1828-1910* (London, 1972), p. 226. The basic source for Miss Cobbe's biography and for most of what follows here is her own *Life.* The second edition (London, 1904) contains an introduction by Blanche Atkinson and brief notes by Miss Cobbe bringing the last two chapters up to 1898; this additional material is chiefly useful for her relationship with Mary C. Lloyd and the schism within the Victoria Street Society in 1898. The chapter on Miss Cobbe in Jennie Chappell, *Women of Worth* (London, n.d. [1908]), pp. 93-194, is little more than a condensation of the autobiography. Briefer but slightly more valuable is the long obituary notice by F. B. Sanborn, "Frances Power Cobbe: A Life Devoted to the Promotion of Social Science," *Journal of Social Science, containing the Proceedings of the American* [Social Science] *Association,* no. 42 (September 1904), pp. 63-68. Jo Manton has sketched an excellent brief portrait of Miss Cobbe, though one which makes her lesbian inclinations rather more overt than I would, in *Mary Carpenter and the Children of the Streets* (London, 1976), pp. 147-52.

40. Cobbe, *Life,* vol. 2, pp. 254-62; [John Colam], *Vivisection: The Royal Society for the Prevention of Cruelty to Animals and the Royal Commission* (London, 1876), pp. li-liii; RSPCA Minute Book No. 13, pp. 100-102. In her autobiography, Miss Cobbe remembered this subcommittee as a collection of nonentities calculated to serve as a ceremonial wastebasket for her petition. Her memory failed her. The subcommittee included two very influential politicians, both of whom played leading roles in the vivisection controversy:

William Cowper-Temple, soon to be a leader of Miss Cobbe's Victoria Street Society, and Edward Viscount Cardwell, chairman of the 1876 Royal Commission.

41. French, *Antivivisection,* pp. 66-80, 91-111.

42. Cobbe, *Life,* vol. 2, pp. 270-75; French, *Antivivisection,* pp. 85-89; Thomas Huxley to Michael Foster, May 25, 1876, in Huxley Papers, vol. 4, p. 120. Other antivivisection societies were formed about this time—the London and International societies the largest —but Victoria Street remained far and away the most influential. French, *Antivivisection,* pp. 89-90.

43. This story is detailed in French, *Antivivisection,* chap. 5; the provisions of the Act are outlined on pp. 143-44.

44. Cobbe, *Life,* vol. 2, pp. 279-94, French, *Antivivisection,* pp. 177-92.

45. Donald Fleming, *William Henry Welch and the Rise of Modern Medicine* (Boston, 1954), p. 7; H. C. Wood, "The Value of Vivisection," *Scribner's Magazine* 20 (1880): 770; James H. Cassedy, *Charles V. Chapin and the Public Health Movement* (Cambridge, Mass., 1962), p. 39. Cf. the medical testimony in U.S. Senate, *Report and Hearing* (1896). Some information about institutional aspects of the growth of American physiology in the nineteenth century is available in Richard H. Shryock, *American Medical Research Past and Present* (New York, 1947), chap. 2.

46. WSPCA Minute Book No. 1, November 22, 1871, and September 29, 1875; Mary F. Lovell, *Outline of the History of the Women's Pennsylvania Society for the Prevention of Cruelty to Animals* (Philadelphia, 1908), p. 13; *Our Dumb Animals* 10 (1877-78): 68; PSPCA Minute Book No. 1, June 17 and September 17, 1878; George T. Angell, *Autobiographical Sketches and Personal Recollections* (Boston, n.d. [1908]), p. 76; RSPCA Minute Book No. 14, p. 300; *Animal World* 13 (1882): 7.

47. *Proceedings of the International Anti-Vivisection and Animal Protection Congress held at Washington, D.C., December 8th to 11th, 1913* (New York, n.d. [1914?], pp. 27-28; *Journal of Zoophily* 1 (1892): 9, and 25 (1916): 131; WSPCA Minute Book No. 2, January 31 and February 14, 1883; *Our Dumb Animals* 15 (1882-83): 177, 184, 194, and 17 (1884-85): 108; American Antivivisection Society, *1897 Annual Report,* p. 2; Sydney H. Coleman, *Humane Society Leaders in America* (Albany, N.Y., 1924), pp. 204-6; Albert Leffingwell, *An Ethical Problem, or Sidelights upon Scientific Experimentation on Man and Animals* (London and New York, 1914), p. 217.

48. MSPCA, *1882 Annual Report,* p. 10; *Our Dumb Animals* 13 (1880-81): 18-19, 26-27, 34-35; 14 (1881-82): 45, 66, 74; 18 (1885-86): 276, 296; and 22 (1889-90): 42; clipping from Boston *Evening Transcript,* November 20, 1886, in Walter B. Cannon Papers (Countway Library, Harvard Medical School). E. H. Clement, editor of the *Transcript,* eventually headed the New England Antivivisection Society.

49. *Journal of Zoophily* 1 (1892): 67-68, 99-100, 131, and 4 (1895): 51.

50. Speech by Caroline White to Worcester, Mass., League of Unitarian Women, January 18, 1893, quoted in Worcester *Daily Telegram,* January 19, 1893; U.S. Senate, *Report and Hearing* (1896), passim.

51. Cobbe, *Life,* vol. 2, pp. 294-95; French, *Antivivisection,* pp. 164-65.

52. Details of the Massachusetts bills and of scientific reaction to them are most readily available in the papers of Harold C. Ernst, in the Cannon Papers.

53. The Washington state bill, killed by veto in 1895, was finally enacted in 1897, but it seems to have been repealed the next year: *Journal of Zoophily* 4 (1895): 27, 37; 6 (1897): 39-40; and 8 (1899): 4. For the D.C. bill, see U.S. Senate, *Report and Hearing* (1896); its more prominent supporters are listed on pp. vi-vii and 140-51.

54. Sanderson, *Sir John Burdon Sanderson,* pp. 102, 115-20; French, *Antivivisection,* pp. 278-84.

55. *Animal World* 6 (1875): 84, 180.

Chapter VI

1. Frances Power Cobbe, "The Rights of Man and the Claims of Brutes," in *Studies New and Old of Ethical and Social Subjects* (London, 1865), p. 245; [Anthony Ashley Cooper, 7th Earl of Shaftesbury], *The Total Prohibition of Vivisection: Substance of a Speech of the Earl of Shaftesbury, K.G., in Support of Lord Truro's Bill* (London, n.d. [1879?], p. 7. Victorian faith in progress is discussed in Walter Houghton, *The Victorian Frame of Mind* (New Haven, 1957), chap. 2, secs. 1-2, and in Richard D. Altick, *Victorian People and Ideas* (New York, 1973), chap. 3, sec. 4.

2. Frances Power Cobbe, *The Moral Aspects of Vivisection* (London, 1875), p. 6; *Journal of Zoophily* 4 (1895): 1; U.S. Senate Committee on the District of Columbia, *Report and Hearing on the Bill (S.1552) for the Further Prevention of Cruelty to Animals in the District of Columbia* (Washington, 1896), p. 11; *Report of the American Humane Association on Vivisection and Dissection in Schools* (Chicago, 1895), p. 25.

3. Ouida [Marie Louise de la Ramée], *The New Priesthood* (London, 1882), p. 28. The best discussion of medical practice in the nineteenth century is William G. Rothstein, *American Physicians in the Nineteenth Century: From Sects to Science* (Baltimore, 1972). Most of what he says about the limitations of American medical therapies applies to Britain. On the image of physician as consoler, cf. U.S. Senate, *Report and Hearing* (1896), p. 122.

4. Ibid., p. 151; Ouida, *New Priesthood,* p. 28. This sense of betrayal by doctors may have been exacerbated by the scientists' constant reminders of the use of anesthesia in vivisection. Antivivisectionists viewed this as the rankest perversion of the great blessing that had conquered pain in surgery.

5. The most concentrated sample of this pervasive theme is [Frances Power Cobbe?], *Scientific Medicine* (London, n.d. [1881]).

6. U.S. Senate, *Report and Hearing* (1896), pp. 55-56; Richard D. French, *Antivivisection and Medical Science in Victorian Society* (Princeton, 1975), pp. 328-31. Cf. Hubert Bretschneider, *Der Streit um die Vivisektion im 19. Jahrhundert* (Stuttgart, 1962), p. 11.

7. George Macilwain, *Vivisection, Being Short Comments on Certain Parts of the Evidence Given Before the Royal Commission* (London, 1877), p. 7; *Journal of Zoophily* 2 (1893): 74-75, and 4 (1895): 44. An excellent example of the mild hostility toward science pervading large reaches of the medical profession was provided by Sir William Fergusson, sergeant-surgeon to the Queen and a man of great eminence in his day. See his testimony in the *Report of the Royal Commission on the Practice of Subjecting Live Animals to Experiments for Scientific Purposes; with Minutes of Evidence and Appendix* (London, 1876), pp. 48-55 (hereafter cited as *Royal Commission 1876*).

8. This bore considerable resemblance to developments in the same period in natural-history-becoming-biology. Lloyd Stevenson attributes part of the suspicion of vivisection among English physicians to the continuing influence of Sir Charles Bell, the great early-nineteenth-century English physiologist who put his faith in comparative anatomy in opposition to Magendie's vivisection: "Anatomical Reasoning in Physiological Thought," in *The Historical Development of Physiological Thought,* ed. Chandler McC. Brooks and Paul F. Cranefield (New York, 1959), p. 33. Stevenson's argument has merit, but he seems to me to put too much weight on it.

9. Oliver Wendell Holmes, Sr., *Medical Essays, 1842-1882,* quoted in Rothstein, *American Physicians,* p. 178. Richard Shryock opined that cynicism about medical practice had grown "beyond ordinary bounds during the early Victorian decades": *The Development of Modern Medicine* (Philadelphia, 1936), p. 241.

10. See, for example, John C. Dalton, *Vivisection: What It Is, and What It Has Accomplished* (New York, 1867) and *Experimentation on Animals as a Means of Knowledge in Physiology, Pathology, and Practical Medicine* (New York, 1875).

11. J[ohn]. Collins Warren, *To Work in the Vineyard of Surgery: The Reminiscences of J. Collins Warren (1842-1927)*, ed. Edward D. Churchill (Cambridge, Mass., 1958), pp. 135-39; I. Harvey Flack, *Lawson Tait, 1845-1899* (London, 1949), pp. 80-91; Lloyd Stevenson, "Science Down the Drain: On the Hostility of Certain Sanitarians to Animal Experimentation, Bacteriology, and Immunology," *Bulletin of the History of Medicine* 29 (1955): 16-17; Rothstein, *American Physicians,* pp. 267-72.

12. *Royal Commission 1876,* p. 326; Stevenson, "Science Down the Drain," pp. 2-3; broadside headed "Vivisection," in Thomas Henry Huxley Papers (Imperial College Archives, London), vol. 49, p. 143 (the work, I suspect, of George Jesse, who *was* irrational and obscurantist).

13. Herbert J. Reid, *Science on "Ticket of Leave"* (London, 1889), p. 18; Edward Berdoe, *Listerism—One of the Triumphs of Vivisection* (London, n.d. [1890?]); idem, *Report of the Asylums Board on Anti-Toxin* (London, n.d. [1896?]); U.S. Senate, *Report and Hearing* (1896), pp. iii-iv; *Journal of Zoophily* 4 (1895): 2; Ernest Bell, *A Clincher for Anti-Toxin* (London, n.d. [1895]).

14. *Monsieur Pasteur's Treatment for the Prevention of Hydrophobia* (Exeter, 1886); *M. Pasteur: An Examination of His Work* (n.p., n.d.); U.S. Senate, *Report and Hearing* (1896), p. iv; *Our Dumb Animals* 30 (1897): supplement following p. 16; *Animal World* 19 (1888): 3.

15. Stevenson, "Science Down the Drain"; Mark Thornhill, *The Morality of Vivisection* (London, 1885), pp. 13-14; Arthur de Noé Walker, *The Right Reverend Father in God the Bishop of Peterborough, on Vivisection* (Norwich, 1882), p. 14; U.S. Senate, *Report and Hearing* (1896), p. 41; Barbara Gutman Rosenkrantz, *Public Health and the State: Changing Views in Massachusetts, 1842-1936* (Cambridge, Mass., 1972), chap. 4.

16. U.S. Senate, *Report and Hearing* (1896), p. iii; George M. Gould, "Vivisection," in *Borderland Studies* (Philadelphia, 1896), p. 22. A good example is Ouida, *New Priesthood.* Cf. French, *Antivivisection,* pp. 349-50. Not all antivivisectionists were hostile to science. A small but vocal group of radical animal lovers included vivisection in their sweeping denunciation of all human exploitation of beasts, yet many of them embraced a rather abstract "Science" as the transforming wave of the future. However, they were interested in science primarily as a solvent of the social and intellectual *status quo;* they had little concern for and less interest in specific scientific disciplines or actual working scientists. Typical of these radicals were Henry Salt and J. Howard Moore, mentioned in Chapter VII.

17. See, for example, Albert Leffingwell, "An Ethical Basis for Humanity to Animals," *Arena* 10 (1894): 477-78. Some antivivisectionists utterly rejected Darwin and all his pomps, but they were clearly a small minority. The most outspoken of them was the Rev. F. O. Morris, the bird protector discussed in Chapter VII.

18. Wesley Mills, "The Cultivation of Humane Ideas and Feelings," *Popular Science Monthly* 43 (1893): 46-51 (address to American Humane Association, October 27, 1892). Mills combined the unlikely posts of professor of physiology at McGill University and honorary member of the Canadian SPCA. Another case of the recognized indebtedness of animal protection to science was the teaching of natural history as the core of humane education.

19. Houghton, *Victorian Frame of Mind,* p. 34; Stevenson, "Science Down the Drain," pp. 24-25.

20. Frances Power Cobbe, "The Scientific Spirit of the Age," in *The Scientific Spirit of the Age and Other Pleas and Discussions* (London, 1888), p. 7; Albert Leffingwell, "Vivisection in America," in *The Vivisection Question* (New Haven, 1901), pp. 52-57.

21. Frances Power Cobbe, *The Moral Aspects of Vivisection* (London, 1875), p. 4; *Thoughts on Vivisection* (broadside dated March 22, 1875), in Huxley Papers, vol. 49, p. 152. Richard French makes the argument about envy in *Antivivisection,* p. 371. Cf. Noel Annan, "Science, Religion, and the Critical Mind," in *1859: Entering an Age of Crisis,* ed. Philip Appleman et al. (Bloomington, 1959), p. 32.

22. Charles Adams, *The Coward Science: Our Answer to Professor Owen* (London, 1882), p. iii; speech by Caroline White, quoted in Worcester *Daily Telegram,* January 19, 1893. Perhaps this explains why all twenty-five honorary members of the AAVS about this time were clergymen: *Journal of Zoophily* 1 (1892): 14.

23. Cobbe, "Scientific Spirit," p. 26; Leffingwell, "A Dangerous Ideal," in *Vivisection Question,* p. 92.

24. Cobbe, "Scientific Spirit," pp. 6, 16.

25. For extended and intelligent consideration of these issues, see Houghton, *Victorian Frame of Mind,* especially chaps. 3, 4, and 11. There is a good brief treatment of the Victorian crisis of faith in Altick, *Victorian People and Ideas,* chap. 6, secs. 3-4, and a discussion of the effects of Darwinism on the bases of ethical belief in Richard Hofstadter, *Social Darwinism in American Thought,* rev. ed. (Boston, 1955), chap. 5. I am not arguing here that there is a necessary conflict between the scientific outlook and the claims of the "heart," but that Victorians generally thought so.

26. *Our Dumb Animals* 2 (1869-70): 38; *Animal World* 11 (1880): 34.

27. *Our Dumb Animals* 20 (1887-88): 118. Von Max's painting is reproduced in Bretschneider, *Streit um die Vivisektion,* between pp. 32 and 33.

28. Rosenkrantz, *Public Health,* p. 5; Stevenson, "Science Down the Drain." Cf. Charles E. and Carroll S. Rosenberg, "Pietism and the Origins of the American Public Health Movement," *Journal of the History of Medicine and Allied Sciences* 23 (1968): 16-35.

29. U.S. Senate Committee on the District of Columbia, *Hearing on the Bill (S.34) for the Further Prevention of Cruelty to Animals in the District of Columbia* (Washington, 1900), p. 24; Rosa G. Abbott, "The Higher Civilization Versus Vivisection," *Arena* 19 (1898): 128. This is an extension of Stevenson's argument in "Science Down the Drain"; see especially pp. 2-3, 14.

30. Henry Childs Merwin, "Vivisection," *Atlantic Monthly* 89 (1902): 324; Cobbe, "Scientific Spirit," p. 24; idem, "Hygeiolotry," in *The Peak in Darien* (London, 1882), pp. 77-86; John Henry Newman, "Christianity and Medical Science," in *The Idea of a University* (1873; New York, 1959), p. 456; Frances Power Cobbe, "The British Medical Manifesto," in *The Modern Rack: Papers on Vivisection* (London, 1889), p. 170; Cobbe, *Life of Frances Power Cobbe by Herself* (London, 1894), vol. 2, pp. 291-92.

31. Edward Maitland, "An Appeal to Hearts and Heads," in *Cruelties of Civilization: A Program of Humane Reform,* ed. Henry S. Salt, vol. 2 (London, n.d. [1896]), pp. 21-22. The aggressive mechanistic materialism of many physiologists in Germany, then the center of medical research, probably helped to make this charge stick.

32. [William James], "Vivisection," *Nation* 20 (1875): 128-29; U.S. Senate, *Report and Hearing* (1896), pp. 12, 50; Charles S. Meyer and Albert Leffingwell, *The Vivisection Problem* (n.p. [New York?], 1907), pp. 25-29; *Royal Commission 1876,* p. 92. Adams, *Coward Science,* and Ouida, *New Priesthood,* exemplify the medical ignorance of antivivisectionists.

33. For instances of wild charges by antivivisectionists, see Leonard Huxley, *Life and Letters of Thomas Henry Huxley,* 2d ed. (London, 1903), vol. 2, pp. 153-57, and Francis Darwin to *Nature* 13 (1876): 384-85. Typical antivivisectionist notions about the structure of science can be found in Adams, *Coward Science,* pp. 58-59, and *Royal Commission 1876,* pp. 89-90.

34. *Journal of Zoophily* 1 (1892): 59; Ouida, *New Priesthood,* p. 23; Auberon Herbert to *The Times* [London], January 17, 1876, in RSPCA Records, vol. 17, p. 187, Edward A.

Freeman, "Field Sports and Vivisection," *Fortnightly Review* 21 (1874): 623; Albert Leffingwell, *Some Mistakes of Scientists* (n.p. [Providence, R.I.?], 1900), p. 1. The conventions of gothic horror novels were doubtless familiar to many antivivisectionists. One wonders whether the images of monks and priests therein subliminally colored this conception of the scientific priesthood—especially since the latter was frequently compared to the Inquisition. The similarities were certainly remarkable, though attributable also to the traditional rhetoric of anti-Popery.

35. Adams, *Coward Science,* p. 21.

36. French, *Antivivisection,* chap. 7. This cozy arrangement continued until 1913, when, on the recommendation of a second Royal Commission, the role of the AAMR Council was assumed by an official advisory body chosen by the Home Secretary from names submitted by the Royal Society and the Royal College of Physicians and Surgeons.

37. John C. Dalton to Henry P. Bowditch, February 13, 1881, and June 29, 18[81?], in the Walter B. Cannon papers (Countway Library, Harvard Medical School); Michael Foster to H. P. Bowditch, November 3, 1890, and November 8, 1900, in Cannon Papers. Examples of English scientists reprinted in *Popular Science Monthly* on the subject include Michael Foster, "Vivisection," 4 (1874): 672-85; Samuel Wilks (a physician), "The Ethics of Vivisection," 21 (1882): 344-50; Gerald F. Yeo, "Vivisection and Practical Medicine," 22 (1883): 615-21. *Nature*'s account of the vivisection debate at Oxford was reprinted in *Science* 5 (1885): 315-16, and in *The American* 9 (1885): 474-76.

38. The organizing in defense of research can be most conveniently followed in Cannon Papers; for Massachusetts, see especially the correspondence of H. C. Ernst therein. Keen's role appears in his correspondence in the American Philosophical Society (photocopy in Countway Library, Harvard Medical School). For Washington, see U.S. Senate, *Report and Hearing* (1896), passim. The formal organization of the Pennsylvania Society was apparently prompted by Stephen Paget, head of the British Research Defence Society: Paget to Cannon, January 14, 1914, in Cannon Papers.

39. Research Defence Society, *Report of Inaugural Meeting, June 19th, 1908* (London, n.d. [1908]); Charles Richet, *The Pros and Cons of Vivisection* (London, 1908), appendix C: The Research Defence Society, pp. 130-36. For a collection of typical RDS pamphlets, see *The Truth about Vivisection* (London, 1910).

40. Walter B. Cannon, *The Way of an Investigator: A Scientist's Experiences in Medical Research* (New York, 1945), pp. 154-59; *Walter Bradford Cannon: Exercises celebrating twenty-five years as George Higginson Professor of Physiology* (Cambridge, Mass., 1932), p. 70. For examples of Cannon's tactics, see following in Cannon Papers: Claude L. Wheeler to Cannon, May 18, 1914 (and similar letters); Cannon-Norman Hapgood correspondence, January-May 1915; Cannon to Prof. August Krogh, October 4, 1921; Cannon to John F. Anderson, February 26, 1914; and Anderson to Cannon, February 28, 1914.

41. Charles Darwin to Lyon Playfair, May 26, 1875, in *More Letters of Charles Darwin,* ed. Francis Darwin and A. C. Seward (London, 1903), vol. 2, p. 436.

42. Robert McDonnell, *What Has Experimental Physiology Done for the Advancement of the Practice of Surgery?* (London, 1882), p. 3; Samuel Wilks, *The Value and Necessity of Experiments for the Acquirement of Knowledge* (London, 1882), p. 6; Joint Committee of the American Physiological Society, etc., *"Vivisection"—A Statement in Behalf of Science* (1896), reprinted in U.S. Senate, *Report and Hearing* (1896), p. 57; U.S. Senate, *Report and Hearing* (1896), p. 48; H. C. Wood, "The Value of Vivisection," *Scribner's* 20 (1880): 766.

43. E. Ray Lankester to *The Times* [London], January 1874, in RSPCA Records, vol. 14, pp. 78-79; John Cleland, *Experiment on Brute Animals* (London, 1883), p. 4; A. L. Loomis, "The Influence of Animal Experimentation on Medical Science," reprinted in U.S. Senate, *Report and Hearing* (1896), p. 69.

44. Lyon Playfair, *Speech Delivered in the House of Commons . . . April 4, 1883* (London, 1883), p. 13; John Simon, *Experiments on Life, as Fundamental to the Science of Preventive Medicine and as of Question Between Man and Brute* (London, 1882), p. 23; G[eorge]. Gore, *The Scientific Basis of National Progress, Including That of Morality* (London, 1882), especially pp. [vi]-[viii]; James Peter Warbasse, *The Conquest of Disease through Animal Experimentation* (New York, 1910), dedication and pp. 7-8.

45. U.S. Senate, *Report and Hearing* (1896), p. 48; William W. Keen, *Our Recent Debts to Vivisection* (Philadelphia, 1885), p. 12; Warbasse, *Conquest of Disease,* p. 14; Cleland, *Experiment on Animals,* pp. 10-12; [G. Stanley Hall?], "The Vivisection Question in Germany," *Nation* 28 (1879): 417. Warbasse's figure was no doubt simply pulled out of the air. Yeo's had a statistical basis in the reports filed under the Act of 1876. However, even Yeo's claim was disingenuous, to say the least. He automatically classified all inoculation experiments as virtually painless, ignoring the after-effects of the injection, which could include contracting a painful disease or the like.

46. J. H. Hildreth to H. C. Ernst, March 2, 1905, in Cannon Papers; French, *Antivivisection,* pp. 130-33, 157; Loomis, "Influence of Animal Experimentation," p. 69; *Journal of Zoophily* 4 (1895): 57.

47. Lionel J. Wallace, "Vivisection," *Westminster Review* 137 (1892): 256.

48. Cleland, *Experiment on Animals,* pp. 5-6, 14; U.S. Senate, *Report and Hearing* (1896), pp. 48, 102; *Royal Commission 1876,* p. 215.

49. [James], "Vivisection," 128-29; Rothstein, *American Physicians,* pp. 256-58, 281.

50. "A Vivisection Instance," *The American* 9 (1885): 268 (reprinted from *The Times* [London]); William W. Keen, "Recent Progress in Surgery" (1889) and "Vivisection and Brain Surgery" (1893), in *Addresses and Other Papers* (Philadelphia, 1905), pp. 101-8, 166-93.

51. Humphry Davy Rolleston, *The Endocrine Organs in Health and Disease, with an Historical Review* (London, 1936), pp. 29-30; Chandler McC. Brooks and Harold A Levey, "Humorally-Transported Integrators of Body Function and the Development of Endocrinology," in *Historical Development of Physiological Thought,* pp. 208-9; Stephen Paget, *Experiments on Animals* (New York, 1900), pp. 191-95.

52. U.S. Senate, *Report and Hearing* (1896), passim.

53. Ibid., pp. 55-61, 87-88, 92; correspondence of H. P. Bowditch, December 1895, in Cannon Papers. Welch's role is discussed in Donald Fleming, *William Henry Welch and the Rise of Modern Medicine* (Boston, 1954), pp. 145-51.

54. U.S. Senate, *Report and Hearing* (1896), pp. i-xxii, 88-89, 127-40.

55. Papers of H. C. Ernst and Welch to H. P. Bowditch, February 14, 189[8?], in Cannon Papers; U.S. Senate Committee on the District of Columbia, *Report on S.1063, a Bill for the Further Prevention of Cruelty to Animals in the District of Columbia,* May 13, 1897 (*Senate Report 116,* 55th Congress, 1st Session, vol. 2).

56. U.S. Senate, *Report and Hearing* (1896), pp. 115-18. Statistics of the Prudential Insurance Company showed that, in fifteen large American cities, the rate of mortality from diphtheria declined from an average of 96 deaths per 100,000 population in the period 1890-1894 to an average of 21 deaths per 100,000 in the period 1910-1914. William W. Keen, *Medical Research and Human Welfare* (Boston, 1917), p. 97.

57. *Journal of Zoophily* 4 (1895) ff.: passim; H. O[?]. Haughton to George B. Shattuck, November 30, 1902, and William H. Welch to H. P. Bowditch, February 14, 189[8?], in Cannon Papers.

58. Brooks and Levey, "Humorally-Transported Integrators," pp. 184-86, 191, 201-2; Walter B. Cannon, *Bodily Changes in Pain, Hunger, Fear and Rage* (New York, 1915); E. H. Starling, "On the Chemical Correlation of the Functions of the Body" (Croonian Lectures for 1905), *Lancet,* 1905, vol. 2, 339-41, 423-25, 501-3, 579-83. An antivivisectionist

tract attacking the work of Bayliss and Starling occasioned both a libel suit by Bayliss against Stephen Coleridge of the National Antivivisection Society (won by Bayliss) and the Brown Dog Riots of 1907-10 in Battersea. There is nothing to indicate that the antivivisectionists had any inkling of the significance of the experiments that they were denouncing. See John Vyvyan, *The Dark Face of Science* (London, 1971), pp. 53-65.

59. Brooks and Levey, "Humorally-Transported Integrators," pp. 199-200; Paget, *Experiments on Animals;* William W. Keen, *Animal Experimentation and Medical Progress* (Boston, 1914); Francis A. Tondorf, ed., *A Vindication of Vivisection: A Course of Lectures on Animal Experimentation,* 2d ed. (Washington, 1923).

60. U.S. Senate, *Hearing on the Bill (S.34)*; papers of H. C. Ernst, 1900 ff., and correspondence of Walter B. Cannon, 1919, in Cannon Papers; Mark N. Ozer, "The British Vivisection Controversy," *Bulletin of the History of Medicine* 40 (1966): 159; Vyvyan, *Dark Face of Science,* pp. 91, 95, 127.

61. Albert Leffingwell, *Is Science Advanced by Deceit?* (n.p. [Providence, R.I.], 1900), p. [33]; French, *Antivivisection,* pp. 212-14. and the following in the Cannon Papers: William D. Chapple to H. C. Ernst, March 17, 1905, and [Ernst?] to Senator Harvey, March 9, 1909; clipping from Brooklyn *Eagle,* February 10, 1912; Walter B. Cannon to John F. Anderson, February 26, 1914, and Anderson to Cannon, February 28, 1914; Frederic Lee to Cannon, June 12, 1919.

62. Obituary of Frances Power Cobbe in *The Times* [London], April 7, 1904; Frances Power Cobbe, *Life of Frances Power Cobbe by Herself,* 2d ed. (London, 1904), pp. 689-92.

63. *Journal of Zoophily* 7 (1898): 13, 25; Albert Leffingwell, *An Ethical Problem, or Sidelights upon Scientific Experimentation on Man and Animals* (London and New York, 1914), pp. v, 218-19.

64. *Animal World* 6 (1875): 84, 180; Colam to Angell, July 17, 1878, in Angell Scrapbook No. 18 (MSPCA archives); *Our Dumb Animals* 24 (1891-92): 26; *Journal of Zoophily* 1 (1892): 37, 45-47, 52, 71-72, 163-65; RSPCA Minute Books No. 17, pp. 330-31, and No. 18, pp. 52-53.

65. RSPCA Minute Book No. 20, pp. 182-88, 196, 203-7, 394-95; R. M. Pearce to Walter B. Cannon, October 26, 1914, in Cannon Papers.

66. Anna Harris Smith to Walter B. Cannon, April 25, 1912, and R. M. Pearce to Frederick R. Green, October 9, 1914, in Cannon Papers; Harold C. Ernst, "Animal Experimentation," *Journal of Social Science, containing the Proceedings of the American* [Social Science] *Association,* no. 42 (September 1904), p. 105.

67. *New England Anti-Vivisection Society Quarterly* 1 (October 1895): 4-6; *Journal of Zoophily* 8 (1899): 3, and 9 (1900): 90; *Proceedings of the International Anti-Vivisection and Animal Protection Congress held at Washington, D.C. December 8 to 11th, 1913* (New York, n.d. [1914?]), pp. 170-76; Vyvyan, *Dark Face of Science,* pp. 82-83, 120; Stephen Paget to Walter Cannon, September 30, 1909, in Cannon Papers. Frances Cobbe provided in her will for elaborate precautions against premature burial.

68. *Journal of Zoophily* 2 (1893): 120, and 5 (1896): 41. The best account of the triumph of scientific medicine over the medical sectarianism of the nineteenth century is Rothstein, *American Physicians.*

69. Fleming, *Welch,* p. 11; Warbasse, *Conquest of Disease,* dedication.

Chapter VII

1. James Crewdson Turner, "Kindness to Animals: The Animal-Protection Movement in England and America during the Nineteenth Century" (unpub. diss., Harvard University, 1975), pp. 251-54. On the original animal shelter, see Gloria Cottesloe, *Lost, Stolen, or Strayed: The Story of the Battersea Dogs' Home* (London, 1971). There is nothing similar

on the work in America, which has to be traced through SPCA records, but see Sydney H. Coleman, *Humane Society Leaders in America* (Albany, N.Y., 1924), especially pp. 181, 208-10.

2. ASPCA, *1909 Annual Report,* p. 7; Animal Rescue League (Boston), *1902 Annual Report,* membership list at end. Of all major societies, the RSPCA and MSPCA probably retained the broadest vision of their responsibilities, but even they became pet-dominated. The thoroughness of this transformation is suggested by the fact that even today SPCA officers, typically businesslike and unsentimental in their commitment to animal welfare, still have a hard time shaking off the public image of mawkish poodle huggers.

3. Anne Allen and Arthur Morton, *This is Your Child: The Story of the National Society for the Prevention of Cruelty to Children* (London, 1961); Roswell C. McCrea, *The Humane Movement: A Descriptive Survey* (New York, 1910), pp. 13-15 and passim.

4. I may seem here to exaggerate the historic importance of kindness to animals. Yet the RSPCA became the largest and perhaps the most influential voluntary organization in Britain during the second half of the century. (See Brian Harrison, "Animals and the State in nineteenth-century England," *English Historical Review* 88 (1973): 786-820, for a general assessment of its influence.) The decentralization of American animal protection makes it harder to measure the status of American SPCAs, but they enjoyed influence of the same order of magnitude.

5. Robert Henry Welker, *Birds and Men: American Birds in Science, Art, Literature, and Conservation, 1800-1900* (Cambridge, Mass., 1955), pp. 160-61; *The Times* [London], October 9, 1865, quoted in RSPCA Records, vol. 9, pp. 27-33; M.C.F. Morris, *Francis Orpen Morris, A Memoir* (London, 1897), pp. 135, 142-46; Francis O. Morris, *Letters to the "Times" about Birds, Etc.* (London, n.d. [1880]), pp. 42, 73, 116; RSPCA Minute Books No. 11, p. 344, and No. 12, pp. 56, 284; *Animal World* 1 (1869-70): 143. The subject was extensively considered in *The Times* during 1868 and 1869 and was the subject of a committee report of the British Association for the Advancement of Science in 1872 (RSPCA Records, vol. 10, pp. 68-76, 91-116, and vol. 12, pp. 111-14).

6. *Our Dumb Animals* 1 (1868-69): 11-12, and 9 (1876-77): 81; George T. Angell, *Autobiographical Sketches and Personal Recollections* (Boston, n.d. [1908]), p. 81; Mary F. Lovell, *Outline of the History of the Women's Pennsylvania Society for the Prevention of Cruelty to Animals* (Philadelphia, 1908), p. 33; Coleman, *Humane Leaders,* p. 183; McCrea, *Humane Movement,* pp. 127-34, 247-55. Welker, *Birds and Men,* surveys the rise of bird protection in America in chaps. 12-16. For contemporary popular enthusiasm for bird watching and bird lore, see Peter J. Schmitt, *Back to Nature: The Arcadian Myth in Urban America* (New York, 1969), chap. 3.

7. McCrea, *Humane Movement,* p. 130; Lovell, *History of WSPCA,* p. 33; Morris, *Morris,* p. 296; *Animal World* 22 (1891): 174; Margaret Mead, *Blackberry Winter* (New York, 1972), p. 25; *Our Animal Friends* 22 (1895): 218. For the history of these specialist efforts and, in general, for the relationship of fashion to bird protection, see Robin W. Doughty, *Feather Fashions and Bird Preservation: A Study in Nature Protection* (Berkeley, 1975).

8. Ralph Waldo Trine, *Every Living Creature, or Heart-Training through the Animal World* (New York, 1899), pp. 9-10; *Animal World* 6 (1875): 104, and 16 (1885): 136; *Our Dumb Animals* 1 (1868-69): 11-12, 9 (1876-77): 81, and 16 (1883-84): 96.

9. For the survival of belief in the Great Chain of Being well into the nineteenth century, see Chapter IV.

10. T[homas] Forster, *Philozoia* (Brussels, 1839), p. 51; William H. Drummond, *The Rights of Animals* (London, 1838), pp. 6, 77, 130; RSPCA, *1833 Annual Report,* p. 29. On the history of natural theology, of which the argument from design was the most influential eighteenth and nineteenth-century manifestation, see Charles Raven, *Natural Religion and Christian Theology* (Cambridge, Eng., 1953). Chaps. 7-9 of volume 1 deal with the eighteenth and nineteenth centuries.

11. Richard Dean, *An Essay on the Future Life of Brutes* (Manchester, 1767), vol. 2, p. 80; Drummond, *Rights of Animals,* pp. 27, 128; *Our Dumb Animals* 1 (1868-69): 50; Forster, *Philozoia,* p. 45; Caroline Bray, *Our Duty to Animals* (London, n.d.), p. 67.

12. *Hansard,* vol. 14, pp. 554-55; W[illiam] Youatt, *The Obligation and Extent of Humanity to Brutes* (London, 1839), p. 35; RSPCA, *Domestic Animals and Their Treatment* (London, 1857), p. [iii]; *Our Dumb Animals* 1 (1868-69): 73; Henry Bergh, "The Cost of Cruelty," *North American Review* 133 (1881): 75-76; Mary F. Lovell, *Woman's Responsibility toward the Animal Creation* (n.p., n.d. [1895?]), p. 3.

13. *Animal World* 6 (1875): 13, 110, and 12 (1881): 38.

14. The first extended public discussion of the question that I have come across was in *The Times* of London—chiefly in its correspondence columns—in 1863 (reproduced in RSPCA Records, vol. 8, pp. 107-18). Even here the preservation of the balance of nature was the central argument.

15. Letter from C. W. Bayly in *Animal World* 1 (1869-70): 59. In 1866 Ernst Haeckel, taking Darwin as his starting point, had outlined "a new science concerned with 'Nature's Economy'" and coined the word ecology (Öcologie): Donald Fleming, "Roots of the New Conservation Movement," *Perspectives in American History* 6 (1972): 23. It was not impossible that Bayly had read Haeckel's prescient sketch, but I should think it highly unlikely.

16. *Animal World* 4 (1873): 6, and 14 (1883): 68; *Our Animal Friends* 21 (1893): 36-38; E. B. Hamley, *Our Poor Relations: A Philozoic Essay* (Boston, 1872), pp. 24-27; George M. Gould, "Vivisection," in *Borderland Studies* (Philadelphia, 1896), pp. 38-39.

17. On conservationist ideology, I have relied chiefly on James B. Trefethen, *Crusade for Wildlife: Highlights of Conservation Progress* (Harrisburg, Pa., 1961); John F. Reiger, ed., *The Passing of the Great West: Selected Papers of George Bird Grinnell* (New York, 1972); Roderick Nash, *Wilderness and the American Mind,* rev. ed. (New Haven, 1973), especially chaps. 6-9; and Fleming, "New Conservation Movement." Trefethen's book, a broadly conceived history of the Boone and Crockett Club, bears most directly on conservation of animal life.

18. For Muir's Transcendentalist nature ethic, see Nash, *Wilderness,* chap. 8.

19. Although the best-known exemplar of this position was Theodore Roosevelt, the theme also resounded in the writings of George Bird Grinnell, second in importance only to T.R. in the Boone and Crockett Club and the chief mover behind the Audubon Society. See Reiger, ed., *Passing of the Great West,* passim, esp. p. 22.

20. Trefethen, *Crusade for Wildlife,* p. 79.

21. Alfred Tennyson, "In Memoriam" (1850), LV-LVI, in *Complete Poetical Works* (Boston, 1883), p. 300.

22. Cf. Fleming, "New Conservation Movement," p. 27.

23. John Lawrence, *A Philosophical and Practical Treatise on Horses, and on the Moral Duties of Man towards the Brute Creation* (London, 1796), vol. 1, pp. 83-84, 120-21; *Hansard,* vol. 14, pp. 555-56; Edward Byron Nicholson, *The Rights of an Animal: A New Essay in Ethics* (London, 1879), p. viii; Noah K. Davis, "The Moral Aspects of Vivisection," *North American Review* 140 (1885): 215; Sarah Ellen Blackwell, "The Moral Aspect of Vivisection," *Journal of Zoophily* 1 (1892): 58; Frances Power Cobbe, *The Ethics of Zoophily* (London, n.d. [1895]), p. 8.

24. Lawson Tait, *The Uselessness of Vivisection upon Animals as a Method of Scientific Research* (Birmingham, 1882), p. 123.

25. *Our Dumb Animals* 1 (1868-69): 84, and 4 (1871-72): 194; Angell, *Autobiographical Sketches,* appendix, p. 5. This point of view had its difficulties. Where did one draw the line, not necessarily between rights and no rights, but between superior rights and inferior rights? One writer, who found it hard to take this whole business very seriously, claimed that if animals could be assigned rights on this basis, then so could vegetables: Rupert Hughes, "Animal and Vegetable Rights," *Harper's Monthly Magazine* 103 (1901): 852-53.

26. "Illustrations of Instinct," *Christian Remembrancer* 14 (1847): 436.

27. *Our Dumb Animals* 1 (1868-69): 31, and 3 (1870-71): 17; Thomas C. Laws, "The Rights of Animals," *Open Court* 7 (1893): 3793.

28. James Fenimore Cooper's revulsion from the wholesale slaughter of pigeons in the celebrated scene in *The Pioneers* (New York, 1823), vol. 2, chap. 3, is, among other things, an early instance of this thriftiness applied to nature. It is also one of the relatively rare expressions of concern at this time for the suffering of birds.

29. Henry Bergh to Thurlow Weed, April 2, 1873, quoted in Buffet, vol. 1, "Vivisection"; Bergh to Morris Waln, April 18, 1868, in Letterbook No. 3 (ASPCA archives), p. 391; [D. C. Lathbury], "Cruelty to Animals," *Cornhill Magazine* 29 (1874): 213; *Address to the Committee appointed by the Pennsylvania Society for the Prevention of Cruelty to Animals, held May 6, 1867* (Philadelphia, 1867), p. 4.

30. Ronald Pearsall, *The Worm in the Bud: The World of Victorian Sexuality* (London, 1969), p. 313, quoting the Rev. S. Barnett; RSPCA, *Domestic Animals,* pp. 44-45; Buffet, vol. 2, "Bergh's Attack."

31. Anna Sewell, *Black Beauty* (Boston, n.d. [1890]), p. 57; Frances Power Cobbe, "The Rights of Man and the Claims of Brutes," in *Studies New and Old of Ethical and Social Subjects* (London, 1865), p. 241; Henry S. Salt, "Humanitarianism: Its General Principles and Progress," in *Cruelties of Civilization: A Program of Humane Reform,* ed. Henry S. Salt, vol. 1 (London, n.d. [1894]), p. 19.

32. Charles Darwin, *On the Origin of Species* (London, 1859), p. 31; W[illiam] Youatt, *On Canine Madness* (London, 1830), p. 14; *Voice of Humanity* 1 (1830): 37; *Hansard,* 3d ser., vol. 67, p. 1287; RSPCA, *1850 Annual Report,* p. 28; *The Times* [London], July 26, 1870, reproduced in RSPCA Records, vol. 12, pp. 24-25.

33. RSPCA, *1836 Annual Report,* p. 12; *Albany Daily Advertiser,* n.d., quoted in *The Spirit of Humanity and Essence of Morality* (Albany, N.Y., 1835), pp. 246-49; *Our Dumb Animals* 1 (1868-69): 34; Bergh, "Cost of Cruelty," 75-81; *Animal World* 2 (1870-71): 124; RSPCA Minute Book No. 20, p. 93; George T. Angell, "The Protection of Animals," *Journal of Social Science: containing the Transactions of the American* [Social Science] *Association,* no. 6 (July 1874), pp. 164-80, especially pp. 166-72.

34. *Our Dumb Animals* 1 (1868-69): 8; T. W. Moffett, *A Letter to the Right Hon. the Lord Mayor of Dublin on Cruelty to Animals with special reference to the Cattle Traffic of the United Kingdom* (Dublin, 1867), p. 4.

35. Henry Bergh to Messrs. Allenton, Dutcher, and Moore (a New York cattle trading firm), October 26, 1866, in ASPCA Letterbook No. 1, p. 283; RSPCA, *1850 Annual Report,* p. 28; *Our Dumb Animals* 1 (1868-69): 6. A somewhat similar though more narrowly conceived argument about the moral outlook of antivivisectionists was sketched twenty-five years ago in an excellent article by Lloyd G. Stevenson, "Science Down the Drain: On the Hostility of Certain Sanitarians to Animal Experimentation, Bacteriology, and Immunology," *Bulletin of the History of Medicine* 29 (1955): 2-3.

36. For broadly similar, though not specifically religious, attitudes on the part of twentieth-century environmentalists, see Fleming, "New Conservation Movement."

37. Henry S. Salt, "Literae Humaniores: An Appeal to Teachers," in *Cruelties of Civilization,* ed. Henry S. Salt, vol. 3 (London, 1897), pp. 9-12; idem, *Animals' Rights Considered in Relation to Social Progress* (London, 1892), pp. 32-33. Salt's own cat is mentioned in his autobiography, *Seventy Years Among Savages* (New York, 1921), p. 130. The best summary of Salt's position is his *Animals' Rights.* There is a recent biographical study by George Hendrick, *Henry Salt: Humanitarian Reformer and Man of Letters* (Urbana, Ill., 1977).

38. J. Howard Moore, *The Universal Kinship* (Chicago, 1908), pp. 4-5, 17, 107, 239, 245-46. On Salt's friendship with Moore, see Salt's memoir, *Company I Have Kept* (London, 1930), pp. 110-12. Moore published extensively; *The Universal Kinship* is the fullest development of his position. For more on both of these radical animal lovers, see Turner, "Kindness to Animals," pp. 405-21.

Bibliographic Note

The foregoing notes to each chapter will guide interested readers through the printed literature, both primary and secondary, bearing on the animal protection movement during the nineteenth century. Scholars requiring a fuller bibliography are referred to the unpublished dissertation on which this book is based: "Kindness to Animals: The Animal-Protection Movement in England and America during the Nineteenth Century" (Harvard University, 1975). The locations of the most important archival materials are listed below.

RSPCA archives, Horsham, Sussex: Manuscript Minute Books, complete. Printed *Annual Reports,* complete. Seventeen-volume typescript, compiled anonymously around 1900, entitled "Records of Proceedings in Parliament, Letters and Articles in the 'Times' and other Publications, and of the general Progress of Public Opinion, with reference to the Prevention of Cruelty to Animals and the Promotion of their proper Care and Treatment, 1800-1895" (actually ends in 1876); this draws principally on *Hansard* and *The Times* but includes material from a wide range of other publications.

ASPCA archives, New York: Manuscript Minute Books, complete; unfortunately, I was unable to obtain permission to use them. Printed *Annual Reports,* complete. Manuscript diaries of Henry Bergh. Newspaper scrapbooks of Henry Bergh. Letter books for parts of 1866-68 and 1871-72. Edward P. Buffet, "Bergh's War on Vested Cruelty" (8 vols., typescript, c. 1930); contains voluminous primary materials.

MSPCA archives, Boston: Minute Books for the period of this study are lost, and only six printed *Annual Reports* prior to 1914 survive. Ten of George Angell's personal scrapbooks (press clippings, pamphlets, a few letters) remain. Virtually complete set of *Our Dumb Animals.*

PSPCA archives, Philadelphia: Manuscript Minute Books from 1877. Miscellaneous newspaper clippings and a few letters.

WSPCA archives, Philadelphia. Manuscript Minute Books, complete. Printed *Annual Reports,* complete. A volume of newspaper clippings and photographs.

Historical Society of Pennsylvania, Philadelphia: PSPCA Papers; a haphazard collection of correspondence, record books, and pamphlets. Diaries of Adele Biddle of the WSPCA and AAVS.

Francis A. Countway Library, Harvard Medical School: Walter B. Cannon Papers; Cannon's voluminous correspondence on vivisection and scores of pamphlets, newspaper clippings, and magazine articles; also similar material dealing with antivivisection in Massachusetts, apparently inherited from Harold C. Ernst.

Archives of Imperial College of Science and Technology, London: Thomas Huxley Papers and Lyon Playfair Papers both contain material relating to antivivisection.

Acknowledgments

One hopes for many readers; one writes for a few friends. First among them has been Donald Fleming. Unstinting of his time, he has kept his eye on this book—and its author—from the beginning. His extraordinary erudition, discriminating literary sensibility, keen intelligence, and fertile imagination have left their mark on every page. His encouragement, friendship, and example have meant more. He is a scholar's scholar, and I should like to think that my book is tribute to his work.

Neil Harris, Bernard Bailyn, and Oscar Handlin had no direct hand in shaping this book but a great deal to do with shaping me; I should like to thank them here. Richard French, Brian Harrison, and Laurence Tribe helped me to chart my course when I first began thinking about this study. John Clive, Martin Pernick, Pauline Maier, Jack Censer, and Thomas Brown read drafts, their efforts issuing in apt advice about style and substance. Jack Censer and Thomas Brown, in particular, combed through the manuscript, applying the acute and jaundiced eye that is the surest proof of friendship. I also want to express my appreciation to my editor, Henry Tom, and manuscript editor, Joyce Latham. This book is very much the better for all this help.

Harvard University, the College of Charleston, and the Charles Warren Center for American History helped with expenses. Many of the actual burdens of research were borne by the staffs of the Bodleian Library of Oxford University; the Boston Public Library; the British Museum; the College of Charleston Library; the Countway Library of the Harvard Medical School; the Harvard College Library; the Historical Society of Pennsylvania; the Houghton Library of Harvard University; the Institute of Historical Research, University of London; the Library of Congress; the University of London Library; and the Wellcome Institute of the History of Medicine. Katharine Kane, Helen Needham, and Dorothy Winchel typed various versions.

Officers and staff members of several organizations made archival material available: American Antivivisection Society, Philadelphia; American Society for the Prevention of Cruelty to Animals, New York; Massa-

183

chusetts SPCA, Boston; Pennsylvania SPCA, Philadelphia; Women's SPCA of Pennsylvania, Philadelphia; Royal SPCA, Horsham, Sussex; and the National Society for the Prevention of Cruelty to Children (NSPCC), London. Richard Cowan of the Massachusetts SPCA and William Pimm of the Royal SPCA were especially helpful over long periods of time. My friend Marion Bones, formerly of the Royal SPCA and now with the NSPCC, deserves a special word of thanks. For three months she helped me every day to find my way through the Royal SPCA archives. Even more, she offered open-handed hospitality and friendship to a stranger and his family in London.

My wife, Julianne Turner, urged me on, pointed out lapses into incomprehensibility, and at critical periods assumed responsibility for our household and children so that I could be alone with the animals. I am grateful.

More than to anyone else, I owe this book to my mother. The debt being too large for my grasp, I shall simply say thank you.

Index

The Johns Hopkins University Press

This book was composed in Alphacomp Times Roman text by David Lorton and Benguiat display by The Composing Room, from a design by Charles West. It was printed on 50-lb. Bookmark Natural Text Stock paper and bound by Thomson-Shore, Inc.